Lecture Notes in Computer Science   **11951**

More information about this series at http://www.springer.com/series/7408

Nan Guan · Joost-Pieter Katoen ·
Jun Sun (Eds.)

Dependable
Software Engineering

Theories, Tools, and Applications

5th International Symposium, SETTA 2019
Shanghai, China, November 27–29, 2019
Proceedings

 Springer

Editors
Nan Guan
Hong Kong Polytechnic University
Kowloon, Hong Kong

Joost-Pieter Katoen 🆔
RWTH Aachen University
Aachen, Germany

Jun Sun
Singapore Management University
Singapore, Singapore

ISSN 0302-9743   ISSN 1611-3349   (electronic)
Lecture Notes in Computer Science
ISBN 978-3-030-35539-5   ISBN 978-3-030-35540-1   (eBook)
https://doi.org/10.1007/978-3-030-35540-1

LNCS Sublibrary: SL2 – Programming and Software Engineering

This Springer imprint is published by the registered company Springer Nature Switzerland AG
The registered company address is: Gewerbestrasse 11, 6330 Cham, Switzerland

Preface

This volume contains the papers presented at the 5th Symposium on Dependable Software Engineering: Theories, Tools, and Applications (SETTA 2019) series of conferences – held during November 27–29, 2019, in Shanghai, China. The purpose of SETTA is to provide an international forum for researchers and practitioners to share cutting-edge advancements and strengthen collaborations in the field of formal methods and its interoperability with software engineering for building reliable, safe, secure, and smart systems. Past SETTA symposiums were successfully held in Nanjing (2015), Beijing (2016), Changsha (2017), and Beijing (2018).

SETTA 2019 attracted 26 submissions co-authored by researchers from 12 countries. Each submission was reviewed by at least three Program Committee members with help from additional reviewers. The Program Committee discussed the submissions online and decided to accept eight papers for presentation at the conference. The program also included three invited talks given by Prof. Wang Yi from Uppsala University, Sweden, Dr. Kuldeep S. Meel from National University of Singapore, Singapore, and Haibo Chen from Shanghai Jiaotong University, China. The 4th National Conference on Formal Methods and Applications in China was also co-located with SETTA 2019 during November 30–December 1, 2019.

We would like to express our gratitude to the authors for submitting their papers to SETTA 2019. We are particularly thankful to all members of Program Committee and the additional reviewers, whose hard and professional work in the review process helped us prepare the high-quality conference program. Special thanks go to our invited speakers for presenting their research at the conference. We would like to thank the Steering Committee for their advice. Finally, we thank the conference general chair, Prof. Yuxi Fu, and the publicity chairs, Dr. Yu Pei and Dr. Tom van Dijk.

October 2019

Jun Sun
Joost-Pieter Katoen
Nan Guan

Organization

Program Committee

Étienne André	Université Paris 13, LIPN, CNRS, UMR 7030, France
Mohamed Faouzi Atig	Uppsala University, Sweden
Ezio Bartocci	Vienna University of Technology, Austria
Sanjoy Baruah	Washington University in St. Louis, USA
Yan Cai	State Key Laboratory of Computer Science and Institute of Software, Chinese Academy of Sciences, China
Milan Ceska	Brno University of Technology, Czech Republic
Sudipta Chattopadhyay	Singapore University of Technology and Design, Singapore
Mingsong Chen	East China Normal University, China
Taolue Chen	Birkbeck, University of London, UK
Yu-Fang Chen	Academia Sinica, Taiwan
Alessandro Cimatti	Fondazione Bruno Kessler (FBK-irst), Italy
Yuxi Fu	Shanghai Jiao-tong University, China
Nan Guan	The Hong Kong Polytechnic University, Hong Kong SAR, China
Tingting Han	Birkbeck, University of London, UK
Arnd Hartmanns	University of Twente, The Netherlands
Nils Jansen	Radboud University, The Netherlands
Ran Ji	Carnegie Mellon University, USA
Yu Jiang	Tsinghua University, China
Lei Ju	Shandong University, China
Joost-Pieter Katoen	RWTH Aachen University, Germany
Guoqiang Li	Shanghai Jiao Tong University, China
Di Liu	Yunnan University, China
Shuang Liu	Singapore Institute of Technology, Singapore
Federico Olmedo	University of Chile, Chile
Yu Pei	The Hong Kong Polytechnic University, Hong Kong SAR, China
Mickael Randour	F. R .S.-FNRS and UMONS, Université de Mons, France
Anne Remke	WWU Münster, Germany
Philipp Ruemmer	Uppsala University, Sweden
Fu Song	School of Information Science and Technology, ShanghaiTech University, China
Jeremy Sproston	University of Turin, Italy
Jun Sun	Singapore Management University, Singapore

Cong Tian	Xidian University, China
Tarmo Uustalu	Reykjavik University, Iceland
Jaco van de Pol	Aarhus University, Denmark
Bow-Yaw Wang	Academia Sinica, Taiwan
Ji Wang	National Laboratory for Parallel and Distributed Processing, China
Xue-Yang Zhu	Institute of Software, Chinese Academy of Sciences, China

Additional Reviewers

Boiret, Adrien
Budde, Carlos
Budde, Carlos E.
Delgrange, Florent
Li, Xin
Lin, Hsin-Hung
Perelli, Giuseppe
Ramparison, Mathias
Sun, Youcheng
Xue, Jianxin
Zhao, Hengjun

Abstracts

The Rise of Model Counting: A Child of SAT Revolution

Kuldeep S. Meel

School of Computing, National University of Singapore, Singapore

Abstract. The paradigmatic NP-complete problem of Boolean satisfiability (SAT) is a central problem in Computer Science. The past 20 years have witnessed a *SAT revolution* with the development of conflict-driven clause-learning (CDCL) SAT solvers. Such solvers combine a classical backtracking search with a rich set of effective heuristics. While 20 years ago SAT solvers were able to solve instances with at most a few hundred variables, modern SAT solvers solve instances with up to millions of variables in a reasonable time. The SAT revolution opens up opportunities to design practical algorithms with rigorous guarantees for problems in complexity classes beyond NP by replacing a NP oracle with a SAT Solver. In this talk, we will discuss how we use SAT revolution to design practical algorithms for one of the fundamental problems in formal methods and artificial intelligence: model counting.

Model counting is a fundamental computational problem with applications in diverse areas spanning neural network verification, reliability estimation, explainable AI, probabilistic inference, security vulnerability analysis, and the like. While counting has been studied extensively by theoreticians for the past three decades. Yet, in spite of this extensive study, it has been extremely difficult to reduce this theory to practice. We examine how the process of revisiting and refining the theory to leverage the SAT revolution has led to the development of the first scalable framework for model counting: ApproxMC [1–4]. ApproxMC[1] can handle industrial-scale problem instances involving hundreds of thousands of variables, while providing provably strong approximation guarantees.

References

1. Chakraborty, S., Meel, K.S., Vardi, M.Y.: A scalable approximate model counter. In: Proceedings of CP (2013)
2. Chakraborty, S., Meel, K.S., Vardi, M.Y.: Algorithmic improvements in approximate counting for probabilistic inference: from linear to logarithmic SAT calls. In: Proceedings of IJCAI (2016)
3. Ivrii, A., Malik, S., Meel, K.S., Vardi, M.Y.: On computing minimal independent support and its applications to sampling and counting. Constraints, 1–18 (2016)
4. Soos, M., Meel, K.S.: BIRD: Engineering an efficient CNF-XOR SAT solver and its applications to approximate model counting. In: Proceedings of AAAI (2019)

---

[1] https://github.com/meelgroup/approxmc.

Building and Updating Safety-Critical Embedded Systems with Deterministic Timing and Functional Behaviours

Wang Yi

Uppsala University, Sweden

Today, the functionality as well as economical value of industrial systems and products, such as cars, air planes, and medical equipment, is defined and realized by software as embedded systems. Dynamical software updates are critical for security updates, new features, and customization, but are not supported for today's safety-critical systems, since we lack techniques to guarantee that the updated system remains safe.

In this talk, I will present a model for embedded systems with deterministic timing and functional behaviours. The model provides a foundation for a new design paradigm for building embedded systems which can be updated on demand dynamically, safely, and efficiently over their operational life-time.

Contents

A Bounded Model Checking Technique for Higher-Order Programs

Yu-Yang Lin and Nikos Tzevelekos[(✉)]

Queen Mary University of London, London, UK
nikos.tzevelekos@qmul.ac.uk

Abstract. We present a Bounded Model Checking technique for higher-order programs based on defunctionalization and points-to analysis. The vehicle of our study is a higher-order calculus with general references. Our technique is a symbolic state syntactic translation based on SMT solvers, adapted to a setting where the values passed and stored during computation can be functions of arbitrary order. We prove that our algorithm is sound and provide a prototype implementation with experimental results showcasing its performance. The first novelty of our technique is a presentation of defunctionalization using nominal techniques, which provides a theoretical background to proving soundness of our technique, coupled with SSA adapted to higher-order values. The second novelty is our use of defunctionalization and points-to analysis to directly encode general higher-order functional programs.

1 Introduction

Bounded Model Checking [3] (BMC) is a model checking technique that allows for highly automated and scalable SAT/SMT-based verification and has been widely used to find errors in C-like languages [1,6,10,16]. BMC amounts to bounding the executions of programs by unfolding loops only up to a given bound, and model checking the resulting execution graph. Since the advent of CBMC [6], the mainstream approach additionally proceeds by symbolically executing program paths and gathering the resulting path conditions in first-order formulas which can then be passed on to SAT/SMT solvers. Thus, BMC performs a syntactic translation of program source code into a first-order formula, and uses the power of SAT/SMT solvers to check the bounded behaviour of programs. Being a Model Checking technique, BMC has the ability to produce *counterexamples*, which are execution traces that lead to the violation of desired properties. A specific advantage of BMC over unbounded techniques is that it avoids the full effect of state-space explosion at the expense of full verification. On the other hand, since BMC is inconclusive if the formula is unsatisfiable, it is generally regarded as a bug-finding or underapproximation technique.

The above approach has been predominantly applied to imperative, first-order languages and, while tools like CBMC can handle C++ (and, more recently,

Research funded by EPSRC (EP/P004172/1).

N. Guan et al. (Eds.): SETTA 2019, LNCS 11951, pp. 1–18, 2019.
https://doi.org/10.1007/978-3-030-35540-1_1

JAVA bytecode), the treatment of higher-order programs is currently limited. In particular, there is no direct analogue of the syntactic translations available for imperative languages in the higher-order case. This is what we address herein. We propose a symbolic BMC procedure for higher-order functional and imperative programs that may contain free variables of ground type based on *defunction-alization* [21] and *points-to analysis* [2]. Our contributions include: (a) a novel syntactical translation to apply BMC to languages with higher-order methods and state; (b) a proof that the approach is sound; (c) an optimisation based on points-to analysis to improve scalability; and (d) a prototype implementation of the procedure with experimental results showcasing its performance.

As with most approaches to software BMC, we translate a given program into a first-order formula for an SMT solver to check for satisfiability, where formulas are satisfiable only if a violation is reachable within a given bound. While in first-order programs BMC places a bound on loop unfolding, in the higher-order setting we place the bound on nested method applications. The main challenge for the translation then is the symbolic execution of paths which involve the flow of higher-order terms, by either variable binding or use of the store. We first adapt the standard technique of Static Single Assignment (SSA) to a setting where variables and references can be of higher order. To handle higher-order terms in particular, we use an approach from operational semantics whereby each method is identified by a unique value, which we call a *name*. During execution, methods are passed and stored as names. Similarly to defunctionalization, application of each method is performed through a method repository.We capture program behaviour by also uniquely identifying every sub-term in the program tree with a return variable; analogously to how CBMC [6] captures the behaviour of sequencing commands in ANSI-C programs.

To illustrate the approach, consider the following code where r is a reference of type int $\rightarrow$ int, f is a variable of type int $\rightarrow$ (int $\rightarrow$ int) $\rightarrow$ (int $\rightarrow$ int) $\rightarrow$ (int $\rightarrow$ int), g, h are variables of type int $\rightarrow$ int, and n, x are variables of type int.

```
1   let f = λ x,g,h. if (x <= 0) then g else h
2   in
3   r := f n (λ x. x−1) (λ x. x+1);
4   assert(!r n >= n)
```

We build a formula capturing the violation of the assertion on line 4. In a symbolic setting, it is not immediately obvious which function to call when dereferencing r in line 4. Luckily, we know that when calling f in line 3, its value can only be the one bound to it in line 1. Thus, a first transformation of the code could be:

```
3   r := if (n <= 0) then (λ x. x−1) else (λ x. x+1);
4   assert(!r n >= n)
```

The assignment in line 3 can be facilitated by using a return variable *ret* and method names for $(\lambda x.x - 1)$ and $(\lambda x.x + 1)$:

```
1   let m1 = λ x. x−1 in let m2 = λ x. x+1 in
2   let ret = if (n <= 0) then m1 else m2 in
3   r := ret;
4   assert(!r n >= n)
```

Here lies the challenge as we now need to decide how to symbolically dereference r. The simplest solution is try to match $!r$ with all existing functions of matching type, in this case $m1$ and $m2$:

```
1   let m1 = λ x. x−1 in let m2 = λ x. x+1 in
2   let ret = if (n <= 0) then m1 else m2 in
3   r := ret;
4   let ret' = match !r with
5                | m1 −> m1 n
6                | m2 −> m2 n in
7   assert(ret' >= n)
```

Performing the substitutions of $m1, m2$, we can read off the following formula for checking falsity of the assertion:

$$(ret' < n) \land (r = m1 \Rightarrow ret' = n - 1) \land (r = m2 \Rightarrow ret' = n + 1) \land (r = ret)$$
$$\land (n <= 0 \Rightarrow ret = m1) \land (n > 0 \Rightarrow ret = m2)$$

The above is true e.g. for $n = 0$, and hence the code violates the assertion.

These ideas underpin the core of our BMC translation, which is presented in Sect. 3 and proven sound later on. The language we examine, HOREF, is a higher-order language with general references and integer arithmetic. While correct, one can quickly see that the translation is inefficient when trying to resolve the flow of functions to references and variables. In effect, it explores all possible methods of the appropriate type that have been created so far, and relies on the solver to pick the right one. This is why a data-flow analysis is required, which we present in Sect. 4. We optimise the translation by restricting such choices according to a simple points-to analysis. In Sect. 5 we present an implementation of our technique in a BMC tool for a higher-order OCAML-like syntax extending HOREF, and test it on several example programs adapted from the MoCHi benchmark [15]. Finally, we compare our tool with MoCHi and an implementation of our bounded operational semantics in ROSETTE [25].

Related Work

While common in symbolic evaluation, defunctionalization with points-to analysis, to our knowledge, has not been used to translate entire general higher-order programs into SAT/SMT-based BMC encodings. As such, we believe we present a different and sound approach to model checking higher-order terms. BMC being a common technique, there exist several similar encodings. For example, [8,9,11] are bounded approaches based on relational logic that verify JAVA programs using SAT/SMT solvers. Being applied to JAVA, and especially prior to JDK 8, these approaches do not cope with terms and store of arbitrary order. In every case, methods are inlined statically, which is not always possible with function abstractions. In [8] we observe a case of exhaustive method application that restricts concrete method invocations by their type. This is similar in concept to our approach, but is only applied to resolve dynamic dispatch.

More common are verification tools for general higher-order programs that are not based on a direct syntactical BMC encoding. Two main techniques followed are higher-order recursion schemes modelling [14,19], and symbolic execution [4,12,13]. In the first category, MoCHi [15] performs full verification of OCaml programs by translating them into higher-order recursion schemes checked with specialised tools. In the second category, ROSETTE [25] and RUBICON [17] perform symbolic evaluation for RACKET and RUBY respectively by using solver-aided languages for functional and imperative higher-order programs. On the other hand, the tool implemented in [18] performs a contracts-based symbolic execution that allows evaluating symbolically *arbitrarily open* higher-order programs. From these approaches, we choose MoCHi and ROSETTE as representatives for a comparison in Sect. 5. Particularly, ROSETTE was selected due to the similarity of RACKET and HOREF, and for its ability to implement our bounding mechanism in RACKET, which provides a more direct comparison of the underlying techniques.

Finally, tools based on CBMC [16,20,22] are inherently similar to our BMC encoding and procedure as we take inspiration from the CBMC translation, and add symbolic defunctionalization to cope with higher-order syntax. Overall, tools based on symbolic execution are able to produce the most extensionally similar implementations, while intentionally our approach is closer in idea to CBMC with defunctionalization.

2   The Language: HORef

Here we present a higher-order language with higher-order global state. The syntax consists of a call-by-value λ-calculus with global references. Its types are given by the grammar: $\theta ::= \texttt{unit} \mid \texttt{int} \mid \theta \times \theta \mid \theta \to \theta$.

We use countably infinite sets Meths, Refs and Vars for methods, global references and variables, ranged over by m, r and x respectively, and variants thereof; while i is for ranging over the integers. Each of these sets is typed, that is, it can be expressed as a disjoint union as follows: $\texttt{Meths} = \biguplus_{\theta,\theta'} \texttt{Meths}_{\theta,\theta'}$, $\texttt{Refs} = \biguplus_{\theta} \texttt{Refs}_{\theta}$, $\texttt{Vars} = \biguplus_{\theta} \texttt{Vars}_{\theta}$.

The syntax and typing rules are given in Fig. 1. We assume a set of arithmetic operators $\oplus$, which we leave unspecified as they do not affect the analysis. Assertions are used for the specification of safety properties to be checked. We extend the syntax with usual constructs: $r{+}{+}$ is $r := {!}r + 1$, and $T;T'$ stands for $\texttt{let } \_ = T \texttt{ in } T'$. Booleans are represented by 0 and $i \neq 0$.

As usual, a variable occurrence is *free* if it is not in the scope of a matching $(\lambda/\texttt{let}/\texttt{letrec})$-binder. Terms are considered modulo α-equivalence and, in particular, we may assume that no variable occurs both as free and bound in the same term. We call a term *closed* if it contains no free variables.

$$\text{Terms} \ni T ::= \mathbf{assert}(T) \mid x \mid m \mid i \mid () \mid \langle T, T \rangle \mid T \oplus T \mid r := T \mid !r \mid \pi_1 T \mid \pi_2 T \mid \lambda x.T$$
$$\mid T\,T \mid \mathbf{if}\ T\ \mathbf{then}\ T\ \mathbf{else}\ T \mid \mathbf{let}\ x = T\ \mathbf{in}\ T \mid \mathbf{letrec}\ x = \lambda x.T\ \mathbf{in}\ T$$

$$\text{Vals} \ni v ::= x \mid m \mid i \mid () \mid \langle v, v \rangle$$

$$\text{ECxts} \ni E ::= \bullet \mid \mathbf{assert}(E) \mid r := E \mid E \oplus T \mid v \oplus E \mid \langle E, T \rangle \mid \langle v, E \rangle \mid \pi_j E \mid E\,T \mid v\,E$$
$$\mid \mathbf{let}\ x = E\ \mathbf{in}\ T \mid \mathbf{if}\ E\ \mathbf{then}\ T\ \mathbf{else}\ T \mid (\!|E|\!)$$

$$\text{CForms} \ni M ::= \mathbf{assert}(v) \mid v \mid r := v \mid !r \mid v \oplus v \mid \pi_1 v \mid \pi_2 v \mid x\,v \mid m\,v \mid \lambda x.M$$
$$\mid \mathbf{if}\ v\ \mathbf{then}\ M\ \mathbf{else}\ M \mid \mathbf{let}\ x = M\ \mathbf{in}\ M \mid \mathbf{letrec}\ x = \lambda x.M\ \mathbf{in}\ M$$

$$\frac{T : \text{int}}{\mathbf{assert}(T) : \text{unit}} \quad \overline{() : \text{unit}} \quad \overline{i : \text{int}} \quad \frac{x \in \text{Vars}_\theta}{x : \theta} \quad \frac{m \in \text{Meths}_{\theta, \theta'}}{m : \theta \to \theta'} \quad \frac{T : \text{int} \quad T_0, T_1 : \theta}{\mathbf{if}\ T\ \mathbf{then}\ T_1\ \mathbf{else}\ T_0 : \theta}$$

$$\frac{T_1, T_2 : \text{int}}{T_1 \oplus T_2 : \text{int}} \quad \frac{T_1 : \theta_1 \quad T_2 : \theta_2}{\langle T_1, T_2 \rangle : \theta_1 \times \theta_2} \quad \frac{\langle T_1, T_2 \rangle : \theta_1 \times \theta_2}{\pi_i \langle T_1, T_2 \rangle : \theta_i} \quad \frac{r \in \text{Refs}_\theta}{!r : \theta} \quad \frac{r \in \text{Refs}_\theta \quad T : \theta}{r := T : \text{unit}}$$

$$\frac{T' : \theta \to \theta' \quad T : \theta}{T'\,T : \theta'} \quad \frac{T : \theta' \quad x : \theta}{\lambda x.T : \theta \to \theta'} \quad \frac{x, T : \theta \quad T' : \theta'}{\mathbf{let}\ x = T\ \mathbf{in}\ T' : \theta'} \quad \frac{x, \lambda y.T : \theta \to \theta'' \quad T' : \theta'}{\mathbf{letrec}\ x = \lambda y.T\ \mathbf{in}\ T' : \theta'}$$

Fig. 1. Grammar and typing rules for HOREF.

Remark 1. By typing variable, reference and method names, we do not need to provide a context in typing judgements, this choice made for simplicity.

The references we use are **global**: a term can use references from the set Refs but not create them locally or pass them as arguments, and in particular there is no **ref** type. Adding ML-like local references is orthogonal to our analysis and it does not seem to present inherent difficulties (we would be treating the dynamic creation of references similarly to how we deal with method names).

On the other hand, methods are dynamically created during execution, and for that reason we will be frequently referring to them simply as names. On a related note, λ-abstractions are not values in our language. This is due to the fact that in the semantics these get evaluated to method names.

Bounded Operational Semantics. We next present a bounded operational semantics for HOREF, which we capture with our bounded BMC routine. The semantics is parameterised by a bound k which, similarly to loop unwinding in procedural languages, limits the depth of method (i.e. function) calls within an execution. A bound $k = 0$ in particular means that, unless no method calls are made, execution will terminate with no return value. Consequently, in this bounded operational semantics, all programs must halt. Note at this point that the unbounded semantics of HOREF, allowing arbitrary recursion, can be obtained e.g. by allowing bound values $k = \infty$.

A **configuration** is a quadruple (T, R, S, k) where T is a typed term and: (a) $R : \text{Meths} \rightharpoonup \text{Terms}$ is a finite map, called a **method repository**, such that for all $m \in \text{dom}(R)$, if $m \in \text{Meths}_{\theta \to \theta'}$ then $R(m) = \lambda x.T : \theta \to \theta'$; (b) $S : \text{Refs} \rightharpoonup \text{Vals}$ is a finite map, called a **store**, such that for all $r \in \text{dom}(S)$, if $r \in \text{Refs}_\theta$ then $S(r) : \theta$; and (c) $k \in \{\text{nil}\} \cup \mathbb{N}$ is the nested calling bound, where decrementing k below zero results in nil. A closed configuration is one

$$(\texttt{assert}(j), R, S, k) \to ((), R, S, k) \qquad (!r, R, S, k) \to (S(r), R, S, k)$$

$$(r := v, R, S, k) \to ((), R, S[r \mapsto v], k) \qquad (\pi_i \langle v_1, v_2 \rangle, R, S, k) \to (v_i, R, S, k)$$

$$(i_1 \oplus i_2, R, S, k) \to (i, R, S, k) \quad (i = i_1 \oplus i_2) \qquad (\lambda x.T, R, S, k) \to (m, R[m \mapsto \lambda x.T], S, k)$$

$$(\texttt{if } j \texttt{ then } T_1 \texttt{ else } T_0, R, S, k) \to (T_1, R, S, k) \qquad (\texttt{if } 0 \texttt{ then } T_1 \texttt{ else } T_0, R, S, k) \to (T_0, R, S, k)$$

$$(\texttt{let } x = v \texttt{ in } T, R, S, k) \to (T\{v/x\}, R, S, k) \qquad ((\!|v|\!), R, S, k) \to (v, R, S, k + 1)$$

$$(mv, R, S, k) \to ((\!|T\{v/x\}|\!), R, S, k - 1) \quad (R(m) = \lambda x.T)$$

$$(\texttt{letrec } f = \lambda x.T \texttt{ in } T', R, S, k) \to (T'\{m/f\}, R[m \mapsto \lambda x.T\{m/f\}], S, k)$$

$$(E[T], R, S, k) \to (E[T'], R', S', k') \quad \text{where } (T, R, S, k) \to (T', R', S', k')$$

Fig. 2. Bounded operational semantics rules. In all cases, $k \neq \texttt{nil}$ and $j \neq 0$.

whose components are all closed. We call a configuration (T, R, S, k) **valid** if all methods and references appearing in T, R, S are included in $\mathrm{dom}(R)$ and $\mathrm{dom}(S)$ respectively.

The bounded operational semantics is given in Fig. 2. It is defined by means of a small-step transition relation with transitions of the form:

$$(T, R, S, k) \to (T', R', S', k')$$

It uses *values* and *evaluation contexts*, which are in turn defined in Fig. 1. By abuse of notation, we extended the term syntax to be able to mark nested method calls explicitly, by use of *evaluation boxes* of the form $(\!|...|\!)$. We use this to correctly bound nested function calls. We also call a transition sequence $(T, R, S, k) \twoheadrightarrow (T', R', S', k')$ *valid*, where $\twoheadrightarrow$ is the reflexive and transitive closure of $\to$, if T' is a value. Note that failing an assertion results in a stuck configuration. Thus, no assertions can be violated in a valid transition sequence. Moreover, we can see that all terms must eventually evaluate to a value, or fail an assertion, or consume the bound and reach $\texttt{nil}$.

3   A Bounded Translation for HORef

We next present an algorithm which, given an initial configuration, produces a tuple containing (quantifier-free) first-order formulas and context components that capture its bounded semantics. Without loss of generality, we define the translation on terms in **canonical form**, ranged over by M and variants, which are presented in Fig. 1. This provision is innocuous as transforming a term in canonical form can be achieved in linear time with standard methods.

The algorithm receives a valid configuration (M, R, S, k) as input, where M is in canonical form and may only contain free variables of ground type, and proceeds to perform the following sequence of transformations:

$$(M, R, S, k) \xmapsto{\ init\ } (M, R, C_S, C_S, \phi_S, \top, \top, k) \xmapsto{\ [\![\cdot]\!]\ } (ret, \phi, R', C, D, \alpha, pc)$$

The first step is an initialisation step that transforms the tuple in the form appropriate for the main translation $[\![\cdot]\!]$, which is the essence of the entire bounded translation. We proceed with $[\![\cdot]\!]$ and will be returning to $init$ later on.

$[\![\cdot]\!]$ operates on symbolic configurations of the form $(M, R, C, D, \phi, \alpha, pc, k)$, where M and R are a term and a repository respectively, k is the bound, and:

- C, D : Refs $\rightharpoonup$ SSAVars are single static assignment (SSA) maps where SSAVars is the set of variables of the form r_i (for each $r \in$ Refs), such that i is the number of times that r has been assigned to so far. The map C is counting all the assignments that have taken place so far, whereas D only counts those in the current path. E.g. $C(r) = r_5$ if r has been assigned to five times so far in every path looked at. We write $C[r]$ to mean *update C with reference r*: if $C(r) = r_i$, then $C[r] = C[r \mapsto r_{i+1}]$, where r_{i+1} is fresh.
- ϕ is a first-order formula containing the (total) behaviour so far.
- α is a first-order formula consisting of a conjunction of statements representing assertions that have been visited by $[\![\cdot]\!]$ so far.
- pc is the path condition that must be satisfied to reach this configuration.

The translation returns tuples of the form $(ret, \phi, R, C, D, \alpha, pc)$, where:

- $\phi, R, C, D, \alpha, pc$ have the same reading as above, albeit for *after reaching the end of all paths from the term M*.
- ret is a logic variable representing the return value of the initial configuration.

Finally, returning to *init*, we have that:

- the initial SSA maps C_S simply map each r in the domain of S to the SSA variable r_0, i.e. $C_S = \{r \mapsto r_0 \mid r \in dom(S)\}$;
- ϕ_S stipulates that each r_0 be equal to its corresponding value $S(r)$, i.e. $\phi_S = \bigwedge_{r \in dom(S)}(r_0 = S(r))$;
- since there is no computation preceding M, its α and pc are simply $\top$ (true).

The BMC translation is given in Fig. 3. In all cases in the figure, ret is a fresh variable and $k \neq$ nil. We also assume a common domain $\Pi = dom(C) = dom(D) \subseteq$ Refs, which contains all references that appear in M and R.

The translation stops when either the bound is nil, or when every path of the given term has been explored completely. The base cases add clauses mapping return variables to actual values of evaluating M. Inductive cases build the symbolic trace of M by recording in ϕ all changes to the store, and adding clauses for return variables at each sub-term of the program, thus building a control flow graph by relating said return variables and chaining them together in the formula. Wherever branching occurs, the chaining is guarded.

In the translation, defunctionalization occurs because every method call is replaced with a call to the repository using its respective name as an argument. Because this is a symbolic setting, however, it is possible to lose track of the specific name desired. Particularly, when applying variables as methods (xv, with $x : \theta$), we encode in the behaviour formula an n-ary decision tree where n is the number of methods to consider. In such cases, we assume that x could be any method in the repository R. We call this case ***exhaustive method application***. This case seems to be fundamental for applying BMC to higher-order terms with defunctionalization. To explore plausible paths only, we restrict R to type

θ (denoted $R \restriction \theta$). In Sect. 4 we will be applying a points-to analysis to restrict this further.

To illustrate the algorithm, we look at a few characteristic cases:

[nil case] When the translation consumes its bound, we end up translating some $[\![M, R, C, D, \phi, \alpha, pc, \mathtt{nil}]\!]$. In this case, we simply return a fresh variable ret representing the final value, and stipulate in the program behaviour that ret is equal to some default value (the latter is needed to ensure a unique model for ret). Breaching of the bound is recorded as a possible assertion violation, and a reserved logic variable $\mathtt{inil}$ is used for that purpose: a breach counts as an assertion violation iff $\mathtt{inil}$ is false. The returned path condition is set to false.

[let case] In $[\![\mathtt{let}\ x = M\ \mathtt{in}\, M', R, C, D, \phi, \alpha, pc, k]\!]$, we first compute the translation of M. Using the results of said translation, we can substitute in M' the fresh variable ret_1 for x, and compute its translation. In the latter step, we also feed the updated repository R_1, SSA maps C_1 and D_1, program behaviour ϕ_1, assertions α_1 (actually, a conjunction of assertions), and the accumulated path condition $pc \wedge pc_1$. To finish, we return ret_2 and the newly updated repository R_2, SSA maps, C_2 and D_2, assertions α_2. The path condition returned is $pc_1 \wedge pc_2$, reflecting the new path conditions gathered.

[xv case] In $[\![xv, R, C, D, \phi, \alpha, pc, k]\!]$ we see method application in action. We first restrict the repository R to type θ to obtain the set of names identifying all methods of matching type for x. If no such methods exist, this means that the binding of x had not succeeded due to breaching the bound earlier on, so $\mathtt{dval}$ is returned. Otherwise, for each method m_i in this set, we obtain the translation of applying m_i to the argument v. This is done by substituting v for y_i in the body of m_i. After translating all method applications, all paths are joined in ψ, by constructing an n-ary decision tree that includes the state of the store in each path. We do this by incrementing all references in C_n, and adding the clauses $C'_n = D_i(r)$ for each path. These paths are then guarded by the clauses $(x = m_i)$. Finally, we return a formula that includes ψ and the accumulation of all intermediate ϕ_i's, the accumulation of repositories, the final SSA map, accumulation of assertions and new path conditions. Note that we return C'_n as both the C and D resulting from translating this term. This is because all branches have been joined, and any term sequenced after this one should have all updates available to it.

Remark 2. The difference between reading (D) and writing (C) is noticeable when branching. Branching can occur in two ways: through a conditional statement, and by performing symbolic method application where we have lost track of the concrete method; more precisely, when M is of the form xv. In the former case, we branch according to the return value of the condition (denoted by ret_b), and each branch translates M_0 and M_1 respectively. In this case, both branches read from the same map D_b, but may contain different assignments, which we accumulate in C. The formula $\psi_0 \wedge \psi_1$ then encodes a binary decision node in the control flow graph through guarded clauses that represent the path conditions. Similar care is taken with branching caused by symbolic method application.

Base Cases:

- $[\![\texttt{assert}(v), R, C, D, \phi, \alpha, pc, k]\!] = (ret, (ret = ()) \wedge \phi, R, C, D, (pc \implies (v \neq 0)) \wedge \alpha, \top)$
- $[\![M, R, C, D, \phi, \alpha, pc, \texttt{nil}]\!] = (ret, (ret = \texttt{dval}) \wedge \phi, R, C, D, \alpha \wedge (pc \implies \texttt{inil}), \bot)$
- $[\![v, R, C, D, \phi, \alpha, pc, k]\!] = (ret, (ret = v) \wedge \phi, R, C, D, \alpha, \top)$
- $[\![!r, R, C, D, \phi, \alpha, pc, k]\!] = (ret, (ret = D(r)) \wedge \phi, R, C, D, \alpha, \top)$
- $[\![\lambda x.M, R, C, D, \phi, \alpha, pc, k]\!] = (ret, (ret = m) \wedge \phi, R', C, D, \alpha, \top)$

  where $R' = R[m \mapsto \lambda x.M]$ and m fresh
- $[\![\pi_i v, R, C, D, \phi, \alpha, pc, k]\!] = (ret, (ret = \pi_i v) \wedge \phi, R, C, D, \alpha, \top)$
- $[\![v_1 \oplus v_2, R, C, D, \phi, \alpha, pc, k]\!] = (ret, (ret = v_1 \oplus v_2) \wedge \phi, R, C, D, \alpha, \top)$
- $[\![r := v, R, C, D, \phi, \alpha, pc, k]\!] = $ let $C' = C[r]$ in let $D' = D[r \mapsto C'(r)]$ in

  $(ret, ((ret = ()) \wedge (D'(r) = v)) \wedge \phi, R, C', D', \alpha, \top)$

Inductive Cases:

- $[\![\texttt{let } x = M \texttt{ in } M', R, C, D, \phi, \alpha, pc, k]\!] =$

  let $(ret_1, \phi_1, R_1, C_1, D_1, \alpha_1, pc_1) = [\![M, R, C, D, \phi, \alpha, pc, k]\!]$ in

  let $(ret_2, \phi_2, R_2, C_2, D_2, \alpha_2, pc_2) = [\![M'\{ret_1/x\}, R_1, C_1, D_1, \phi_1, \alpha_1, pc \wedge pc_1, k]\!]$ in

  $(ret_2, \phi_2, R_2, C_2, D_2, \alpha_2, pc_1 \wedge pc_2)$
- $[\![\texttt{letrec } f = \lambda x.M \texttt{ in } M', R, C, D, \phi, \alpha, pc, k]\!] =$

  let m be fresh in

  let $R' = R[m \mapsto \lambda x.M\{m/f\}]$ in $[\![M'\{m/f\}, R', C, D, \phi, \alpha, pc, k]\!]$
- $[\![m\, v, R, C, D, \phi, \alpha, pc, k]\!] =$

  let $R(m)$ be $\lambda x.N$ in $[\![N\{v/x\}, R, C, D, \phi, \alpha, pc, k-1]\!]$
- $[\![\texttt{if } v \texttt{ then } M_1 \texttt{ else } M_0, R, C, D, \phi, \alpha, pc, k]\!] =$

  let $(ret_0, \phi_0, R_0, C_0, D_0, \alpha_0, pc_0) = [\![M_0, R, C, D, \phi, \alpha, pc \wedge (v = 0), k]\!]$ in

  let $(ret_1, \phi_1, R_1, C_1, D_1, \alpha_1, pc_1) = [\![M_1, R_0, C_0, D, \phi_0, \alpha_0, pc \wedge (v \neq 0), k]\!]$ in

  let $C' = C_1[r_1] \cdots [r_n]\ (\Pi = \{r_1, \ldots, r_n\})$ in

  let $\psi_0 = (v = 0) \implies ((ret = ret_0) \wedge \bigwedge_{r \in \Pi}(C'(r) = D_0(r)))$ in

  let $\psi_1 = (v \neq 0) \implies ((ret = ret_1) \wedge \bigwedge_{r \in \Pi}(C'(r) = D_1(r)))$ in

  $(ret, \psi_0 \wedge \psi_1 \wedge \phi_1, R, C', C', \alpha_1, ((pc_0 \wedge (v = 0)) \vee (pc_1 \wedge (v \neq 0))))$
- $[\![x^\theta v, R, C, D, \phi, \alpha, pc, k]\!] =$

  if $R \upharpoonright \theta = \emptyset$ then $(ret, (ret = \texttt{dval}) \wedge \phi, R, C, D, \alpha, \bot)$ else

  let $R \upharpoonright \theta$ be $\{m_1, ..., m_n\}$ and (R, C, ϕ, α) be $(R_0, C_0, \phi_0, \alpha_0)$ in

  for each $i \in \{1, ..., n\}$:

  let $R(m_i)$ be $\lambda y_i.N$ in let $(ret_i, \phi_i, R_i, C_i, D_i, \alpha_i, pc_i) =$

  $\quad [\![N_i\{v/y_i\}, R_{i-1}, C_{i-1}, D, \phi_{i-1}, \alpha_{i-1}, pc \wedge (x = m_i), k-1]\!]$ in

  let $C'_n = C_n[r_1] \cdots [r_j]\ (\Pi = \{r_1, \ldots, r_j\})$ in

  let $\psi = \bigwedge_{i=1}^{n} \left((x = m_i) \implies ((ret = ret_i) \wedge \bigwedge_{r \in \Pi}(C'_n(r) = D_i(r))) \right)$ in

  let $pc'_n = \bigvee_{i=1}^{n} (pc_i \wedge (x = m_i))$ in $(ret, \psi \wedge \phi_n, R_n, C'_n, C'_n, \alpha_n, pc'_n)$

Fig. 3. The BMC translation.

Example 3. Consider the following program, where n is an open variable and the reference r is initialised to 0.

letrec f =
   λ x. **if** x **then** (r++; f (x − 1))
   else (λ y. **assert** (y = !r + x))
in let g = f n **in** g n

When applied to this code, using $k = 2$, the translation follows the steps depicted on the RHS diagram. Each rectangular box represents a recursive call of the translation. The code examined is placed on the top half of the box, while the updates in R, k, ϕ and α are depicted in the bottom half (e.g. $\phi : r_0 = 0$ means that we attach $r_0 = 0$ to ϕ as a conjunct). Rounded boxes, on the other hand, represent joining of branches spawned by conditional statements or by exhaustive method applica-

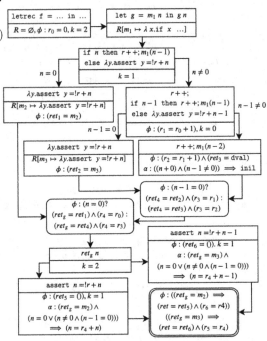

tion. In those boxes we include the updates to ϕ which encode the joining. The first two rounded boxes (single-lined) correspond to the joins of the two conditional statements examined. The last rounded box is where the branches spawned by examining $ret_g\, n$ are joined: ret_g could be either of m_2 or m_3. The resulting behaviour and assertions are given as follows.

$$\phi = (r_0 = 0) \wedge (ret_1 = m_2) \wedge (r_1 = r_0 + 1) \wedge (ret_2 = m_3) \wedge (r_2 = r_1 + 1) \wedge (ret_3 = \mathsf{dval})$$
$$\wedge ((n - 1 = 0)?((ret_4 = ret_2) \wedge (r_3 = r_1)) : ((ret_4 = ret_3) \wedge (r_3 = r_2)))$$
$$\wedge ((n = 0)?((ret_g = ret_1) \wedge (r_4 = r_0)) : ((ret_g = ret_4) \wedge (r_4 = r_3)))$$
$$\wedge (ret_5 = ()) \wedge (ret_6 = ()) \wedge ((ret_g = m_2) \implies (ret = ret_6) \wedge (r_5 = r_4))$$
$$\wedge ((ret_g = m_3) \implies (ret = ret_7) \wedge (r_5 = r_4))$$

$$\alpha = (((ret_3 = m_2) \wedge (n = 0 \vee (n \neq 0 \wedge (n - 1 = 0)))) \implies (n = r_4 + n))$$
$$\wedge (((ret_3 = m_3) \wedge (n = 0 \vee (n \neq 0 \wedge (n - 1 = 0)))) \implies (n = r_4 + n - 1))$$
$$\wedge (((n + 0) \wedge (n - 1 \neq 0)) \implies \mathsf{inil})$$

Bounded Model Checking with the Translation. The steps to do a k-bounded model checking of some initial configuration (M, R, S, k), where M has free ground-type variables $\vec{x}$, using the algorithm described previously are:

1. Build $init(M, R, S, k) = (M, R, C_S, C_S, \phi_S, \top, \top, k)$.
2. Compute the translation: $[\![M, R, C_S, C_S, \phi_S, \top, \top, k]\!] = (ret, \phi, R', C, D, \alpha, pc)$.
3. Check $\phi \wedge \mathsf{inil} \wedge \neg\alpha$ for satisfiability:

(a) If satisfiable, we have a model for $\phi \wedge \mathtt{inil} \wedge \neg\alpha$ that provides values for all open variables $\vec{x}$ and, therefore, a reachable assertion violation.
(b) Otherwise, check $\phi \wedge \neg\mathtt{inil} \wedge \neg\alpha$ for satisfiability. If satisfiable, the bound was breached. Otherwise, the program has been exhaustively explored with no errors, i.e. has been fully verified.

Remark 4. Note how bound breaches are regarded as assertion violations only if $\mathtt{inil}$ is false (so $\mathtt{inil}$ means: ignore nils). Analysing Example 3 for a fixed $k = 2$, we obtain $\phi \wedge \mathtt{inil} \wedge \neg\alpha$ unsatisfiable, but $\phi \wedge \neg\mathtt{inil} \wedge \neg\alpha$ satisfiable: we cannot violate an assertion, but our analysis is not conclusive as we breach the bound.

Soundness. Intuitively, soundness states that, within a given bound, the algorithm reports either an error or the possibility of exceeding the bound, if and only if a corresponding concrete execution within that bound exists such that the error is reached or the bound is exceeded respectively. Soundness of the algorithm depends on its correctness, which states that every reduction reaching a final value via the operational semantics is captured by the BMC translation.

We start off with some definitions. We first set $[\![M, R, S, k]\!] = [\![init(M, R, S, k)]\!]$. Moreover, an **assignment** $\sigma : \mathtt{Vars} \rightharpoonup \mathtt{CVals}$ is a finite map from variables to closed values. Given a term M, we write $M\{\sigma\}$ for the term obtained by applying σ to M. On the other hand, applying σ to a method repository R, we obtain the repository $R\{\sigma\} = \{m \mapsto R(m)\{\sigma\} \mid m \in dom(R)\}$ – and similarly for stores S. Then, given a valid configuration (M, R, S, k), we have $(M, R, S, k)\{\sigma\} = (M\{\sigma\}, R\{\sigma\}, S\{\sigma\}, k)$. Using program variables as logic variables, we can use assignments as logic assignments. Given a formula ϕ, we let $\sigma \models \phi$ mean that the formula $\phi\{\sigma\}$ is valid (its negation is unsatisfiable). We say σ **represents** ϕ, and write $\sigma \simeq \phi$, if $\sigma \models \phi$ and $\phi \implies x = \sigma(x)$ is valid for all $x \in dom(\sigma)$.

Theorem 5 (Soundness). *Given a valid configuration (M, R, S, k) whose open variables are of ground type, suppose $[\![M, R, S, k]\!] = (ret, \phi, R'', C, D, \alpha, pc)$. Then, for all assignments σ closing (M, R, S, k), 1 and 2 are equivalent:*

1. $\exists E, R', S'. (M, R, S, k)\{\sigma\} \twoheadrightarrow (E[\mathtt{assert}(0)], R', S', k')$
2. $\exists \sigma' \supseteq \sigma. \; \sigma' \models \phi \wedge \mathtt{inil} \wedge \neg\alpha.$

Moreover, if $\phi \wedge \mathtt{inil} \wedge \neg\alpha$ is not satisfiable then 3 and 4 are equivalent:

3. $\exists M', R', S'. (M, R, S, k)\{\sigma\} \twoheadrightarrow (M', R', S', \mathtt{nil})$
4. $\exists \sigma' \supseteq \sigma. \; \sigma' \models \phi \wedge \neg\mathtt{inil} \wedge \neg\alpha.$

Proof (sketch). (1) $\implies$ (2) and (3) $\implies$ (4) follow directly from Lemma 6 below. For the reverse directions, we rely on the fact that the semantics is bounded so, in every case, $(M, R, S, k)\{\sigma\}$ should either reach a value, or a failed assertion, or breach the bound. Moreover, the semantics is deterministic, in the sense that the final configurations reached may only differ in the choice of fresh names used in the process. This allows us to employ Lemma 6 also for the reverse directions. □

Lemma 6 (Correctness). *Given* $M, R, C, D, \phi, \alpha, pc, k, \sigma$ *such that* $\sigma \simeq \phi$, $(M, R, D, k)\{\sigma\}$ *is valid, and* $[\![M, R, C, D, \phi, \alpha, pc, k]\!] = (ret, \phi', R', C', D', \alpha', pc')$ *there exists* $\sigma' \supseteq \sigma$ *such that* $\sigma' \simeq \phi'$ *and:*

- *if* $(M, R, D, k)\{\sigma\} \twoheadrightarrow (v, \hat{R}, \hat{S}, \hat{k})$ *then* $\sigma' \vDash (pc \implies (pc' \wedge (ret = v))) \wedge ((\alpha \wedge pc) \implies \alpha'), R'\{\sigma'\} \supseteq \hat{R}$ *and* $D'\{\sigma'\} = \hat{S}$
- *if* $(M, R, D, k)\{\sigma\} \twoheadrightarrow (E[\texttt{assert}(0)], \hat{R}, \hat{S}, \hat{k})$ *then* $\sigma' \vDash (\texttt{inil} \wedge \alpha \wedge pc) \implies \neg \alpha'$
- *if* $(M, R, D, k)\{\sigma\} \twoheadrightarrow (\hat{M}, \hat{R}, \hat{S}, \texttt{nil})$ *then* $\sigma' \vDash (pc \implies \neg pc') \wedge ((\texttt{inil} \wedge \alpha \wedge pc) \implies \alpha') \wedge ((\neg\texttt{inil} \wedge \alpha \wedge pc) \implies \neg\alpha').$

Base Cases:

$PT(M, R, pt, nil) = (ret, \varnothing, R, pt)$ $PT(\langle v_1, v_2 \rangle, R, pt, k) = (ret, \langle pt(v_1), pt(v_2) \rangle, R, pt)$
$PT(m, R, pt, k) = (ret, \{m\}, R, pt)$ $PT(\lambda x.M, R, pt, k) = (ret, \{m\}, R[m \mapsto \lambda.M], pt)$
$PT(x, R, pt, k) = (ret, pt(x), R, pt)$ $PT(r := v, R, pt, k) = (ret, \varnothing, R, pt[r \mapsto pt(v)])$
$PT(!r, R, pt, k) = (ret, pt(r), R, pt)$ $PT(\pi_i \, v, R, pt, k) = (ret, \pi_i \, (pt(v)), R, pt)$
$PT(v_1 \oplus v_2, R, pt, k) = (ret, \varnothing, R, pt)$ $PT(v, R, pt, k) = (ret, \varnothing, R, pt)$ where $v = i, ()$
$PT(\texttt{assert}(v), R, pt, k) = (ret, \varnothing, R, pt)$

Inductive Cases:

$PT(\texttt{let } x = M \texttt{ in } M', R, pt, k) =$
   let $(ret_1, A_1, R_1, pt_1) = PT(M, R, pt, k)$ in $PT(M'\{ret_1/x\}, R_1, pt_1[ret_1 \mapsto A_1], k)$
$PT(\texttt{letrec } f = \lambda x.M \texttt{ in } M', R, pt, k) =$
   let m be fresh in $PT(M'\{m/f\}, R[m \mapsto \lambda x.M\{m/f\}], pt, k)$
$PT(m \, v, R, pt, k) = $ let $R(m)$ be $\lambda x.N$ in $PT(N\{v/x\}, R, pt, k - 1)$
$PT(\texttt{if } v \texttt{ then } M_1 \texttt{ else } M_0, R, pt, k) =$
   let $(ret_0, A_0, R_0, pt_0) = PT(M_0, R, pt, k)$ in
   let $(ret_1, A_1, R_1, pt_1) = PT(M_1, R_0, pt_b, k)$ in $(ret, A_0 \cup A_1, R_1, merge(pt_0, pt_1))$
$PT(x^\theta \, v, R, pt, k) =$
   let R be R_0 and $pt(x)$ be $\{m_1, ..., m_n\}$ in
   if $n = 0$ then $(ret, \emptyset, R_0, pt)$ else: for each $i \in \{1, ..., n\}$:
      let $R(m_i)$ be $\lambda y_i.N$ in let $(ret_i, A_i, R_i, pt_i) = PT(N_i\{v/y_i\}, R_{i-1}, pt, k - 1)$ in
      $(ret, A_1 \cup ... \cup A_n, R_n, merge(pt_1, \ldots, pt_n))$

Fig. 4. The points-to analysis algorithm.

4   A Points-To Analysis for Names

The presence of exhaustive method application in our BMC translation is a primary source of state space explosion. As such, a more precise filtering of R is necessary for scalability. In this section we describe a simple analysis to restrict the number of methods considered. We follow ideas from points-to analysis [2], which typically computes an overapproximation of the *points-to set* of each variable inside a program, that is, the set of locations that it may point to.

Our analysis computes the set of methods that may be bound to each variable while unfolding. We do this via a finite map $pt : (\text{Refs} \cup \text{Vars}) \rightharpoonup \text{Pts}$ where **Pts** contains all *points-to sets* and is given by: $\text{Pts} \ni A ::= X \mid \langle A, A \rangle$ where $X \subseteq_{fin} \text{Meths}$. Thus, a points-to set is either a finite set of names or a pair of points-to sets. These need to be updated whenever a method name is created, and are assigned to references or variables according to the following cases:

$$
\begin{array}{ll}
r := M & \text{add in pt: } r \mapsto pt(M) \\
\texttt{let } x = M \texttt{ in } M' & \text{add in pt: } x \mapsto pt(M) \\
xM & \text{add in pt: } ret(M) \mapsto pt(M)
\end{array}
$$

where $ret(M)$ is the variable assigned to the result of M. The **letrec** binder follows a similar logic. The need to have sets of names, instead of single names, in the range of pt is that the analysis, being symbolic, branches on conditionals and applications, so the method pointed to by a reference cannot be decided during the analysis. Thus, when joining after branching, we merge the pt maps obtained from all branches.

The points-to algorithm is presented in Fig. 4. Given a valid configuration (M, R, S, k), the algorithm returns $PT(M, R, S, k) = (ret, A, R, pt)$, where A is the points-to set of ret, and pt is the overall points-to map computed. The merge of points-to maps is given by:

$$
merge(pt_1, \ldots, pt_n) = \{x \mapsto \bigcup_i \hat{pt}_i \mid x \in \bigcup_i dom(pt_i)\}
$$

where $\hat{pt}_i(x) = pt_i(x)$ if $x \in dom(pt_i)$, $\emptyset$ otherwise, and $A \cup B$ is defined by $\langle A_1 \cup B_1, A_2 \cup B_2 \rangle$ if $A, B = \langle A_1, A_2 \rangle, \langle B_1, B_2 \rangle$, and just $A \cup B$ otherwise.

The Optimised BMC Translation. We can now incorporate the points-to analysis in the BMC translation to get an optimised translation which operates on symbolic configurations augmented with a points-to map, and returns:

$$
[\![M, R, C, D, \phi, \alpha, pc, pt, k]\!]_{PT} = (ret, \phi', R', C', D', \alpha, pc, A, pt')
$$

The optimised BMC translation is defined by lock-stepping the two algorithms presented above (i.e. $[\![\cdot]\!]$ and $PT(\cdot)$) and letting $[\![\cdot]\!]$ be informed from $PT(\cdot)$ in the xM case, which now restricts the choices of names for x to the set $pt(x)$. Its soundness is proven along the same lines as the basic algorithm.

To illustrate the significance of reducing the set of names, consider the program on the right which recursively generates names to compute triangular numbers. Without points-to analysis, since f creates a new method per call, and the translation considers all methods of matching type per recursive call, the number of names to apply at depth $m \le n$ when

```
letrec f = λ x.
   if x ≤ 0 then 0
   else let g = (λ y.x + y) in
     g (f (x−1))
in
letrec f' = λ x.if x ≤ 0 then 0
               else x + (f' (x−1))
in assert(f n = f' n)
```

translating $f(n)$ is approximately $m!$. This means that the number of paths explored grows by the factorial of n, with the total number of methods created being the left factorial sum $!n$. In contrast, $f'(n)$ only considers n names with a linear growth in number of paths. With points-to analysis, the number of names considered and created in f is reduced to that of f'.

5   Implementation and Experiments

We implemented the translation algorithm in a prototype tool to model check higher-order programs called BMC-2. The implementation and benchmarks can be found at: https://github.com/LaifsV1/BMC-2.

The tool takes program source code written in an ML-like language, and produces a propositional formula in SMT-LIB 2 format. This is then be fed to an SMT solver such as Z3 [7]. Syntax of the input language is based on the subset of OCAML that corresponds to HOREF. Differences between OCAML and our concrete syntax are for ease of parsing and lack of type checking. For instance, all input programs must be either written in "Barendregt Convention", meaning all bound variables must be distinct, and different from free variables. Additionally, all bound variables are annotated with types. Internally, BMC-2 implements an abstract syntax that extends HOREF with vector arguments and integer lists. This means that functions can take multiple arguments at once. Lists are handled for testing, but not discussed here as they are not relevant to the theory. BMC-2 itself was written in OCAML.

To illustrate our input language, on the right is sample program mc91-e from [15] translated from OCAML to our syntax. The keyword Methods is used to define all methods in the repository. The keyword Main is used to define the main method. For this sample program, our tool builds a translation with $k = 1$ for which Z3 correctly reports that the assertion fails if $n = 102$.

```
Methods:
mc91 (x:Int) :(Int) =
  if x >= 101 then x + −10
  else mc91 (mc91 (x + 11));
Main (n:Int) :(Unit):
  if n <= 102
  then assert((mc91 n)==91)
  else skip
```

Benchmarks. We tested our implementation on a set of 40 programs that include a selection from the MoCHi benchmark [15]. This is a set of higher-order programs written in OCAML, originally used to test the higher-order model checking tool MoCHi [15] and subsequently used for benchmarking [5,23,24]. We added custom samples with references (ref-1, ref-1-e, ref-2, ref-2-e, ref-3), as well as programs of varying lengths–100, 200 and 400 lines of code–constructed by combining the other samples. To combine programs, we refactored and concatenated methods and main methods from different files into a single file, and switch between the methods based on user input, thus forcing BMC-2 to consider all mains. In this set we have unsafe versions of safe programs denoted by the -e termination in their filename. Unsafe programs were constructed by slight modifications to the assertions of the original safe programs. For our experiment, the programs were manually translated to our input language and checked using our tool and Z3. Care was taken to keep all sample programs as close to the original source code as our concrete syntax allows. All experiments ran on an UBUNTU machine equipped with an Intel Core i7-6700 CPU clocked at 3.40 GHz and 16 GB RAM. All tests were set to time-out after 3 min, and up to a maximum bound $k = 15$. These limits were chosen due to the combinatorial nature of model checking and the sample programs used. BMC-2 ran twice per program per bound, and the average was recorded.

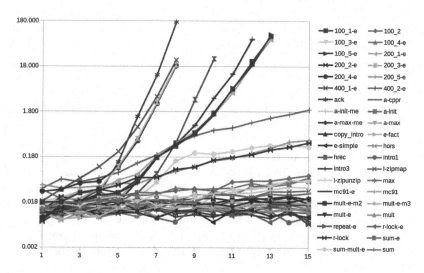

Fig. 5. Average execution time (s) for BMC-2 on bounds $k = 1..15$.

Figure 5 plots the average time taken for BMC-2 to check all the benchmark programs. We can observe that performance of BMC-2 heavily depends on the program it is checking, making the possibility of full verification entirely dependent on the nature of the program. For example, `ack`, which is an implementation of the Ackermann function, is a deeply recursive program that diverges rapidly, and thus cannot be translated by our algorithm any better than its normal growth. This agrees with the intuition that BMC is not appropriate to find bugs in deep recursion. As mentioned before, however, BMC has been shown to be effective on shallow bugs in industry. This can be seen with our examples for 100 to 400 lines of code, which were correctly shown to have bugs, with little difficulty despite the increase in program size.

In addition to testing BMC-2, we also ran comparison experiments on prior tools MoCHi [15] and ROSETTE [25]. All experiments ran on the same machine used to test BMC-2. These tools will be described in more detail in the following section. For ROSETTE, we used an implementation of our bounded semantics in ROSETTE provided to us by an anonymous reviewer. With the semantics implemented, we compare ROSETTE's symbolic execution of HOREF, to BMC-2 with Z3's translation and solving of the same terms.

Comparison with MoCHi. Though the goals of each tool are different, we attempted to compare our approach to MoCHi. Being unable to build from source, we decided to used the Docker-file on the UBUNTU machine from before. In Table 1, we have the time taken for BMC-2 and MoCHi for a smaller set of programs–the full range of results can be found in the tool page. We noticed that MoCHi is very sensitive to the operators and functions used in the assertions, while BMC-2 appears to be less dependent on these. For instance, checking mult-e with assert(mult m m <= mult n n) was three orders of magnitude slower than the original, while, at $k = 1$, BMC-2 takes 0.012 s; an increase of 20% from the original 0.010 s to find a bug. We

Table 1. Time taken (s) for BMC-2 ($k = 4..15$) and MoCHi, where $-$, c, m and u respectively indicate *time-out*, *crash*, *out-of-memory* and *unsupported*

	4	7	10	13	15	MoCHi
100_1-e	0.034	0.173	1.661	84.130	–	c
100_2	0.020	0.028	0.032	0.053	0.071	c
100_3-e	0.021	0.027	0.028	0.040	0.051	10.734
200_1-e	0.034	0.188	1.572	71.296	–	m
200_2-e	0.033	0.063	0.151	0.259	0.372	–
200_3-e	0.034	2.849	–	–	m	1.742
400_1-e	0.108	3.805	–	–	m	m
400_2-e	0.061	0.196	0.696	1.321	1.991	–
ack	0.027	11.519	–	–	–	0.525
a-cppr	0.031	0.020	0.026	0.027	0.028	28.584
a-init	0.018	0.016	0.032	0.042	0.053	c
e-fact	0.009	0.014	0.016	0.021	0.022	0.629
e-simple	0.010	0.008	0.007	0.009	0.009	0.098
hrec	0.020	0.075	26.175	–	–	0.867
r-lock-e	0.009	0.013	0.013	0.007	0.011	0.216
ref-2	0.013	0.008	0.011	0.012	0.010	u
ref-2-e	0.011	0.013	0.010	0.013	0.011	u
ref-3	0.019	0.018	0.047	0.211	0.211	u

also noticed that MoCHi is less consistent with larger programs. For 100 to 400 lines of code, MoCHi correctly found bugs in 4 out of 12 samples, but halted unexpectedly on the remaining 8. BMC-2 found all 11 bugs of the 12 programs, and found no bugs in the safe program. Finally, we included 5 examples with references, which BMC-2 correctly checked (MoCHi does not support state).

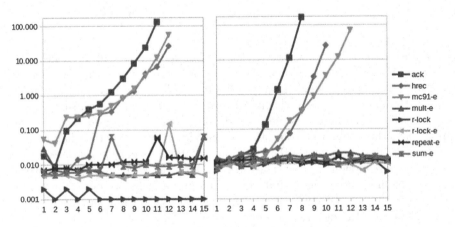

Fig. 6. Execution time (s) of $k = 1 \ldots 15$ for ROSETTE (left) and BMC-2 (right).

Comparison with ROSETTE for RACKET. We found that BMC-2 and ROSETTE are very similar in their ability to check higher-order programs. Since RACKET is a stateful higher-order language like HOREF, and ROSETTE employs a symbolic virtual machine with symbolic execution techniques for RACKET, we can expect this similarity. Fundamentally, ROSETTE and BMC-2 provide different approaches to verification as the former is related to symbolic evaluation, while the latter is a monolithic BMC translation. We were particularly interested in ROSETTE's ability to implement bounded verification for higher-order programs. With our bounding mechanism defined in ROSETTE, we compared its symbolic evaluation to BMC-2 on the UBUNTU machine. Figure 6 showcases this comparison. We found that ROSETTE and BMC-2 are comparable in scalability, with BMC-2 being less optimised for some diverging programs such as ack. This could be due to the way ROSETTE performs *type-driven state merging*, which provides opportunities for concretization. In contrast, we perform a suboptimal SSA transformation which could benefit from *dominance frontiers* for optimal merging of control flow. BMC, however, has the theoretical advantage of faster compilation time over symbolic execution [25]. Since testing in ROSETTE involves manually (re)translating our examples into RACKET, our comparison is based on a sample of 8 programs from the MoCHi benchmarks.

References

1. Amla, N., Kurshan, R., McMillan, K.L., Medel, R.: Experimental analysis of different techniques for bounded model checking. In: Garavel, H., Hatcliff, J. (eds.) TACAS 2003. LNCS, vol. 2619, pp. 34–48. Springer, Heidelberg (2003). https://doi.org/10.1007/3-540-36577-X_4
2. Andersen, L.O.: Program analysis and specialization for the C programming language. Ph.D. thesis, DIKU, University of Copenhagen, May 1994. (DIKU report 94/19)
3. Biere, A., Cimatti, A., Clarke, E., Zhu, Y.: Symbolic model checking without BDDs. In: Cleaveland, W.R. (ed.) TACAS 1999. LNCS, vol. 1579, pp. 193–207. Springer, Heidelberg (1999). https://doi.org/10.1007/3-540-49059-0_14
4. Boyer, R.S., Elspas, B., Levitt, K.: SELECT-a formal system for testing and debugging programs by symbolic execution. ACM SIGPLAN Not. **10**, 234–245 (1975)
5. Burn, T.C., Ong, C.L., Ramsay, S.J.: Higher-order constrained horn clauses for verification. In: PACMPL, 2(POPL), pp. 11:1–11:28 (2018)
6. Clarke, E., Kroening, D., Lerda, F.: A tool for checking ANSI-C programs. In: Jensen, K., Podelski, A. (eds.) TACAS 2004. LNCS, vol. 2988, pp. 168–176. Springer, Heidelberg (2004). https://doi.org/10.1007/978-3-540-24730-2_15
7. de Moura, L., Bjørner, N.: Z3: an efficient SMT solver. In: Ramakrishnan, C.R., Rehof, J. (eds.) TACAS 2008. LNCS, vol. 4963, pp. 337–340. Springer, Heidelberg (2008). https://doi.org/10.1007/978-3-540-78800-3_24
8. Dennis, G., Chang, F.S., Jackson, D.: Modular verification of code with SAT. In: Pollock, L.L., Pezzè, M. (eds.) Proceedings of the ACM/SIGSOFT International Symposium on Software Testing and Analysis, ISSTA 2006, Portland, Maine, USA, 17–20 July 2006, pp. 109–120. ACM (2006)
9. Dolby, J., Vaziri, M., Tip, F.: Finding bugs efficiently with a SAT solver. In: Crnkovic, I., Bertolino, A. (eds.) Proceedings of the 6th joint meeting of the European Software Engineering Conference and the ACM SIGSOFT International Symposium on Foundations of Software Engineering, Dubrovnik, Croatia, 3–7 September 2007, pp. 195–204. ACM (2007)
10. D'Silva, V., Kroening, D., Weissenbacher, G.: A survey of automated techniques for formal software verification. IEEE Trans. CAD Integr. Circ. Syst. **27**(7), 1165–1178 (2008)

11. Galeotti, J.P., Rosner, N., Pombo, C.G.L., Frias, M.F.: TACO: efficient SAT-based bounded verification using symmetry breaking and tight bounds. IEEE Trans. Softw. Eng. **39**(9), 1283–1307 (2013)
12. Howden, W.E.: Symbolic testing and the DISSECT symbolic evaluation system. IEEE Trans. Softw. Eng. **SE-3**, 266–278 (1977)
13. King, J.C.: A new approach to program testing. In: Proceedings of the International Conference on Reliable Software, pp. 228–233. ACM (1975)
14. Kobayashi, N.: Types and higher-order recursion schemes for verification of higher-order programs. In: Proceedings of the 36th Annual ACM SIGPLAN-SIGACT Symposium on Principles of Programming Languages, POPL 2009, pp. 416–428. ACM, New York (2009)
15. Kobayashi, N., Sato, R., Unno, H.: Predicate abstraction and CEGAR for higher-order model checking. In: Hall, M.W., Padua, D.A. (eds.) Proceedings of the 32nd ACM SIGPLAN Conference on Programming Language Design and Implementation, PLDI 2011, pp. 222–233. ACM (2011)
16. Morse, J., Ramalho, M., Cordeiro, L., Nicole, D., Fischer, B.: ESBMC 1.22. In: Ábrahám, E., Havelund, K. (eds.) TACAS 2014. LNCS, vol. 8413, pp. 405–407. Springer, Heidelberg (2014). https://doi.org/10.1007/978-3-642-54862-8_31
17. Near, J.P., Jackson, D.: Rubicon: bounded verification of web applications. In: Tracz, W., Robillard, M.P., Bultan, T. (eds.) 20th ACM SIGSOFT Symposium on the Foundations of Software Engineering (FSE-20), SIGSOFT/FSE 2012, Cary, NC, USA, 11–16 November 2012, p. 60. ACM (2012)
18. Nguyen, P.C., Horn, D.V. (eds.) Relatively complete counterexamples for higher-order programs. In: Grove, D., Blackburn, S. (eds.) Proceedings of the 36th ACM SIGPLAN Conference on Programming Language Design and Implementation, Portland, OR, USA, 15–17 June 2015, pp. 446–456. ACM (2015)
19. Ong, C.-H.L.: On model-checking trees generated by higher-order recursion schemes. In: 21st Annual IEEE Symposium on Logic in Computer Science (LICS 2006), pp. 81–90, August 2006
20. Rabinovitz, I., Grumberg, O.: Bounded model checking of concurrent programs. In: Etessami, K., Rajamani, S.K. (eds.) CAV 2005. LNCS, vol. 3576, pp. 82–97. Springer, Heidelberg (2005). https://doi.org/10.1007/11513988_9
21. Reynolds, J.C.: Definitional interpreters for higher-order programming languages. High. Order Symb. Comput. **11**(4), 363–397 (1998)
22. Rocha, W., Rocha, H., Ismail, H., Cordeiro, L., Fischer, B.: DepthK: A k-induction verifier based on invariant inference for C programs. In: Legay, A., Margaria, T. (eds.) TACAS 2017. LNCS, vol. 10206, pp. 360–364. Springer, Heidelberg (2017). https://doi.org/10.1007/978-3-662-54580-5_23
23. Sato, R., Unno, H., Kobayashi, N.: Towards a scalable software model checker for higher-order programs. In: Albert, E., Mu, S. (eds.) Proceedings of the ACM SIGPLAN 2013 Workshop on Partial Evaluation and Program Manipulation, PEPM 2013, pp. 53–62. ACM (2013)
24. Terao, T., Kobayashi, N.: A ZDD-based efficient higher-order model checking algorithm. In: Garrigue, J. (ed.) APLAS 2014. LNCS, vol. 8858, pp. 354–371. Springer, Cham (2014). https://doi.org/10.1007/978-3-319-12736-1_19
25. Torlak, E., Bodík, R.: A lightweight symbolic virtual machine for solver-aided host languages. In: O'Boyle, M.F.P., Pingali, K. (eds.) ACM SIGPLAN Conference on Programming Language Design and Implementation, PLDI 2014, Edinburgh, United Kingdom, 09–11 June 2014, pp. 530–541. ACM (2014)

Fault Trees from Data: Efficient Learning with an Evolutionary Algorithm

Alexis Linard[1,3]([⊠]), Doina Bucur[2], and Mariëlle Stoelinga[1,2]

[1] Institute for Computing and Information Science, Radboud University,
Nijmegen, The Netherlands
`a.linard@cs.ru.nl`
[2] University of Twente, Enschede, The Netherlands
`{d.bucur,m.i.a.stoelinga}@utwente.nl`
[3] KTH Royal Institute of Technology, Stockholm, Sweden

Abstract. Cyber-physical systems come with increasingly complex architectures and failure modes, which complicates the task of obtaining accurate system reliability models. At the same time, with the emergence of the (industrial) Internet-of-Things, systems are more and more often being monitored via advanced sensor systems. These sensors produce large amounts of data about the components' failure behaviour, and can, therefore, be fruitfully exploited to learn reliability models automatically. This paper presents an effective algorithm for learning a prominent class of reliability models, namely fault trees, from observational data. Our algorithm is evolutionary in nature; i.e., is an iterative, population-based, randomized search method among fault-tree structures that are increasingly more consistent with the observational data. We have evaluated our method on a large number of case studies, both on synthetic data, and industrial data. Our experiments show that our algorithm outperforms other methods and provides near-optimal results.

Keywords: Fault tree induction · Safety-critical systems ·
Cyber-physical systems · Evolutionary algorithm

1 Introduction

Reliability engineering is an important field that provides methods, tools and techniques to evaluate and mitigate the risks related to complex systems such as drones, self-driving cars, production plants, etc. Fault tree analysis is one of the most prominent technique in this field. It is widely deployed in the automotive, aerospace and nuclear industry, by companies and institutions like NASA, Ford, Honeywell, Siemens, the FAA, and many others.

This research is supported by the Dutch Technology Foundation (STW) under the Robust CPS program (project 12693), the EU project SUCCESS, the Smart Industries program (project SEQUOIA 15474), and the Wallenberg AI, Autonomous Systems and Software Program (WASP) funded by the Knut and Alice Wallenberg Foundation.

ⓒ Springer Nature Switzerland AG 2019
N. Guan et al. (Eds.): SETTA 2019, LNCS 11951, pp. 19–37, 2019.
https://doi.org/10.1007/978-3-030-35540-1_2

Fault trees [32] (FTs) belong to analytical techniques for safety, security, and dependability. They are graphical models that represent how component failures arise and propagate through the system, leading to system-level failures. Component failures are modelled in the leaves of the tree as *basic events*. Fault tree *gates* model how combinations of basic events lead to a system failure, represented by the top event in the FT. The analysis of such FTs [29] is multifold: they can be used to compute dependability metrics such as system reliability and availability; understand how systems can fail; identify the best ways to reduce the risk of system failure, etc. A key bottleneck in fault tree analysis is, however, the effort needed to construct a faithful fault tree model. FTs are usually built manually by domain experts. Given the complexity of today's systems, industrial FTs often contain thousands of gates. Hence, their construction is a very intricate task, and also error-prone, since their soundness and completeness largely depends on domain expertise. With the emergence of the industrial Internet-of-Things, Cyber-physical systems are more and more equipped with smart sensor systems, monitoring whether a system component is in a failed state or not. Even though such a monitoring system is often designed to detect failures during operations, their data can be very fruitfully deployed to learn reliability models. Such data can be crucial for the engineers to build an FT [14]. Recent work focused on learning FTs from observational data, identifying causalities from data [25].

In this paper, we focus on FT generation from data, using an evolutionary algorithm (EA). EAs approximate stochastic learning by mimicking biological evolution, and have been successfully applied to a wide plethora of applications; examples include the scheduling of flexible manufacturing systems [11], automata learning [10], induction of Boolean functions [28], and many more. In our case, each stage of the EA keeps a population of candidate FTs. New fault trees are generated by mimicking biological evolution. That is, new FTs are created by reproduction (e.g., adding or deleting FT gates), crossover (e.g. swapping FT branches), and mutation (e.g. changing an AND gate into an OR gate). In total, we have identified seven (parametric) generation rules, which are equally applied. Finally, we select the new population by only keeping those FTs with the best *fitness*, i.e. FTs that best fit to the observational data. We have experimentally verified the applicability of our algorithm, on synthetic data, an industrial case study, and a benchmark of FTs previously studied in the literature. Our experiments show that the algorithm is fast and accurate (>99%). Further, we have investigated the robustness of our method to noisy data. Here we found that our EA handles noisy records. We also developed a variation of our EA in order to take expert knowledge into account. When domain experts partially know the structure of the FT, then the task is reduced to evolve *sub*-Fault Trees, given the known *skeleton* of the FT.

Being a first step, our algorithm focuses on *static* fault trees, featuring only Boolean gates. An important topic for future work is the extension to dynamic fault trees. These come with additional gates, catering for common dependability patterns like spare management and functional dependencies. Static fault trees, however, have appeal as relatively simple yet powerful formalism and are often used in practice. Furthermore, dynamic fault trees strongly depend on the temporal order in which failures occur, and their learning will, therefore, require more complex data, such as time series.

This paper is organized as follows. Sections 2 and 3 review related work on learning FTs from data as well as preliminary definitions. We present then in Sect. 4 our technique to infer an FT using an EA. In Sect. 5, the variation of our EA that takes expert knowledge into account. In Sect. 6, we show the results we achieved. Finally, we discuss and conclude about further research. We refer to the full version of our paper for missing technical details.[1]

2 Related Work

Related work on learning fault trees spans three areas of research: the synthesis of fault trees from other graphical models of the system under study; recent work on the generation of fault trees from observational data describing the system; and, since fault trees are in essence Boolean functions, literature on learning Boolean functions from observational data.

Model-Based Synthesis. While state-of-the-art fault tree design is often performed manually by domain specialists [15], several methods have been proposed to synthesize FTs automatically from other models of the system [3,30]. Thus, these methods require the pre-construction of a system model in a suitable model description language, which varies with each method for FT synthesis. For example, the HiP-HOPS framework [27] synthesizes an FT from a system model describing transactions among the system components, annotated with failure information. Similar synthesis methods were developed from the AltaRica system description language, which models the causal relations between system variables and events using transitions [20]. Specific system control models in the form of directed graphs have also been shown to suit the synthesis of fault trees [1,12], as well as Go models [33]. Furthermore, system models described in the model language NuSMV also enable the synthesis of FTs. A limitation of this method is, however, the fact that the resulting FTs show the relation between top events and basic events, but do not show how failure propagates in the system via system components [4]. Static FTs can also be synthesized from models in the Architectural Analysis and Design Language AADL [21].

As a special case, FT generation has been attempted so that the learning method includes explicit reasoning about the causal relations between events in the system. For this type of FT generation, [18] requires a probabilistic system model, from which a model-checking step obtains a set of probabilistic counterexamples. When the system is concurrent, the order of events in these counterexamples does not necessarily signify causality, so logical combinations of events are separately validated for causality. Similarly, in [22] a cause-effect graph (and from that, an FT) is extracted by model checking a process already modelled by a finite-state machine, against safety and liveness requirements, using failure

---

[1] See http://arxiv.org/abs/1909.06258.

injection. Since model-based FT learning requires prior modelling of the system under study, these methods do not *adapt* well in applications where the systems evolve and thus need to be remodelled, e.g., components are replaced, or the interactions between components change, thus changing the failure modes and their probability of occurrence.

Learning Causal Models from Data. Supervised *automated learning* of dependability models using *system data*, unlike the model-based methods described above, will adapt to system change, under the assumption that all the system components remain monitored by sensors throughout their lifetime, also after a change of components. Here, we take "learning" to mean broadly any autonomous computational intelligence method able to infer (or even approximate) high-level models of knowledge from data. Causal Bayesian Networks [19] are standard graphical models which have been learnt from data examples. These models have straightforward translations into FTs, but are themselves NP-hard or require exponential time to synthesize accurately [8,16]. These networks will model a limited form of causality, namely global causal relationships, rather than a sequence of causal relationships among events local to the components of a system.

LIFT [25] is a recent approach for learning static FTs with Boolean event variables, n-ary AND/OR gates, annotated with event failure probabilities. The input to the algorithm is untimed observational data, i.e., a dataset where each row is a single observation over the entire system, and each column records the value of a system event. All intermediate events to be included in the FT must be present in the dataset, but not all may be needed in the FT, and a small amount of noise in the dataset can be tolerated. LIFT also includes a causal validation step (the Mantel-Haenszel statistical test) to filter for the most likely causal relationships among system events, but the worst-case complexity is exponential in the number of system events in the data. Its main advantage is that of being one of the few automated FT-learning methods which validate causality.

Learning Boolean Formulas and Classifiers from Data. Before LIFT, observational data were used to generate FTs with the IFT algorithm [24] based on standard decision-tree statistical learning. The advantage of learning a graphical decision tree out of data is the inherent interpretability of decision-tree models and their ease of translation into other graphical models. Boolean formulas or networks were also machine-learnt using a similar tree-based method [16,26]. The classic C4.5 learning algorithm yields a Boolean decision tree that is easily translatable into a Boolean formula by constructing the conjunction of all paths leading to a leaf modelling a True value (i.e., system failure), and then simplifying the Boolean function. The resulting models encode the same information as a decision tree (i.e., a classifier for the observational data), so lack the validation of causal relations, but are expected to preserve their predictive power about the system. This retained our attention: indeed, static FTs (in opposition to dynamic FTs, where time-dependence of events is considered) can be seen as Boolean functions. Furthermore, Boolean formulas were also

machine-learnt using black-box classifiers (namely, classifiers not easily inter-
pretable as a graphical model). Such methods include SVMs, Logistic Regression
and Naive Bayes.

We propose a novel algorithm to learn an FT that best (most accurately)
classifies records in a tabular dataset composed of observational tuples, in which
values (failures) for each Boolean basic event and Boolean top event in the system
are known. We compare it with these existing learning algorithm, in terms of its
performance when fitting data and robustness to noisy data.

3 Background

In this section, we first define the structure of a static FT (consisting of logic
gates, and also of intermediate events) and a dataset from which an FT is then
inferred. The formulations below follow definitions from [25].

FTs [32] are trees that model how component failures propagate to system
failures. Since subtrees can be shared, FTs are in fact directed acyclic graphs
(DAGs) rather than trees. Essentially, *intermediate events* in the FT are logical
combinations of other intermediate events, with only *basic events* (BE) as the
leaves of the tree, and one special intermediate event called the *top event* as
root. Gates model how BE failures lead to system failures. Standard fault trees
feature two types of gates: AND, and OR.

Definition 1. *A **gate** G is a tuple $(t, \boldsymbol{I}, O)$ such that:*

- *t is the type of G with $t \in \{And, Or\}$.*
- *$\boldsymbol{I}$ is a set of $n \geq 2$ intermediate events $\{i_1, \ldots, i_n\}$ that are inputs of G.*
- *O is the intermediate event that is the output of G.*

*We denote by $I(G)$ the set of intermediate events in the input of G and by
$O(G)$ the intermediate event in the output of G.*

Definition 2. *An **AND** gate is a gate $(And, \boldsymbol{I}, O)$ where output O occurs (i.e.
O is True) if and only if every $i \in \boldsymbol{I}$ occurs.*

Definition 3. *An **OR** gate is a gate $(Or, \boldsymbol{I}, O)$ where output O occurs (i.e. O
is True) if and only if at least one $i \in \boldsymbol{I}$ occurs.*

Definition 2 requires that all system components modelled by the events in
the input of the **AND** gate must fail in order for the system modelled by the
event in the output to fail. Similarly, Definition 3 requires that one of the system
components modelled by the events in the input of the **OR** gate must fail in
order for the system modelled by the event in the output to fail.

Definition 4. *A **basic event** B is an event with no input and one intermediate
event as output. We denote by $O(B)$ the intermediate event in the output of B.*

Sometimes other gates are considered, like the XOR (exclusive OR), the voting gate and the NOT gate [17,32]. For the sake of simplicity, we focus on the AND and OR gates; other gates can be treated in a similar fashion. The root of the tree is called the *top event* (T). The *top event* represents the failure condition of interest, such as the stranding of a train, or the unplanned unavailability of a satellite. Thus, a FT fails if its *top event* fails.

Definition 5. *A* **fault tree** *F is a tuple* ($\boldsymbol{BE}, \boldsymbol{IE}, T, \boldsymbol{G}$) *where:*

- $\boldsymbol{BE}$ *is the set of basic events;* $O(B) \in \boldsymbol{IE}$, $\forall B \in \boldsymbol{BE}$. *A basic event may be annotated with a probability of occurrence p.*
- $\boldsymbol{IE}$ *is the set of intermediate events.*
- *T is the top event,* $T \in \boldsymbol{IE}$.
- $\boldsymbol{G}$ *is the set of gates;* $I(G) \subset \boldsymbol{IE} \cup \boldsymbol{BE}$, $O(G) \in \boldsymbol{IE}$, $\forall G \in \boldsymbol{G}$.
- *The graph formed by* $\boldsymbol{G}$ *should be connected and acyclic, with the top event T as unique root.*

*We denote by IE(**F**) the set of intermediate events in **F** and by IE(G) the intermediate event corresponding to gate G.*

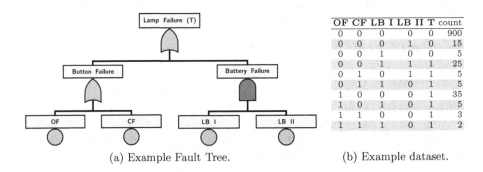

OF	CF	LB I	LB II	T	count
0	0	0	0	0	900
0	0	0	1	0	15
0	0	1	0	0	5
0	0	1	1	1	25
0	1	0	1	1	5
0	1	1	0	1	5
1	0	0	0	1	35
1	0	1	0	1	5
1	1	0	0	1	3
1	1	1	0	1	2

(a) Example Fault Tree.   (b) Example dataset.

Fig. 1. Example of Fault Tree and learning dataset.

We now define a data format from which we learn an FT, as a collection of records. Each record is a valuation for the set of BEs (variable that models the state of one basic, indivisible system component), indicating whether a *failure* was observed for that BE. We assume that our dataset is *labeled*, i.e., also indicates whether the top event T has failed, yielding the predicted outcome of the FT.

Definition 6. *A record R over the set of variables $\boldsymbol{V}$ is a list of length $|\boldsymbol{V}|$ containing tuples $[(V_i, v_i)], 1 \leq i \leq |\boldsymbol{V}|$ where V_i is a variable, $V_i \in V$ and v_i is a Boolean value of V_i.*

Definition 7. *A dataset **D** is a set of $|D|$ records, all over the same set of variables **V**. Each variable in **V** forms a column in **D**, and each record forms a row. When k identical records are present in **D**, a single such record is shown, with a new count column for the value k.*

Figure 1a shows a FT modeling a lamp failure. The top OR-gate shows that a lamp fails if there is either a button failure or a battery failure. A button failure happens if either an operator (**OF**) or a cable (**CF**) fails. The AND-gate indicates that battery failure happens if both batteries are low (**LB I** and **LB II**). Figure 1b shows a corresponding dataset.

4   Learning Fault Trees with Nature-Inspired Stochastic Optimization

Evolutionary algorithms (EAs) were among the earliest artificial intelligence methods, first envisioned by Alan Turing in 1950 [31]. EAs are heuristics that mimic biological evolution: one starts with an initial population, and iteratively generates new individuals through modification and recombination, where only the best individuals are kept in the next generation – mimicking survival of the fittest. EAs are particularly suitable to automatically learn models of some kind, such as trees, graphs or matrix structures, free-form equations, sets and permutations, and synthetic computer programs, etc. Evolutionary algorithms have been very successfully applied in several domains, ranging from antenna designs for spacecrafts [13], graph-like network topologies [5] and matrix-like robot designs [7].

The main challenges in devising EAs are (a) formalizing what is a syntactically correct *solution* to the problem (in our case, a well-formed fault tree), and (b) formalizing what makes, semantically, a solution better than another, i.e., writing a *fitness function* which takes any proposed solution and returns a numerical "goodness" for that solution. In our case, we want the fault tree to be consistent with the observational data. Hence the fitness function is the proportion of records correctly classified. Then, the EA will aim to *maximize* the fitness as close as possible to its optimal value of 100%. The EA consists of an iterative optimization process, which maintains a *population* of candidate solutions at each iteration, and randomly mutates and combines (i.e., applies *genetic operators* to) solutions from a population, such that the fitness of the *best solution* per population improves in time.

1. *Initialization*: The initial population contains two simple FTs; all variables in the input dataset **D** are represented as BEs in these FTs.
2. *Mutation and recombination*: Genetic operations are performed on the FTs and generate new FTs.
3. *Evaluation*: The fitness of each new FT is evaluated.
4. *Selection*: High-fitness FTs from the new generation replace low-fitness FTs from the previous generation.

5. *Termination*: Steps 2 to 4 are repeated until a given termination criterion is met. This can be if at least one solution in the population exceeds a given fitness bound, or if a given maximum number of iterations is reached. Upon termination, the best solution or solutions in the population are returned.

We describe these steps in more detail below.

4.1   Initialization

Our EA takes as input a dataset **D** and aims at computing an FT with maximal fitness to this dataset. The dataset yields the set of BEs, as well as the top level event T. We start with an initial population consisting of the following two FTs, where all BEs are connected to T via an AND and an OR gate respectively F_1 = $(\mathbf{BE}, \{T\}, T, \{(And, \mathbf{BE}, T)\})$ and $F_2 = (\mathbf{BE}, \{T\}, T, \{(Or, \mathbf{BE}, T)\})$, where $\mathbf{BE} \cup \{T\} = \mathbf{V}$, so all the basic events and the top event must be in the dataset **D**. These two FTs are the simplest structures including all the observational variables in the data, with an AND gate and an OR gate, respectively, at the top of the FT, and all BEs as inputs of this gate. These two individuals act as a seed population; later populations are larger in size. The population size is a setting depending on the nature of the FT to learn (namely, the number of BEs). Since the time complexity of the algorithm depends on the population size, increasing the population size may lead to scalability issues. It has also been shown in [6] that increasing the population size does not always perform as well as expected. In our experiments, we limit the population to hundreds of FTs.

4.2   Mutation and Recombination

We define seven stochastic genetic operators (one binary and six unary) which apply to FTs. For each iteration, each of the genetic operators operates on all individuals in the population with a given probability, to create new individuals. The order in which they are applied is randomized at each iteration.

G-create. Given the input FT $\mathbf{F} = (\mathbf{BE}, \mathbf{IE}, T, \mathbf{G})$, create a gate $G \notin \mathbf{G}$, randomly select its nature (AND or OR), then randomly select a gate $G' \in \mathbf{G}$. Randomly select inputs events I' of $I(G')$ to become inputs of G such that $I(G) = I'$ and $I(G') = I(G') \setminus I'$. Then, add $O(G)$ to the input events of G' such that $I(G') = I(G') \cup O(G)$. The new FT is $\mathbf{F} = (\mathbf{BE}, \mathbf{IE} \cup O(G), T, \mathbf{G} \cup \{G\})$ with $G \notin \mathbf{G}$.

G-mutate. Given the input FT $\mathbf{F} = (\mathbf{BE}, \mathbf{IE}, T, \mathbf{G})$, randomly select a gate $G \in \mathbf{G}$ and change its nature (AND to OR, or OR to AND).

G-delete. Given the input FT $\mathbf{F} = (\mathbf{BE}, \mathbf{IE}, T, \mathbf{G})$, randomly select a gate $G \in \mathbf{G}$ such that $O(G) \neq T$ and delete it. We set then, $I(G_p) = \bigcup_{i \in I(G)} IE_i$ such that $O(G) \in G_p$. The new FT is $\mathbf{F} = (\mathbf{BE}, \mathbf{IE} \setminus O(G), T, \mathbf{G} \setminus \{G\})$.

BE-disconnect. Given the input FT $\mathbf{F} = (\mathbf{BE}, \mathbf{IE}, T, \mathbf{G})$ and a randomly chosen basic event $B \in \mathbf{BE}$, disconnect B from its intermediate event $G = O(B)$. The new FT if $\mathbf{F} = (\mathbf{BE} \setminus \{B\}, \mathbf{IE}, T, \mathbf{G})$, where $B \notin I(G)$.

Note here that a gate G left with 0 or 1 input will not be removed: this is to preserve the solution search space and enable the connection of BEs to this gate. Only the genetic operator *G-delete* can remove such a gate.

BE-connect. Given the input FT $\mathbf{F} = (\mathbf{BE}, \mathbf{IE}, T, \mathbf{G})$ and a basic event $B \notin \mathbf{BE}$ and $B \in \mathbf{V} \setminus T$, randomly choose a gate $G \in \mathbf{G}$ and connect B to the input of G. The new FT is $\mathbf{F} = (\mathbf{BE} \cup \{B\}, \mathbf{IE}, T, \mathbf{G})$, where $B \in I(G)$. Note that this operator is essentially the inverse of **BE-disconnect**. The relevance of this operator lies in the fact that some FTs in the population may not contain as many BEs as variables $\mathbf{V}$ in the dataset. Also, our definition of this operator implies that no BE will be input to 2 different gates. However, the connection of the same BE to 2 different gates can occur within a *crossover* operation.

BE-swap. Given the input FT $\mathbf{F} = (\mathbf{BE}, \mathbf{IE}, T, \mathbf{G})$ and a randomly chosen basic event $B \in \mathbf{BE}$ and a randomly chosen gate $G \in \mathbf{G} \setminus O(B)$, disconnect B from $O(B)$ and connect B to G.

Crossover. The crossover operator takes two FTs as input and swaps at random two of their subtrees. This leads to two new FTs, where the first fault tree contains the selected subtree of the second fault tree and vice versa. More precisely, one selects at random an intermediate event $IE_1 \in \mathbf{IE_1}$ from the first fault tree $\mathbf{F_1}$, and one also selects at random an intermediate event $IE_2 \in \mathbf{IE_2}$ from the section fault tree. Then one replaces in $\mathbf{F_1}$ the subtree under $\mathbf{IE_1}$ by the subtree under $\mathbf{IE_2}$. Similarly, one replaces in $\mathbf{F_2}$ the subtree under $\mathbf{IE_2}$ by the subtree under $\mathbf{IE_1}$. Given two input FTs $\mathbf{F_1} = (\mathbf{BE_1}, \mathbf{IE_1}, T_1, \mathbf{G_1})$ and $\mathbf{F_2} = (\mathbf{BE_2}, \mathbf{IE_2}, T_2, \mathbf{G_2})$, randomly select an $IE_1 \in \mathbf{IE_1}$ and $IE_2 \in \mathbf{IE_2}$. Then, we set $I(O(IE_1)) = I(O(IE_1)) \setminus IE_1 \cup IE_2$ and $I(O(IE_2)) = I(O(IE_2)) \setminus IE_2 \cup IE_1$. Finally, $O(IE_1) = O(IE_2)$ and vice versa.

4.3   Evaluation

We define the *fitness* of an FT as the number of records in the dataset for which the value of the top event, given the values of the BEs, is correctly computed. The count of a record, i.e. the number of appearances, give more weight in the fitness function to records that occur often. In this way, noisy data can be better handled, which often happen in real life applications.

Definition 8. *The fitness of a fault tree is its accuracy w.r.t. the dataset $\mathbf{D}$ s.t.*

$$f = \frac{\sum\limits_{r \in D} x}{\sum\limits_{r \in D} k} \quad where \quad \begin{cases} x = k \text{ if } V[T] = P[T] \\ x = 0 \qquad otherwise \end{cases}$$

*where P[T] stands for the predicted value of the top event given the dataset **D** for a given FT, V[T] the real value of the top event and k the number of occurrences of the record r.*

4.4 Selection

The selection strategy of the best individuals to undergo genetic operations is essential to increase the improvement rate of the fitness of the population. Commonly used strategies are roulette wheel, stochastic universal sampling, tournament and random selections. In all our experiments, we use an elitist strategy. The nature of the individuals motivates this choice: best-fitted FTs are the closest in the population to the optimal solution. They consist of Boolean gates and BEs, which means that a least fitted solution needs more genetic operations to become optimal. We thus hope that mutating the best FTs will be less costly in terms of iterations of the EA in order to converge towards the right solution.

4.5 Termination

The decision of whether to return the best FTs in the actual population or to continue the evolutionary process follows the termination criteria. In our experiments, we used the standard termination criteria, which are:

1. at least one solution in the population achieves an accuracy of 1, which means a perfect fitness to the data.
2. a maximum number of allowed iterations is reached.
3. convergence: no improvement of the best FT in the population has been observed for a given number of iterations.

Note that several runs of our EA may return different FTs with the same fitness, especially in terms of structure. Indeed, two FTs with a different structure may be semantically equivalent; FTs, like Boolean formulas, can be factorized to Disjunctive Normal Form (DNF, where a Boolean formula is standardized as a disjunction of conjunctive clauses) or to Conjunctive Normal Form (CNF, where a Boolean formula is standardized as a conjunction of disjunctive clauses). As a result, it may happen that all variables in the dataset do not appear in the FT since they are either not needed or not relevant. In our experiments, we chose to compute the CNF of the best-fitted FT. The transformation of an FT into a CNF is based on the following rules: the double negative law, De Morgan's laws, and the distributive law.

5 Learning of Partial Fault Trees

A fruitful application of learning fault trees is the learning of partial models, where domain experts partially know the structure of the FT, and other parts need to be inferred from data. In this way expert knowledge and data-driven approaches are aggregated. To accommodate this approach, we propose here a variation of our EA. We parameterize our EA with such a partially known structure as input to the algorithm. The task for the EA is then to evolve *sub-Fault Trees*, given the known *skeleton* of the FT. The initial population becomes then the partial structures given as input. Genetic operators are slightly modified to ensure the given skeletons to remain unmodified in each mutated FT. We gather at any moment of the evolutionary process a population composed of FTs containing the allowed skeleton. In this section, we detail the initialization and the genetic operators to take into account the expert knowledge provided as a *skeleton* FT.

5.1   Initialization

In the same way as the procedure described in Sect. 4, our evolutionary algorithm takes as input a dataset $\mathbf{D}$, as well a known FT-*skeleton* F_o. We start then with an initial population consisting of this FT-*skeleton*:

$$F_o = (\mathbf{BE_o}, \mathbf{IE_o}, T_o, \mathbf{G_o})$$

where $\mathbf{BE_o}$ are BEs contained in the skeleton, $\mathbf{IE_o}$ are the intermediate events of the skeleton, T_o is the top event of the skeleton and $\mathbf{G_o}$ is the set of gates contained in the skeleton. This is this structure given as input that will remain in all mutated FTs all along the evolutionary process.

5.2   Mutation and Recombination

In order to preserve the FT-*skeleton* during mutation and recombination operations, we have to adapt the following genetic operators.

G-create-o. Given the input FT $\mathbf{F} = (\mathbf{BE}, \mathbf{IE}, T, \mathbf{G})$, create a gate $G \notin \mathbf{G}$, randomly select its nature (AND or OR), then randomly select a gate $G' \in \mathbf{G}$. Randomly select inputs events I' of $I(G') \setminus \mathbf{IE_o}$ to become inputs of G such that $I(G) = I'$ and $I(G') = I(G') \setminus I'$. Then, add $O(G)$ to the input events of G' such that $I(G') = I(G') \cup O(G)$. The new FT is $\mathbf{F} = (\mathbf{BE}, \mathbf{IE} \cup O(G), T, \mathbf{G} \cup \{G\})$ with $G \notin \mathbf{G}$. In that way, we allow the creation of a gate such that its input events are not in the gates of the skeleton, that is, the skeleton remains unchanged.

G-mutate-o. Given the input FT $\mathbf{F} = (\mathbf{BE}, \mathbf{IE}, T, \mathbf{G})$, randomly select a gate $G \in \mathbf{G} \setminus \mathbf{G_o}$ and change its nature (AND to OR, or OR to AND).

G-delete-o. Given the input FT $\mathbf{F} = (\mathbf{BE}, \mathbf{IE}, T, \mathbf{G})$, randomly select a gate $G \in \mathbf{G} \setminus \mathbf{G_o}$ such that $O(G) \neq T$ and delete it. We set then, $I(G_p) = \bigcup_{i \in I(G)} IE_i$ such that $O(G) \in G_p$.

BE-disconnect-o. Given the input FT $\mathbf{F} = (\mathbf{BE}, \mathbf{IE}, T, \mathbf{G})$ and a randomly chosen basic event $B \in \mathbf{BE} \setminus \mathbf{BE_o}$, disconnect B from its intermediate event $G = O(B)$. The new FT if $\mathbf{F} = (\mathbf{BE} \setminus \{B\}, \mathbf{IE}, T, \mathbf{G})$, where $B \notin I(G)$.

BE-swap-o. Given the input FT $\mathbf{F} = (\mathbf{BE}, \mathbf{IE}, T, \mathbf{G})$ and a randomly chosen basic event $B \in \mathbf{BE} \backslash \mathbf{BE_o}$ and a randomly chosen gate $G \in \mathbf{G} \backslash O(B)$, disconnect B from $O(B)$ and connect B to G.

Crossover-o. Given two input FTs $\mathbf{F_1} = (\mathbf{BE_1}, \mathbf{IE_1}, T_1, \mathbf{G_1})$ and $\mathbf{F_2} = (\mathbf{BE_2}, \mathbf{IE_2}, T_2, \mathbf{G_2})$, randomly select an $IE_1 \in \mathbf{IE_1} \backslash \mathbf{IE_o}$ and $IE_2 \in \mathbf{IE_2} \backslash \mathbf{IE_o}$. Then, we set $I(O(IE_1)) = I(O(IE_1)) \backslash IE_1 \cup IE_2$ and $I(O(IE_2)) = I(O(IE_2)) \backslash IE_2 \cup IE_1$. Finally, $O(IE_1) = O(IE_2)$ and vice versa.

Note that the scenario where expert guidance is used to lead to faster convergence of the FT learning algorithm is realistic: indeed, this variation is helpful to refine existing FTs, or checking if a handmade model is accurate given real-world measurements.

6   Experimental Evaluation

We have evaluated the efficiency and effectiveness of our EA method using a large number of cases. We compared our methods with six other learning techniques: five approaches from the literature, and the variant of our own EA technique for learning partial fault trees. For these methods, we investigated both the accuracy and as well as runtime. Our comparisons were performed for a set of synthetic cases (Sects. 6.2 and 6.3), as well as for industrial benchmarks (Sects. 6.4 and 6.5).

6.1   Experimental Set Up

The first three methods in our evaluation are: (1) Support Vector Machine (abbreviated svm in the figures), (2) Logistic Regression (abbreviated log) and (3) Naive Bayes Classifier (nba). These methods are Boolean classifiers that, given the values of the BEs, predict the value of the top event T. Being classifiers, methods (1)–(3) do not yield FT models, only a prediction for the value of T.

Then, we have used three methods that do learn fault tree models: (4) We have compared our results to the well-known C4.5 algorithm for learning decision trees (abbreviated c45). Decision trees can be transformed to FTs, by first computing in the decision tree the conjunction of all paths leading to failure leaves, and then simplifying the conjunction to CNF. (5) We have also compared to the earlier LIFT approach, which re returns an FT. (6) Finally, we used the variation of the EA for learning partial fault trees (ea-p). Here, we assumed that the two upper layers of the fault trees were fixed.

To compare these methods, the observational data was divided into two sets: one training set, used as input to the EA (with an average of 2/3 of all possible observations), and a test set containing all observational variables (complete boolean table), used to evaluate the solution returned by our algorithms. The parameters of the EA were set as follows: we used a population size of 100. As termination criteria, we used either a maximum number of 100 iterations or an observed convergence (i.e. no improvement of the best individual's fitness) over 10 iterations or an FT with fitness 1 (optimal solution) in the population. Each genetic operator was applied with probability 0.9 in order to increase the mutation rate of the population. The selection and replacement strategy were elitists, to systematically replace least-fitted individuals in the old population by the best individuals in the union of the old population and the set of newly generated individuals. Finally, to homogenize several runs of the EA, the conjunctive normal form (CNF) of the best FT was returned in the termination step. Note that our Python implementations and dataset are available[2], and that we used state-of-the-art implementations of the scikit-learn library for techniques (1)–(5).

6.2   Synthetic Dataset: Accuracy and Runtime

We have first used a large synthetic case. We considered 100 randomly generated fault trees with 6 to 15 BEs, and for each FT, a randomly generated data set, with 200 to 230k records. Figures 2a and b present respectively the average accuracy and the average runtime, both as functions of the number of BEs. Figure 2a shows that the svm and c45 methods have the highest accuracy. However, the svm method only provides a classifier, not a fault tree. Further, the c45 method does not perform well in terms of runtime, see Fig. 2b. Our methods EA and EA-p perform reasonably well in terms of accuracy, as well as in term of run time. Finally, the log and nba method are fast but provide low accuracy. We also see that LIFT obtains less good results. An exponential complexity can explain this, and the fact LIFT requires data about intermediate events.

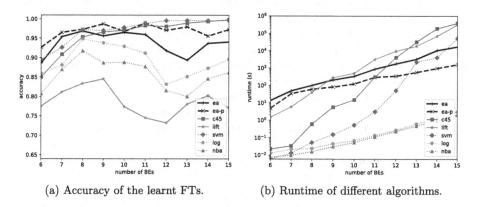

(a) Accuracy of the learnt FTs.   (b) Runtime of different algorithms.

Fig. 2. Comparison of different learning algorithms.

We can also see that the more the FTs contain BEs, the more it is complicated to gather a solution with perfect fitness w.r.t. the training set. This is due to the

---

[2] https://gitlab.science.ru.nl/alinard/learning-ft.

significant number of iterations needed to converge to an optimal solution when dealing with a large number of BEs. However, we can see that expert knowledge is extremely beneficial in the case of ea-p, where the skeleton of the FT is given. It enables us to learn more accurate FTs (accuracy > 95%) and faster (up to 10 times faster than the baseline EA).

6.3   Synthetic Dataset: Other Statistics

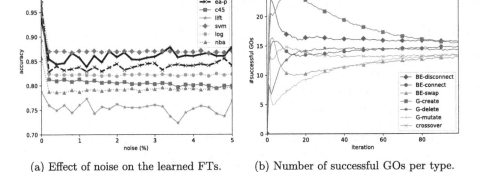

(a) Effect of noise on the learned FTs.   (b) Number of successful GOs per type.

Fig. 3. Statistics on genetic algorithm.

We also carried out an experiment where noise is added in the dataset, in order to test the robustness of the different algorithms. The noise varies from 0 to 5% of noisy records. We call a *noisy* record one where the value of at least one variable has been changed, i.e. measured incorrectly in real life. In the results shown in Fig. 3a, we see that our methods are relatively robust against noise compared to other methods. However, we see that the accuracy of the learned FTs drops whenever noise is present in the dataset.

Further, we also investigated which genetic operations were successful, as a function of the number of iterations, shown in Fig. 3(b). The latter is computed by looking at, for each iteration, the number of individuals issued from the same genetic operator who survived in the next generation, i.e. whose fitness was good enough to be kept in the population. We see that the success of most operations depends on the stage of the EA: this is the case for *BE-disconnect*, and *G-create*, which provide satisfying new individuals during the first iterations of the algorithm. An explanation is that *G-create* will increase the size of the FT, i.e. its complexity. Then, the search space of the solution is increased. In opposition to these gates, *G-mutate* seems to be a less good operator since the number of individuals issued from it tends not to survive in the population. This is mainly due to the change of semantics this operator implies: indeed, when the depth of the mutated gate is small (i.e. close to the top event), the meaning of the resulting FT may drastically change. Hence a small number of successful operations of this type.

6.4   Case Study with Industrial Dataset

We present here an industrial case study based on the dataset from [23]. We consider here a component called the nozzle. The system containing the nozzles records large amounts of data about the state of the components over time, among them the failing of nozzles and nozzle-related factors. The dataset is composed of 9,000 records, 8 basic events being nozzles-related factors and a Boolean top event, standing for nozzle failure. We ran our genetic algorithm 10 times, with a maximum allowed iterations of 100 (convergence criterion of 10), and the fitness of the best FT learnt was of 0.997 (split ratio for train/test set of 80/20). The resulting FT has been validated by domain experts. Even in a practical context, multiple runs of the EA may return different (possibly equivalent) FTs, with different structures. Depending on the applications, expert knowledge can figure out whether one or the other returned FT is the most relevant to the case study. To help the selection process, one can place additional constraints on the FT, such as the number of children.

6.5   Fault Tree Benchmark

We present here the results we obtained for a set of publicly available benchmark suite[3], consisting of industrial fault trees from the literature, containing from 6 to 14 BEs and 4 to 10 gates. The FTs used are Cardiac Assist System (CAS), Container Seal Design Example (CSD), Multiprocessor Computing System (MCS), Monopropellant Propulsion System (MPS), Pressure Tank (PT), Sensor Filter Network (SF14) and Spread Mooring System (SMS_A1). Whereas the fault tree models were given in the literature, no data sets were available. Therefore, we have randomly generated these data sets, containing 10M records per case, in order to cope with low failure rates. Since the benchmark does provide failure probabilities per BEs, we have used those probabilities: If p_e is the failure probability of BE e in the benchmark, then we set, in each data record, $R[e] = 1$ with probability p_e. Figure 4a and b present the accuracy and runtime, respectively. Missing bars stand for experiments for which no result could have been obtained within 1 week of running time. We can see that for all case studies, our method is either the most or the second most efficient. We also see that in all cases, our method is among the most accurate methods.

7   Discussion

Extensions. The definition of gates and genetic operators can be extended. We show how to deal with **K/N** gates, which are gates of type $(k/N, \mathbf{I}, O)$ where

---

[3] https://dftbenchmarks.utwente.nl/.

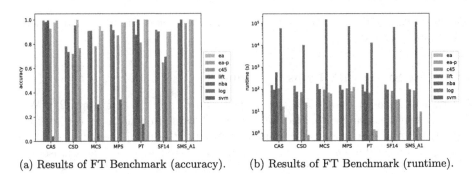

(a) Results of FT Benchmark (accuracy).   (b) Results of FT Benchmark (runtime).

Fig. 4. Results of Fault Tree Benchmark.

output O occurs (i.e. O is True) if at least k input events $i \in \mathbf{I}$ occurs, with $|\mathbf{I}| = N$. The cardinality of a k/N gate is said to be the number k. Note that this gate can be replaced by the OR of all sets of k inputs, but the use of k/N gates is much more compact for the representation of a FT. We can then define new genetic operators, such as **k-n-change** where, given an input FT $\mathbf{F} = (\mathbf{BE}, \mathbf{IE}, T, \mathbf{G})$, randomly select a k/N gate $G \in \mathbf{G}$ and change its cardinality, such that $k \in [1, N-1]$. We also extend the mutate gate operator of **G-mutate**, as follows: Given an input FT $\mathbf{F} = (\mathbf{BE}, \mathbf{IE}, T, \mathbf{G})$, randomly select a gate $G \in \mathbf{G}$ and change its nature (AND to OR or k/N; OR to AND or k/N; k/N to OR or AND). Similarly, we can redefine the create gate operator **C-create** such that the randomly selected nature of the new gate is chosen among AND, OR or k/N.

Our formalism can also handle **NOT** gates so that the FTs can become non-monotonic.

Limitations. While we can accurately learn small fault trees, the main limitation of our method at the moment is scalability. While other techniques, especially naive Bayesian classifiers, score well, techniques that learn models experience slower performance. Therefore, a solution may be to combine both methods. We can also use better heuristics on which GO to deploy, and with what parameters. Such ideas were also the key to the success of EAs in other application domains. The result obtained by the EA does not ensure a perfect fitness of the FT with regards to the data. This is the case when a maximal number of iteration has been reached, and the best FT in the population returned. Hence the near-optimality of our algorithm. In addition, multiple runs of the EA may return different (possibly equivalent) FTs, with different structures. We leave for further work the discovery of which of the returned FT is right, based on the data, figuring out causal relationships between variables using Mantel-Haenszel Partial Association score [2]. Another limitation lies in the growing size of the FTs after iterations: this may lead to overgrown FTs. However, we think that the best fit individuals may be compacted when returned: indeed, some gates in the FTs may contain none of only one input, and some factorization can be applied. We thus recommend performing FT reduction on the returned FTs, such as the calculation of CNFs or DNFs. A first alternative would be to reduce to CNF or DNF the FTs in the population at each iteration of the EA. However, this would drastically reduce the search space of the EA (e.g. by making fewer mutations/recombinations possible, hence leading to a lower fitness) and go against genetic programming principles. A second alternative would be to take into account the size of the solutions as a second fitness function for the selection step. The implementation of such a multi-objective EA [9] is left for further work.

In all cases, learning FTs from an already known *skeleton* FT may suffer less from overgrown FTs after several iterations: the *skeleton* may give, indeed, already enough information on the structure of the FT. Thus, it helps the algorithm to converge faster to a solution.

8   Conclusion and Future Work

We presented an evolutionary algorithm for the automated generation of FTs from Boolean observational data. We defined a set of genetic operators specific to the formalism of FTs. Our results show the robustness and scalability of our algorithm. Our future research will focus on the learning of dynamic FTs, and especially trying to learn their specific gates such as PAND, FDEP and SPARE gates. We will also further look into Bayesian Inference and translating rules from Bayesian Networks to FTs. We also hope to take into account different failure modes of components thanks to INHIBIT gates. Finally, since there are many possible (i.e. logically equivalent) alternatives to an FT, we would like to investigate further what are the features of a good FT. In other words, we think that we need to characterize how much better a particular FT structure is compared to another.

References

1. Allen, D.J.: Digraphs and fault trees. Ind. Eng. Chem. Fundam. **23**(2), 175–180 (1984)
2. Birch, M.: The detection of partial association, i: the 2×2 case. J. R. Stat. Soc. Ser. B (Methodological) **26**, 313–324 (1964)
3. Bozzano, M., Bruintjes, H., Cimatti, A., Katoen, J.-P., Noll, T., Tonetta, S.: COMPASS 3.0. In: Vojnar, T., Zhang, L. (eds.) TACAS 2019. LNCS, vol. 11427, pp. 379–385. Springer, Cham (2019). https://doi.org/10.1007/978-3-030-17462-0_25
4. Bozzano, M., Villafiorita, A.: The FSAP/NuSMV-SA safety analysis platform. Int. J. Softw. Tools Technol. Transf. **9**(1), 5 (2007)
5. Bucur, D., Iacca, G., Squillero, G., Tonda, A.: The impact of topology on energy consumption for collection tree protocols: an experimental assessment through evolutionary computation. Appl. Soft Comput. **16**, 210–222 (2014)
6. Chen, T., Tang, K., Chen, G., Yao, X.: A large population size can be unhelpful in evolutionary algorithms. Theor. Comput. Sci. **436**, 54–70 (2012)

7. Cheney, N., MacCurdy, R., Clune, J., Lipson, H.: Unshackling evolution: evolving soft robots with multiple materials and a powerful generative encoding. In: Proceedings of the 15th Annual Conference on Genetic and Evolutionary Computation, pp. 167–174. ACM (2013)
8. Chickering, D.M., Heckerman, D., Meek, C.: Large-sample learning of Bayesian networks is NP-hard. J. Mach. Learn. Res. **5**, 1287–1330 (2004)
9. Deb, K., Agrawal, S., Pratap, A., Meyarivan, T.: A fast and elitist multiobjective genetic algorithm: NSGA-II. IEEE Trans. Evol. Comput. **6**(2), 182–197 (2002)
10. Dupont, P.: Regular grammatical inference from positive and negative samples by genetic search: the GIG method. In: Carrasco, R.C., Oncina, J. (eds.) ICGI 1994. LNCS, vol. 862, pp. 236–245. Springer, Heidelberg (1994). https://doi.org/10.1007/3-540-58473-0_152
11. Geiger, C.D., Uzsoy, R., Aytuğ, H.: Rapid modeling and discovery of priority dispatching rules: an autonomous learning approach. J. Sched. **9**(1), 7–34 (2006)
12. Henry, J., Andrews, J.: Computerized fault tree construction for a train braking system. Qual. Reliab. Eng. Int. **13**(5), 299–309 (1997)
13. Hornby, G., Globus, A., Linden, D., Lohn, J.: Automated antenna design with evolutionary algorithms. In: Space 2006, p. 7242 (2006)
14. Joshi, A., Gavriloiu, V., Barua, A., Garabedian, A., Sinha, P., Khorasani, K.: Intelligent and learning-based approaches for health monitoring and fault diagnosis of RADARSAT-1 attitude control system. In: 2007 IEEE International Conference on Systems, Man and Cybernetics, pp. 3177–3183 (2007)
15. Kabir, S.: An overview of fault tree analysis and its application in model based dependability analysis. Expert Syst. Appl. **77**, 114–135 (2017)
16. Kearns, M., Li, M., Valiant, L.: Learning boolean formulas. J. ACM **41**(6), 1298–1328 (1994)
17. Lee, W.S., Grosh, D.L., Tillman, F.A., Lie, C.H.: Fault tree analysis, methods, and applications: a review. IEEE Trans. Reliab. **34**(3), 194–203 (1985)
18. Leitner-Fischer, F., Leue, S.: Probabilistic fault tree synthesis using causality computation. Int. J. Crit. Comput. Based Syst. **4**(2), 119–143 (2013)
19. Li, J., Shi, J.: Knowledge discovery from observational data for process control using causal bayesian networks. IIE Trans. **39**(6), 681–690 (2007)
20. Li, S., Li, X.: Study on generation of fault trees from Altarica models. Procedia Eng. **80**, 140–152 (2014)
21. Li, Y., Zhu, Y., Ma, C., Xu, M.: A method for constructing fault trees from AADL models. In: Calero, J.M.A., Yang, L.T., Mármol, F.G., García Villalba, L.J., Li, A.X., Wang, Y. (eds.) ATC 2011. LNCS, vol. 6906, pp. 243–258. Springer, Heidelberg (2011). https://doi.org/10.1007/978-3-642-23496-5_18
22. Liggesmeyer, P., Rothfelder, M.: Improving system reliability with automatic fault tree generation. In: Digest of Papers. Twenty-Eighth Annual International Symposium on Fault-Tolerant Computing, pp. 90–99 (1998)
23. Linard, A., Bueno, M.L.P.: Towards adaptive scheduling of maintenance for cyber-physical systems. In: Margaria, T., Steffen, B. (eds.) ISoLA 2016. LNCS, vol. 9952, pp. 134–150. Springer, Cham (2016). https://doi.org/10.1007/978-3-319-47166-2_9
24. Madden, M.G., Nolan, P.J.: Generation of fault trees from simulated incipientfault case data. WIT Trans. Inf. Commun. Technol. **6** (1994)
25. Nauta, M., Bucur, D., Stoelinga, M.: LIFT: learning fault trees from observational data. In: McIver, A., Horvath, A. (eds.) QEST 2018. LNCS, vol. 11024, pp. 306–322. Springer, Cham (2018). https://doi.org/10.1007/978-3-319-99154-2_19

26. Oliveira, A.L., Sangiovanni-Vincentelli, A.: Learning complex Boolean functions: algorithms and applications. In: Advances in Neural Information Processing Systems, pp. 911–918 (1994)
27. Papadopoulos, Y., McDermid, J.: Safety-directed system monitoring using safety cases. Ph.D. thesis, University of York (2000)
28. Park, M.S., Choi, J.Y.: Logical evolution method for learning Boolean functions. In: 2001 IEEE International Conference on Systems, Man and Cybernetics. e-Systems and e-Man for Cybernetics in Cyberspace, vol. 1, pp. 316–321 (2001)
29. Ruijters, E., Stoelinga, M.: Fault tree analysis: a survey of the state-of-the-art in modeling, analysis and tools. Comput. Sci. Rev. **15–16**, 29–62 (2015)
30. Sharvia, S., Kabir, S., Walker, M., Papadopoulos, Y.: Model-based dependability analysis: state-of-the-art, challenges, and future outlook. In: Software Quality Assurance, pp. 251–278. Elsevier (2016)
31. Turing, A.M.: Computing machinery and intelligence. In: Epstein, R., Roberts, G., Beber, G. (eds.) Parsing the Turing Test, pp. 23–65. Springer, Dordrecht (2009). https://doi.org/10.1007/978-1-4020-6710-5_3
32. Vesely, W.E., Goldberg, F.F., Roberts, N.H., Haasl, D.F.: Fault tree handbook. Technical report, Nuclear Regulatory Commission Washington DC (1981)
33. Zhang, Y., Ren, Y., Liu, L., Wang, Z.: A method of fault tree generation based on go model. In: 2015 First International Conference on Reliability Systems Engineering (ICRSE), pp. 1–5. IEEE (2015)

Simplifying the Analysis of Software Design Variants with a Colorful Alloy

Chong Liu, Nuno Macedo[(✉)], and Alcino Cunha

INESC TEC and Universidade do Minho, Braga, Portugal
nuno.m.macedo@inesctec.pt

Abstract. Formal modeling and automatic analysis are essential to achieve a trustworthy software design prior to its implementation. Alloy and its Analyzer are a popular language and tool for this task. Frequently, rather than a single software artifact, the goal is to develop a full *software product line* (SPL) with many variants supporting different features. Ideally, software design languages and tools should provide support for analyzing all such variants (e.g., by helping pinpoint combinations of features that could break a property), but that is not currently the case. Even when developing a single artifact, support for multi-variant analysis is desirable to explore design alternatives. Several techniques have been proposed to simplify the implementation of SPLs. One such technique is to use background colors to identify the fragments of code associated with each feature. In this paper we propose to use that same technique for formal design, showing how to add support for features and background colors to Alloy and its Analyzer, thus easing the analysis of software design variants. Some illustrative examples and evaluation results are presented, showing the benefits and efficiency of the implemented technique.

Keywords: Formal software design · Variability · Alloy

1 Introduction

Formal methods are crucial in the development of high-assurance software. Their role in early development phases is well established, for example to check the consistency of formally specified requirements before proceeding to design, or that a formal model of the intended design satisfies desirable properties before proceeding to implementation. Among the myriad of formal methods proposed, *lightweight* ones – which rely on automatic analyses to verify (often partial) specifications – are quite popular. That is the case of model checkers like NuSMV [4] or SPIN [13], for verifying temporal logic properties of (behavioral) designs (modeled as transition systems), or model finders like Alloy [14], more geared towards verifying first-order properties of structural designs specified at a high level of abstraction (using simple mathematical concepts like sets and relations).

When developing large-scale software systems it is common to adopt the paradigm of *feature-oriented software development* [2], which organizes software

N. Guan et al. (Eds.): SETTA 2019, LNCS 11951, pp. 38–55, 2019.
https://doi.org/10.1007/978-3-030-35540-1_3

around the key concept of *feature*, a unit of functionality that satisfies some of the requirements and that originates a configuration option. If the implementation is properly decomposed, it is possible to deliver many variants of the system just by selecting the desired features. The set of all those variants is usually called a *software product line* (SPL). Ideally, the design of SPLs should already explicitly take features into account, and formal methods should be adapted to support such *feature-oriented design* [3]. In fact, even when developing a single software product, it is still convenient to explicitly consider features and multi-variant analysis during design to support the exploration of different design alternatives.

Most techniques to organize software implementation around features fall into one of two categories: *compositional* approaches implement features as distinct modules, and some sort of module *composition* technique is defined to generate a specific software variant; *annotative* approaches implement features with explicit (or sometimes implicit) annotations in the source code, that dictate which code fragments will be present in a specific variant. The former are well suited to support coarse-grained extensions, for example adding a complete new class to implement a particular feature, but not to support fine-grained extensions, for example adding a sentence to a method or change the expression in a conditional, to affect the way a code fragment works with different features [15]. Annotative approaches are much better suited for such fine-grained variability points.

Unfortunately, explicit support for feature-oriented design in formal methods, providing a uniform formalism for feature, architectural and behavioral modeling as advocated for SPL engineering [19], is still scarce. Support for features in model checking has been proposed, namely a compositional approach for the SMV modeling language of NuSMV [18] and an annotative approach for the Promela modeling language of SPIN [5]. For structural design, a compositional approach has been proposed to explicit support features in Alloy [3]. Typically, modeling and specifying in Alloy is done at high levels of abstraction, and adding a feature can require only minimal and very precise changes (e.g., adding one new relation to the model or changing part of the specification of a desired property). Compositional approaches such as [3] are not well suited for these fine-grained extensions. This paper addresses precisely this problem, proposing an annotative approach to add explicit support for features to Alloy and its Analyzer.

A classic annotative approach for source code is the use of `#ifdef` and `#endif` C/C++ compiler preprocessor directives to delimit code fragments that implement a specific feature. Unfortunately, such annotation style obfuscates the code and makes it hard to understand and maintain, leading to the well-known `#ifdef` hell [11]. To alleviate this problem, while retaining the advantages of annotative approaches, Kästner et al. [15] proposed to annotate code fragments associated with different features with different background colors, which was later shown to clearly improve SPL code comprehension and be favored by developers [11]. Given these results, we propose to use such annotative technique to support features in Alloy. Our main contribution is thus a colorful extension to Alloy and its Analyzer, that allows users to annotate model and specification fragments with different background colors (denoting different features), and run analysis commands to verify either a particular variant, or several variants at

```
1   fact FeatureModel {
2     // ④ requires ③
3     ④ some none ④ }
4
5   sig StoredModel {
6     ① derivationOf : lone StoredModel ①,
7     public        : lone Link,
8     ② secret       : lone Link ②,
9     ③ command      : lone Command ③ }
10
11  ② sig Secret in StoredModel {} ②
12
13  sig Link {}
14
15  ③ sig Command {} ③
16
17  ③④ sig Instance {
18    instanceOf : one Command,
19    model      : set StoredModel,
20    link       : one Link } ④ ③
21
22  fact {
23    // Links are not shared between artifacts
24    all l : Link | one (public+ ② secret ② + ③ link ③ ).l
25    // All models have public links, unless commands are stored
26    ③ all m : StoredModel | one m.public ③
27    // The model derivations form a forest
28    ① no m : StoredModel | m in m.^derivationOf ①
29    // Private and public links must be different
30    ② all m : StoredModel | m.public != m.secret ②
31    ... }
32
33  run {some command} with ③ for 3
34  run {some command} with exactly ②, ③ for 3
35
36  assert OneDerivation {
37    // Stored models without a public link can have at most one derivation
38    ① all m : StoredModel | no m.public implies lone derivationOf.m ① }
39  check OneDerivation with ① for 3
```

Fig. 1. Alloy4Fun specification in colorful Alloy.

once, of the design, simplifying the detection of feature combinations that may fail to satisfy the desired specification. To the best of our knowledge, this is the first color-based annotative approach for feature support in a formal method.

The paper is organized as follows. The next section presents an overview of the proposed approach using a simple case study. Section 3 formally presents the new language extension, including the typing rules for the annotations, and Sect. 4 the extensions to the Alloy engine to support multi-variant analysis. Section 5 evaluates the flexibility of the language and the efficiency of the new multi-variant analysis engine using various examples. Section 6 discusses related work. Finally, Sect. 7 concludes the paper, presenting ideas for future work.

2   Overview

Alloy4Fun [17] is a web-platform[1] developed by our team for learning Alloy and sharing models. Besides the online creation, analysis and sharing of models,

---

[1] alloy4fun.inesctec.pt.

Alloy4Fun has two additional goals: to provide a kind of auto-grading feature by marking certain parts of the model as secret, and to collect information regarding usage patterns and typical pitfalls when modeling in Alloy.

Modeling. The structure of an Alloy[2] model is defined by declaring *signatures* and *fields* (of arbitrary arity) within them, possibly with multiplicity constraints. A hierarchy can be imposed on signatures, either through extension or inclusion. These are combined into relational expressions using standard relational and transitive closure operators. Basic formulas over these expressions either compare them or perform simple multiplicity tests, and are combined using first-order logic operators. *Predicates* and *functions* represent re-usable formulas and expressions, respectively. Additional axioms are introduced through *facts*, and properties which are to be checked through *asserts*. In colorful Alloy, parts of the model can be associated with a positive annotation – selecting the feature introduces the element, colored background – or a negative annotation – selecting a feature removes the element, colored strike-through. Both positive and negative annotations can be nested, in which case the colors are mixed. Following the results of [11], we chose colors that would reduce visual fatigue.

Figure 1 depicts an excerpt of the encoding of the Alloy4Fun design variants in colorful Alloy. The base variant (i.e., the parts without annotations) simply stores models when shared by the user, and is thus comprised by stored models (**sig** StoredModel, l. 5) assigned to at most one public link (**sig** Link, l. 11, through field public with **lone** multiplicity, l. 7). Two additional constraints are enforced (by a **fact**, l. 22): a link is assigned to exactly **one** stored model (l. 24) and every stored model has a public link assigned to it (l. 26). To this base, 4 features can be added:

① to collect usage patterns, the derivation tree of the stored models is registered, introducing a new field (derivationOf, l. 6) and an additional constraint to avoid cyclic dependencies (using transitive closure, l. 28);

② stored models can have secrets defined (**sig** Secret as a subset of StoredModel, l. 11), and as a consequence, have private links generated when shared so that they can be recovered (field secret, l. 8); a new constraint forces public and private links to be distinct (l. 30) and the existing constraint on links is relaxed to allow links to be private (l. 24);

③ models are also stored when commands are executed (**sig** Command, l. 14), rather than just when shared by the user, allowing finer data collection; the command that originated such models is also stored (field command, l. 9); moreover, the constraint on the existence of public links is removed (l. 26), since stored models created through command execution are shared;

④ instances (**sig** Instance, l. 17) resulting from command execution can also be stored and shared; the constraint on links (l. 24) is relaxed, which may now point to stored instances (field link, l. 20) rather than just stored models.

Feature-oriented software development is usually accompanied by a *feature model* denoting which feature combinations are acceptable. In our example, instances

---

[2] For a thorough presentation of the Alloy language and the Analyzer, please see [14].

are associated to the commands that created them, so feature 4 requires feature 3. This is enforced by a fact (l. 1) that guarantees that invalid variants are unsatisfiable: if feature 4 without feature 3, an inconsistent formula is imposed (**some none**, since Alloy does not support Boolean constants). Feature models are easily translated into propositional logic [9], and are expected to be simple and easy to encode as this kind of facts at the level of abstraction that (colorful) Alloy is employed. Exploring whether dedicated support to encode feature models is needed is left for future work.

Analysis. Once the colorful Alloy model is defined, the user can instruct the Analyzer to generate scenarios for which a certain property holds through *run* commands, or instruct it to find counter-examples to a property expected to hold through *check* commands. These are assigned a scope, denoting the maximum size to be considered for the model's signatures. The colorful Analyzer supports an additional scope on the variants that should be explored: a set of (positive and negative) feature presence conditions is provided, and analysis will either consider all variants or the smallest variant for which those conditions hold.

In our example, the run in l. 33 allows the user to explore scenarios with stored commands in all 8 variants where feature 3 is selected (without feature 3 command does not exist, so a type error would be thrown). This will generate an arbitrary instance for one of those variants; the user can then ask for succeeding solutions which may vary in variant or in scenario (more controlled enumeration is work in progress). A tighter scope provides a finer control on the explored variants, as the run in l. 34 for the 4 variants with features 2 and 3, which the Analyzer will report as unsatisfiable. This was due to a bug in the constraint on secret links (l. 30), which does not hold when stored models are created from command execution (a possible fix is to enforce instead **all** m : StoredModel | **no** m.public&m.secret). Such issue could go unnoticed without variant-focused analysis since it arises from the interaction of 2 features.

After exploring scenarios, the user can start checking desirable properties. The assert in l. 36 specifies a property that could be expected to hold for all variants that allow derivation trees: if a stored model has no public link, then at most one stored model is derived from it. Through the check in l. 39 for all variants with feature 1, the Analyzer quickly shows that is not the case, generating a counter-example in a variant with features 1, 2 and 3, where command execution allows two stored models to derive the same ancestor. An analysis focused on individual variants could miss this possible issue arising from the interaction of features 1 and 3. Figure 2 presents an overview of the colorful Alloy Analyzer for this scenario, with its editor with feature annotations, and its visualizer with the counter-example and a panel denoting to which variant it belongs.

Discussion. Using regular Alloy, the user would have two alternative ways of encoding these design variants. One would be to try to encode in a single Alloy model all conditional structures and behaviors that the design may have, using a signature (e.g., Variant) to denote which features are under consideration.

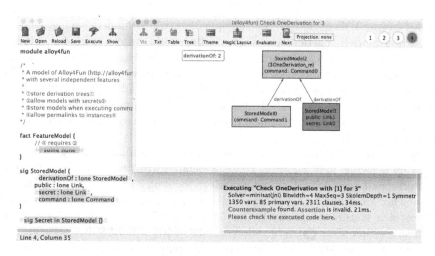

Fig. 2. Counter-example to `OneDerivation`.

This quickly renders the Alloy model intractable, particularly in annotations of small granularity. For instance, the expression in l. 24 could be encoded like

```
public + (F2 in Variant implies secret else none → none) +
(F3 + F4 in Variant implies link else none → none)
```

which can quickly become impenetrable and unmanageable.

The other alternative would be to rely on the Alloy module system and define variants as separate modules that import common elements. Modules are completely included when imported, meaning that existing elements cannot be removed or changed. As a consequence, a base module with the non-annotated parts cannot be extended with fields in existing signatures, requiring less intuitive workarounds. For instance, a module for feature 2 could add signature `Command` with the (arguably less intuitive) inverted field `secret` declared in it; for feature 1, adding field `derivationOf` would require the introduction of a "dummy" singleton signature with a field of type `StoredModel → StoredModel`. Negative annotations are even more troublesome, since they would have to be added by all modules except the ones that would remove them, which quickly becomes unmanageable. These issues are handled by the compositional approach implemented in FeatureAlloy [3], that allows the insertion of fields in existing signatures, as well as replacing existing paragraphs. However, handling variability points of fine granularity is still difficult to manage. For instance, the constraint in l. 24 not only would have to be fully replaced by features 2 and 4, but a new feature merging those two features would have to be created due to feature interaction.

3 Language

One of the reasons behind the initial proposal of color annotations was to avoid obfuscating the code with additional constructs [15]. There, colors are internally handled by the IDE developed for that purpose, which hinders saving, sharing and editing models, particularly when dealing with simple, single-file, models as is typical in Alloy. Our approach aims at a middle ground, using minimal annotations that are colored when using the Analyzer, but that can still be saved and interpreted as a pure text file. Additionally, unlike [15], our language allows elements to be marked with the absence of features. Thus, although not allowing full propositional formulas, elements can be assigned a conjunction of positive/negative literals.

The colorful Alloy language is thus a minimal extension to regular Alloy mainly by allowing, first, elements to be associated with the presence or absence of features; and second, analysis commands to focus on particular sets of features. Features are identified by circled symbols, $ⓒ$ and $●$, denoting the presence and absence of a feature, respectively, for $1 \leq c \leq 9$ (throughout the paper, $ⓒ$ will denote either $ⓒ$ or $●$). This allows models with at most 9 distinct features, which we believe to be adequate since the colorful approach is known to be better suited for models with a small number of features [11], and our own experiments never relied on more than 6 features. Figure 3 presents the syntax of colorful Alloy, highlighting changes with regard to the regular Alloy language.

Features are associated to model elements by using feature marks as delimiters surrounding those elements. An element within a positive delimiter $ⓒ$ will only exist in variants where c is selected, while those within negative delimiters $●$ only exist if c is absent from the variant. Color annotations can be nested, denoting the conjunction of presence conditions (e.g., ④ ❸ **some none** ❸ ④ in Fig. 1, l. 3, **some none** will be present in any variant with feature 4 selected but not feature 3). Likewise [15], only elements of the Alloy AST can be annotated. Thus, features cannot be assigned, for instance, to operators. Another consequence is that the model stripped down of its color marks is still a valid Alloy AST itself.[3] In general, any node whose removal does not invalidate the AST can be marked with features, including all global declarations (i.e., signatures, fields, facts, predicates, functions and asserts) and individual formulas within blocks. The marking of local declarations (i.e., predicate and function arguments, and quantified variables) is left as future work. One exception to the AST validity rule is allowed for binary expressions with a neutral element, in which case the sub-expressions can be annotated even if the whole binary expression is not. For instance, `public+②link②` is interpreted as `public+(none → none)` in variants where feature 2 is not selected.

Run and check commands can then be instructed to focus, possibly **exactly**, on certain features using a **with** scope: if not exact, commands will consider every variant where the scope features are present/absent; otherwise, exactly the variant with the presence features will be considered (negative features are spurious in that case). For instance, **run{} with** ①,❷ will consider every variant with feature 1 selected but not feature 2, while **run {} with exactly** ①,❷ will only consider the variant with exactly feature 1 selected. An additional feature

---

[3] We actually force the stripped model to be a valid Alloy model, forbidding, for instance, declarations with the same identifier associated with different feature sets.

```
spec    ::= module qualName [ [ name,+ ] ] import* paragraph*
import  ::= open qualName [ [ qualName,+ ] ] [ as name ]
paragraph ::= colPara | cmdDecl
colPara ::= ©ₓ colPara ©ₓ | sigDecl | factDecl | funDecl | predDecl | assertDecl
sigDecl ::= [ abstract ] [ mult ] sig name,+ [ sigExt ] { colDecl,* } [ block ]
sigExt  ::= extends qualName | in qualName [ + qualName ]*
mult    ::= lone | some | one
decl    ::= [ disj ] name,+ : [ disj ] expr
colDecl ::= ©ₓ colDecl ©ₓ | decl
factDecl ::= fact [ name ] block
assertDecl ::= assert [ name ] block
funDecl ::= fun name [ [ decl,* ] ] : expr block
predDecl ::= pred name [ [ decl,* ] ] block
expr    ::= const | qualName | @name | this | unOp expr | expr binOp expr
          | colExpr colBinOp colExpr | expr arrowOp expr | expr [ expr,* ]
          | expr [ ! | not ] compareOp expr | expr ( ⇒ | implies ) expr else expr
          | quant decl,+ blockOrBar | ( expr ) | block | { decl,+ blockOrBar }
colExpr ::= ©ₓ colExpr ©ₓ | expr
const   ::= none | univ | iden
unOp    ::= ! | not | no | mult | set | ~ | * | ^
binOp   ::= ⇔ | iff | ⇒ | implies | − | ++ | <: | :> | .
colBinOp ::= || | or | && | and | + | &
arrowOp ::= [ mult | set ] → [ mult | set ]
compareOp ::= in | =
letDecl ::= name = expr
block   ::= { colExpr* }
blockOrBar ::= block | | expr
quant   ::= all | no | mult
cmdDecl ::= [ check | run ] [ qualName ] ( qualName | block ) [ colScope ] [ typeScopes ]
typeScopes ::= for number [ but typeScope,+ ] | for typeScope,+
typeScope ::= [ exactly ] number qualName
colScope ::= with [ exactly ] [ ⊗ | ©ₓ ],+
qualName ::= [ this/ ] ( name/ )* name
```

Fig. 3. Concrete syntax of the colorful Alloy language (additions w.r.t. the Alloy syntax are colored red). (Color figure online)

mark $\otimes$ denotes the empty variant (no features selected), and can be used to analyze every possible variant (if not exact, the default behavior if no color scope is provided) or solely the base variant (if exact).

The grammar of the language restricts which elements can be annotated, but additional type checking rules must be employed to guarantee consistent colorful models. These are formalized in Figs. 4 and 5 for a kernel of expressions and paragraphs, respectively, to which the remainder language features can be converted (except comprehension, omitted for simplicity). Expression arity is also considered, since this is the only rule enforced by the type system of regular Alloy. For a mark, $\neg \text{©}$ converts between the positive and negative version; **c** denotes a set of marks; and $\lfloor \mathbf{c} \rfloor$ expands **c** with all marks **©** such that $\text{©} \notin \mathbf{c}$. The context of the type rules is a mapping Γ from variables to the color (and arity) of their declaration, and a set of marks **c** under which it is being evaluated. We denote a singleton mapping as $v \mapsto (\mathbf{c}, n)$ for a variable v, marks **c** and arity n, while ++ denotes the overriding of mappings. An expression (or declaration) e of arity n is well-typed if $\Gamma, \mathbf{c} \vdash_n e$ (arity 0 denotes formulas), and a paragraph p if $\Gamma, \mathbf{c} \vdash p$. A set of marks **c** is valid, $\vdash \mathbf{c}$, if it does not contain contradictory

$$\frac{\square \in \{\textbf{none},\textbf{univ}\}}{\Gamma,\mathbf{c}\vdash_1 \square} \qquad \frac{}{\Gamma,\mathbf{c}\vdash_2 \textbf{iden}} \qquad \frac{v \mapsto (\mathbf{r},n) \in \Gamma \quad \mathbf{r}\subseteq \mathbf{c}}{\Gamma,\mathbf{c}\vdash_n v}$$

$$\frac{\Gamma,\mathbf{c}\vdash_n e \quad n>0}{\Gamma,\mathbf{c}\vdash_n {}^\wedge e} \qquad \frac{\Gamma,\mathbf{c}\vdash_2 e}{\Gamma,\mathbf{c}\vdash_2 \sim e} \qquad \frac{\Gamma,\mathbf{c}\vdash_0 e}{\Gamma,\mathbf{c}\vdash_0 \textbf{not } e} \qquad \frac{\Gamma,\mathbf{c}\vdash_0 e_1 \quad \Gamma,\mathbf{c}\vdash_0 e_2}{\Gamma,\mathbf{c}\vdash_0 e_1 \textbf{ and } e_2}$$

$$\frac{\Gamma,\mathbf{c}\vdash_n e_1 \quad \Gamma,\mathbf{c}\vdash_n e_2 \quad n>0}{\Gamma,\mathbf{c}\vdash_0 e_1 \textbf{ in } e_2} \qquad \frac{\Gamma,\mathbf{c}\vdash_n e_1 \quad \Gamma,\mathbf{c}\vdash_n e_2 \quad n>0 \quad \square \in \{\&,+,-\}}{\Gamma,\mathbf{c}\vdash_n e_1 \,\square\, e_2}$$

$$\frac{\Gamma,\mathbf{c}\vdash_n e_1 \quad \Gamma,\mathbf{c}\vdash_m e_2 \quad k=n+m-2 \quad n,m,k>0}{\Gamma,\mathbf{c}\vdash_k e_1 \,.\, e_2}$$

$$\frac{\Gamma,\mathbf{c}\vdash_n e_1 \quad \Gamma,\mathbf{c}\vdash_m e_2 \quad k=n+m \quad n,m>0}{\Gamma,\mathbf{c}\vdash_k e_1 \to e_2}$$

$$\frac{\Gamma,\mathbf{c}\vdash_1 d \quad \Gamma,\mathbf{c}+\!\!+ v \mapsto (\emptyset,1)\vdash_0 e}{\Gamma,\mathbf{c}\vdash_0 \textbf{all } v:d \mid e} \qquad \frac{\Gamma,\mathbf{c}\vdash_n e \quad \neg\,\textcircled{c}\notin \mathbf{c}}{\Gamma,\mathbf{c}\cup\{\textcircled{c}\}\vdash_n \textcircled{c}\, e\, \textcircled{c}}$$

Fig. 4. Type rules for kernel expressions.

$$\frac{\Gamma,\mathbf{c}\vdash_{n_1} d_1 \quad \cdots \quad \Gamma,\mathbf{c}\vdash_{n_i} d_i \quad \Gamma,\mathbf{c}\vdash_0 b \quad \Gamma,\mathbf{c}\vdash_1 h \quad n_1\ldots n_i>0}{\Gamma,\mathbf{c}\vdash a\; m\; \textbf{sig } n\; x\; h\; \{\,d_1,\ldots,d_i\,\}\; b}$$

$$\frac{\Gamma,\mathbf{c}\vdash_{n_1} d_1 \quad \cdots \quad \Gamma,\mathbf{c}\vdash_{n_i} d_i \quad \Gamma,\mathbf{c}\vdash_n e \quad \Gamma,\mathbf{c}\vdash_n b \quad n,n_1\ldots n_i>0}{\Gamma,\mathbf{c}\vdash \textbf{fun } n\; [\,d_1,\ldots,d_i\,]\,:e\; b}$$

$$\frac{\Gamma,\mathbf{c}\vdash_{n_1} d_1 \quad \cdots \quad \Gamma,\mathbf{c}\vdash_{n_i} d_i \quad \Gamma,\mathbf{c}\vdash_0 b \quad n_1\ldots n_i>0}{\Gamma,\mathbf{c}\vdash \textbf{pred } n\; [\,d_1,\ldots,d_i\,]\; b} \qquad \frac{\Gamma,\mathbf{c}\vdash_0 b}{\Gamma,\mathbf{c}\vdash \textbf{fact } n\; b}$$

$$\frac{\Gamma,\mathbf{c}\vdash_0 b \quad \square \in \{\textbf{run},\textbf{check}\} \quad \vdash \mathbf{c}}{\Gamma,\emptyset\vdash \square\; n\; b\; \textbf{with } c\; s} \qquad \frac{\Gamma,\lfloor\mathbf{c}\rfloor\vdash_0 b \quad \square \in \{\textbf{run},\textbf{check}\} \quad \vdash \mathbf{c}}{\Gamma,\emptyset\vdash \square\; n\; b\; \textbf{with exactly } c\; s}$$

$$\frac{\Gamma,\mathbf{c}\vdash p \quad \neg\,\textcircled{c}\notin \mathbf{c} \quad \vdash \mathbf{c} \quad \neg\,\textcircled{c}\notin \mathbf{c}}{\Gamma,\mathbf{c}\cup\{\textcircled{c}\}\vdash \textcircled{c}\, p\, \textcircled{c} \quad \vdash \textcircled{c},\mathbf{c}} \qquad \frac{\Gamma,\mathbf{c}\vdash_n e \quad n>0}{\Gamma,\mathbf{c}\vdash_n v:e} \qquad \frac{\Gamma,\mathbf{c}\vdash_n d \quad \neg\,\textcircled{c}\notin \mathbf{c}}{\Gamma,\mathbf{c}\cup\{\textcircled{c}\}\vdash_n \textcircled{c}\, d\, \textcircled{c}}$$

$$\frac{\Gamma = \textsf{decls}(\emptyset,p_1,\ldots,p_n) \quad \Gamma,\emptyset\vdash p_1 \quad \cdots \quad \Gamma,\emptyset\vdash p_i}{\vdash m\; p_1\,\cdots\,p_i}$$

Fig. 5. Type rules for kernel paragraphs.

marks. A complete colorful model m comprised by paragraphs $p_1\ldots p_i$, is well-typed if $\vdash m\; p_1\ldots p_i$. This requires the prior collection of the declarations of global elements, as calculated by function decls:[4]

---

[4] Function arity is an oversimplification, since calculating the arity of a bounding expression requires the arity of other declared sigs and fields.

$$\mathsf{decls}(\mathbf{c}, d_1, \ldots, d_n) = \mathsf{decl}(\mathbf{c}, d_1) + \ldots + \mathsf{decl}(\mathbf{c}, d_n)$$

$$\mathsf{decl}(\mathbf{c}, \textcircled{c}\; d\; \textcircled{c}) = \mathsf{decl}(\mathbf{c} \cup \{\textcircled{c}\}, d)$$

$$\mathsf{decl}(\mathbf{c}, a\; m\; \mathbf{sig}\; n\; x\; \{\; d\; \}\; b) = n \mapsto (\mathbf{c}, 1) + \mathsf{decls}(\mathbf{c}, d)$$

$$\mathsf{decl}(\mathbf{c}, v\; :\; e) = v \mapsto (\mathbf{c}, \mathsf{arity}(e))$$

$$\mathsf{decl}(\mathbf{c}, \mathbf{pred}\; n\; [\; d\;]\; b) = n \mapsto (\mathbf{c}, \#d)$$

$$\mathsf{decl}(\mathbf{c}, \mathbf{fun}\; n\; [\; d\;]\; :\; e\; b) = n \mapsto (\mathbf{c}, \#d + \mathsf{arity}(e))$$

$$\mathsf{decl}(\mathbf{c}, \mathbf{run}\; n\; b\; w\; f) = \emptyset$$

$$\mathsf{decl}(\mathbf{c}, \mathbf{check}\; n\; b\; w\; f) = \emptyset$$

Type rules check mainly for two kinds of coloring issues. First, calls to global elements must occur in a context that guarantees its existence. For instance, signature Secret, declared with feature 1, may not be called in a plain **fact** { **some** Secret } since that fact will be present in variants where secrets do not exist (those without feature 1). This applies to calls in expressions, the class hierarchy (the parent signature must exist in every variant that the children do), and calls to predicates/asserts in run/check commands. Commands are not annotated, their context being instead defined by the color scope (for exact color scopes, the context is expanded with the negation of all marks not present in it, $\lfloor \mathbf{c} \rfloor$). Second, the nesting of negative and positive annotations of the same feature is forbidden, since this conjunction of conditions is necessarily inconsistent (i.e., under ①❶ e❶①, e will never exist). This also applies to color scopes of commands, where the presence and absence of a feature would allow no variant.

4 Analysis

Analysis of colorful Alloy models is achieved through the translation into regular Alloy. There are two main alternative ways to do this: (i) through the generation and analysis, for every feature combination, of a projected version of the model; (ii) through the generation of an 'amalgamated' Alloy model that encompasses the alternative behaviors of the model family. In order to compare their performance (see Sect. 5), we have implemented both translations in our prototype. Since this preliminary evaluation is inconclusive, the current version of the colorful Analyzer relies on the amalgamated translation for non-exact color scopes, and on the projection one otherwise (i.e., for the analysis of a single variant). The resulting models are also provided to the user, which can be used to better understand the model family under development (particularly, the projected versions allow the user to inspect concrete variants).

Figures 7 and 8 present the translation of the colorful model into the amalgamated version for paragraphs and expressions, respectively. It is assumed that the colorful model is well-typed at this stage, and that all unique colorful marks $\mathbf{c}_0$ that occur in it have been collected during that process (i.e., the features relevant for this family of models). Expressions $\mathbf{c}^+$ and $\mathbf{c}^-$ filter the positive or

```
abstract sig Feature {}
one sig F1,F2,F3,F4 extends Feature{}
sig Variant in Feature {}

fact FeatureModel {
  (F3 not in Variant and F4 in Variant) implies
    some none }

sig StoredModel {
  derivationOf : set StoredModel,
  ...,
  command      : set Command }
sig Link, Command {}

fact {
  F3 in Variant implies
    command in StoredModel → lone Command else no command
  F3 not in Variant implies no Command
  ... }

fact Links {
  all : Link | one (public+
  (F2 in Variant implies secret else none → none)+
  (F3+F4 in Variant implies link else none → none)).l
  F3 not in Variant implies all m : StoredModel | one m.public
  ... }
```

(a) Amalgamated translation.

```
sig StoredModel{
  public: lone Link,
  secret: lone Link,
  command: lone Command }

sig Secret in StoredModel{}

sig Link{}

sig Command{}

fact Links {
  all l : Link |
    one (public+secret).l
  all m : StoredModel |
    m.public != m.secret
  ... }
```

(b) ②,③ projection.

Fig. 6. Excerpts of the translations for the Alloy4Fun colorful model.

negative color marks from a set, respectively. For a model $m\ p_1\ \dots\ p_i$, the translation $[\![m\ p_1\ \dots\ p_i]\!]_{c_0}$ starts by introducing an abstract signature Feature, that is extended exactly by singleton signatures that represent each of the relevant features. Signature Variant, a sub-set of Feature, represents particular feature combinations under consideration.[5] Its acceptable valuations are restricted by facts introduced during the translation of the color scope of the commands. To control the existence of structural elements (signatures and fields), their multiplicity is relaxed and additional facts only enforce them if the associated features are present/absent. Even though these elements are always declared, the colorful type checking rules guarantee that they are not referenced in invalid variants. In the kernel language, only sub-expressions of binary operators may be associated with features (blocks of formulas have been converted into binary conjunctions). Depending on the presence/absence of the relevant features, either the expression or its neutral element is returned. Commands are also expanded depending on their color scope, so that only relevant variants are considered. Figure 6a presents an except of the amalgamated Alloy model for the Alloy4Fun colorful model.

The projection translation is straight-forward: given a concrete variant, it projects away elements not relevant in that variant. Paragraphs not associated with a particular variant are completely removed, as are branches of marked

---

[5] To avoid collisions with the identifiers of the colorful model, the translation actually uses obfuscated identifiers these signatures.

$$[\![m \; p_1 \; \cdots \; p_i]\!]_{k \ldots l} \equiv \begin{array}{l} m \\ \textbf{abstract sig } \text{Feature } \{\} \\ \textbf{one sig } \text{Fk, } \ldots, \text{ Fl } \textbf{extends } \text{Feature } \{\} \\ \textbf{sig } \text{Variant } \textbf{in } \text{Feature } \{\} \\ [\![p_1]\!]_\emptyset \; \cdots \; [\![p_i]\!]_\emptyset \end{array}$$

$$[\![a \; m \; \textbf{sig } n \; x \; \{ \; d_1, \ldots, d_i \; \} \; b]\!]_c \equiv \begin{array}{l} a \; \textbf{sig } n \; x \; \{ \; [\![d_1]\!]_c, \ldots, [\![d_i]\!]_c \; \} \; [\![b]\!]_c \\ \textbf{fact } \{ \; ([\![c^+]\!] \textbf{ in } \text{Variant } \textbf{and } [\![c^-]\!] \textbf{ not in } \text{Variant}) \textbf{ implies } m \; n \\ \qquad \textbf{else no } n \; \} \\ \textbf{fact } \{ \; \text{trans}(d_1) \; \ldots \; \text{trans}(d_i) \; \} \end{array}$$

where

$\quad$ trans($\textcircled{c} \; d \; \textcircled{c}$) = trans($d$)

$\quad$ trans($v \; : \; e$) = $([\![c^+]\!]$ **in** Variant **and** $[\![c^-]\!]$ **not in** Variant) **implies** v **in** $n \rightarrow e$
$\qquad$ **else no** v

$[\![\textbf{pred } n \; [\; d \;] \; b]\!]_c \equiv \textbf{pred } n \; [\; [\![d]\!]_c \;] \; [\![b]\!]_c$

$[\![\textbf{fun } n \; [\; d \;] \; : \; e \; b]\!]_c \equiv \textbf{fun } n \; [\; [\![d]\!]_c \;] \; : \; [\![e]\!]_c \; [\![b]\!]_c$

$[\![\textbf{fact } n \; b]\!]_c \equiv \textbf{fact } n \; [\![b]\!]_c$

$[\![\textbf{run } n \; b \; \textbf{with } c \; s]\!]_\emptyset \equiv \textbf{run } n \; \{ \; ([\![c^+]\!] \textbf{ in } \text{Variant } \textbf{and } [\![c^-]\!] \textbf{ not in } \text{Variant}) \textbf{ and } [\![b]\!]_c \; \} \; s$

$[\![\textbf{run } n \; b \; \textbf{with exactly } c \; s]\!]_\emptyset \equiv \textbf{run } n \; \{ \; [\![c^+]\!] = \text{Variant } \textbf{and } [\![b]\!]_c \; \} \; s$

$[\![\textbf{check } n \; b \; \textbf{with } c \; s]\!]_\emptyset \equiv \textbf{check } n \; \{ \; ([\![c^+]\!] \textbf{ in } \text{Variant } \textbf{and } [\![c^-]\!] \textbf{ not in } \text{Variant}) \textbf{ implies } [\![b]\!]_c \; \} \; s$

$[\![\textbf{check } n \; b \; \textbf{with exactly } c \; s]\!]_\emptyset \equiv \textbf{check } n \; \{ \; [\![c^+]\!] = \text{Variant } \textbf{implies } [\![b]\!]_c \; \} \; s$

$[\![\textcircled{c} \; p \; \textcircled{c}]\!]_c \equiv [\![p]\!]_{c \cup \{\textcircled{c}\}}$

$[\![v \; : \; m \; e]\!]_c \equiv v \; : \; \textbf{set } [\![e]\!]_c$

$[\![v \; : \; e_1 \; m_1 \; \rightarrow \; m_2 \; e_2]\!]_c \equiv v \; : \; [\![e_1]\!]_c \; \textbf{set } \rightarrow \; \textbf{set } [\![e_2]\!]_c$

$[\![\textcircled{i}, \ldots, \textcircled{j}]\!] \equiv [\![\textcircled{i}]\!], \ldots, [\![\textcircled{j}]\!]$

$[\![\textcircled{c}]\!] \equiv \text{Fc}$

$[\![\otimes]\!] \equiv \textbf{none}$

Fig. 7. Paragraph translation into the amalgamated model with variability.

binary expressions. Since colorful Alloy does not natively support feature models, the $2^{\#c}$ projected models must be generated and analyzed (although the process can be stopped once one of those models is found to be satisfiable). However, the codification of feature models proposed in Sect. 2 actually renders invalid variants trivially unsatisfiable and instantaneously discharged: the projection of the model for such variants will end up with a fact enforcing **some none**, which is detected during the translation into SAT before the solving process is even launched. Figure 6b presents an excerpt of a projected Alloy model for the Alloy4Fun colorful model under an exact scope ②,③.

5   Evaluation

Our evaluation aimed to answer two questions regarding the feasibility of the approach, prior to developing more advances analysis procedures: (*i*) is the analysis through the amalgamated model feasible? And if so, (*ii*) does it outperform a preprocessing approach that iteratively analyzes all projected variants?

$$[\![k]\!]_c \equiv k$$
$$[\![n]\!]_c \equiv n$$
$$[\![\Box e]\!]_c \equiv \Box[\![e]\!]_c$$
$$[\![e_1 \ \Box \ e_2]\!]_c \equiv \begin{cases} [\![e_1]\!]_c \ \Box \ [\![e_2]\!]_c & \text{if } \Box \notin \{+, \&, \textbf{or}, \textbf{and}\} \\ \text{trans}(e_1) \ \Box \ \text{trans}(e_2) & \text{otherwise} \end{cases}$$

where

$\text{trans}(e) \equiv [\texttt{c}^+]$ in Variant and $[\texttt{c}^-]$ not in Variant implies $[\![e]\!]_c$ else $\text{neutral}(\Box, \text{arity}(e))$

$\text{neutral}(+, a) = \underbrace{\textbf{none} \ \rightarrow \ \dots \ \rightarrow \ \textbf{none}}_{a}$

$\text{neutral}(\&, a) = \underbrace{\textbf{univ} \ \rightarrow \ \dots \ \rightarrow \ \textbf{univ}}_{a}$

$\text{neutral}(\textbf{or}, a) = \textbf{some none}$

$\text{neutral}(\textbf{and}, a) = \textbf{no none}$

$$[\![\Box \ d \ | \ e]\!]_c \equiv \Box[\![d]\!]_c \ | \ [\![e]\!]_c$$
$$[\![\textcircled{c} \ e \ \textcircled{c}]\!]_c \equiv [\![e]\!]_{c \cup \{\textcircled{c}\}}$$
$$[\![v \ : \ e]\!]_c \equiv v \ : \ [\![e]\!]_c$$

Fig. 8. Expression translation into the amalgamated model with variability.

To answer these questions, we applied our technique to 7 model families with different characteristics, including some rich on structural and others on behavioral properties, and mostly encoding variants of system design. This also allowed us to validate the expressibility and flexibility of the language extension.

5.1 Evaluation Subjects

The *OwnGrandpa* model is based on 2 toy models by Daniel Jackson distributed with the Alloy Analyzer that share certain elements, one modeling genealogical relationships and other solving the "I'm My Own Grandpa" puzzle. In [14], the latter is presented in stages to address different concepts, which are distributed as 3 distinct Alloy files. Our base variant considers basic biological facts, which can be extended by (1) introducing Adam and Eve, who are considered as the first man and woman according to the Bible creation myth; (2) introducing social norms regarding marriage; and (3) forbidding incestuous marriages. The feature model forces feature 3 to require 2. The command evaluated checks whether all persons descend from Adam and Eve in variants with feature 1.

The *E-commerce* platform model is adapted from [8] and models variants for the catalog structure of the platform. In the base variant the catalog is a collection of items, which can be enhanced by (1) allowing items to be classified in categories; (2) allowing a hierarchy on categories; (3) allowing the assignment of multiple categories to items; (4) presenting images of items; and (5) presenting thumbnails summarizing categories. The feature model forces features 2, 3 and 5 to require feature 1; feature 5 also requires feature 4. The command evaluated tests whether all items are cataloged in every variant.

Graph is adapted from a compositional version from [1] that explores different classes of graphs. The base simply defines nodes and edges, which can

Table 1. Evaluation of the amalgamated and iterative approaches for the examples.

Model	NF	Command	NP	NV	Scope	TA(s)	TI(s)	SU	SP(s)
OwnGrandpa	3	AllDescend	4	4	9	0.3	1.7	5.67	0.9
					10	1.0	10.9	10.90	4.0
					11	7.3	24.1	3.30	13.4
					12	26.1	132.6	5.08	57.1
E-commerce	5	AllCataloged	32	12	10	6.2	13.6	2.19	3.5
					11	15.5	57.1	3.68	17.4
					12	73.7	182.0	2.47	45.2
Graph	6	Connected	32	6	8	3.2	19.2	6.00	3.4
					9	11.9	80.9	6.80	16.7
		SourcesAndSinks	32	10	8	7.0	62.1	6.99	12.9
					9	187.5	1010.2	5.39	166.0
Alloy4Fun	4	NoCommands	4	4	25	1.8	8.1	4.50	3.1
					30	4.4	17.5	3.98	7.7
		PublicSecretDisjoint	8	6	20	1.1	6.3	5.73	1.9
					25	2.8	19.6	7.00	7.6
					30	5.9	37.9	6.42	11.0
Vending	2	Stock	4	4	6 but 4 Int	4.6	8.5	1.85	5.0
					8 but 4 Int	5.5	9.7	1.76	4.4
					5 but 5 Int	**30.7**	**26.1**	**0.85**	14.8
					7 but 5 Int	19.3	28.6	1.48	13.1
		Selection	4	4	6 but 4 Int	2.1	2.8	1.33	1.1
					8 but 4 Int	2.4	3.7	1.54	1.7
					5 but 5 Int	4.5	5.7	1.27	2.7
					7 but 5 Int	4.0	9.0	2.25	4.5
Bestiary	4	Injective	8	8	25	6.9	12.8	1.86	3.0
					30	9.8	49.6	5.05	16.0
		Functional	8	8	25	2.4	11.1	4.59	2.4
					30	10.2	33.6	3.29	8.4
		Associative	8	8	6	2.8	9.4	3.38	2.5
					7	52.5	211.9	4.04	62.2
					8	230.2	891.9	3.88	309.1

be extended by forcing the graph to be: (1) a multigraph; (2) undirected; (3) a directed acyclic graph; (4) a tree; (5) edge labeled; and (6) a binary search tree. The feature model declares feature 2 as incompatible with 3, feature 4 requiring 3, and 6 requiring both 4 and 5. The evaluated properties are whether the graph is connected and whether non-empty graphs have at least one source and one sink node.

Alloy4Fun has already been thoroughly explored in Sect. 2. The evaluated commands check whether it is possible to create commands, and whether public and private links are always disjoint. *Vending* is inspired by various vending machine examples commonly used in SPL literature (e.g., [10]). The base variant of this dynamic example encodes the process of selecting and serving an item, extensible by introducing two independent features, (1) the notion of price and payment; and (2) the possibility to select multiple items. The first command evaluated tests whether the stock is always non-negative, and the second whether only elements with positive stock can be selected (all commands assume scope 15 on `Time`). Finally, *Bestiary* is a family of very simple models that we use in classes to explore different types of relations. Each feature defines relations as (1) injective; (2) functional; (3) total; and (4) surjective. Commands test alternative definitions of injectivity and functionality, as well as whether relations are associative.

5.2 Results

Table 1 depicts execution times for the examples presented above, for varying scope. The table presents how many features each model has (NF). Then, for each pair command/scope of a model, it presents how many variants are considered by the color scope (NP), how many of those variants are valid according to the feature model (NV), the analysis time under the amalgamated model (TA), under the iterative analysis of all projected variants (TI), and the speedup of the former in relation to the latter (SU). The slowest time for a projected variant (SP) is also presented. All commands were run 50 times on a MacBook with a 2.4 GHz Intel Core i5 and 8GB memory using the MiniSAT solver.

Results show that the amalgamated approach is indeed feasible, since it proves to be always faster than the iterative analysis except for one particular command of *Alloy4Fun* (highlighted as bold). The evaluation did however raise an interesting unexpected question, due to how frequent the analysis of a single projected variant is slower than the full amalgamated analysis. For *Own-Grandpa* we identified the cause as being related to imposing signature multiplicities through the declaration rather than through a fact. Why this affects the underlying procedure, and whether it can be explored to improve performance, is left as future work.

6 Related Work

Several approaches have been proposed for feature-oriented design. We focus on those that provide specification languages supported by automated analyses. *fSMV* [18] is a compositional approach for SMV, where a base system in pure SMV can be extended with features, modeled in new textual units. The base behavior may be overwritten by features, integrated automatically by compilation into pure SMV so that normal SMV model checkers can be employed. *fPromela* [5] provides instead an annotative approach for SPIN's modeling language, where features are introduced by a new user-defined data type structure. Features of a model must be declared as a field of this structure and can be referenced elsewhere by declaring a variable of this type. fPromela is accompanied by a language for the specification of feature models, TVL. *FeatureAlloy* [3] introduces a compositional approach for Alloy. Like fSMV, features are encapsulated and modeled separately from the base system, which are then combined by an external tool in order to produce a final model. This is achieved by recursively superimposing and merging selected features; new fields can be added to signatures, while facts, predicates, or function are overridden, which is unsuited for fine-grained variability points.

The idea to compare some kind of "amalgamated" model checking with the iterative analysis of all variants has been explored in [6], where the analysis of fSMV models through a symbolic algorithm for featured transition systems (FTS) was compared with that of the enumeration of regular SMV models and analysis with NuSMV. Evaluation showed that the former often outperformed the enumerative approach. A similar study was performed for fPromela through a semi-symbolic algorithm for FTS [5], which again proved to be more efficient in general than the enumerative approach using SPIN.

As previously mentioned, background colors have been proposed as an annotative approach for feature-oriented software development [15]. These are similar to `#ifdef` statements, with code fragments only being included when the associated features are selected. Similarly to our approach, it offers a direct mechanism for developers to find whether a code fragment is associated with a feature, but in our approach annotations are part of the model itself, instead being handled by the supporting tool. Extensions to this work [11] also support negative annotations, but color them similarly to positive ones. Colors have also been used to highlight feature annotations in graphical editors for models with variability [7, 12].

Several approaches have used Alloy to formalize and analyze feature models [20], but not models with variability points. These could complement colorful Alloy, if dedicated support for feature models is deemed useful in the future.

Techniques have been proposed for type-checking SPLs. One such technique is proposed in [16] but is tailored for Java programs. [8] proposes checking the well-formedness of a model template against a feature model by mapping OCL well-formedness rules into to propositional formulas verified by a SAT solver.

7   Conclusion and Future Work

This work explores an annotative approach to feature-based design that minimally extends the Alloy language, and its Analyzer, through colorful annotations and variant-focused analysis commands. Two alternative analysis approaches have been explored to execute these commands. A preliminary study has been performed, showing that in general the amalgamated analysis of the model fares better than the enumeration and subsequent analysis of all projected variants.

Future work is planned on several axes. Regarding the language, we intend to expand the support to additional operators, as well as explore whether syntactic features for specifying feature models are needed. Regarding the analysis processes, we plan to continue exploring the relation between the amalgamated and the iterative approach, and whether there is some middle ground that could provide optimal results. We also expect to implement new analysis operations, like run commands that check all variants for consistency.

Acknowledgments. This work is financed by the ERDF - European Regional Development Fund - through the Operational Programme for Competitiveness and Internationalisation - COMPETE 2020 - and by National Funds through the Portuguese funding agency, FCT - Fundação para a Ciência e a Tecnologia, within project POCI-01-0145-FEDER-016826. The third author was also supported by the FCT sabbatical grant with reference SFRH/BSAB/143106/2018.

References

1. Apel, S., Kästner, C., Lengauer, C.: Language-independent and automated software composition: the featurehouse experience. IEEE Trans. Softw. Eng. **39**(1), 63–79 (2013)
2. Apel, S., Kästner, C.: An overview of feature-oriented software development. J. Object Technol. **8**(5), 49–84 (2009)
3. Apel, S., Scholz, W., Lengauer, C., Kästner, C.: Detecting dependences and interactions in feature-oriented design. In: Proceedings of the IEEE 21st International Symposium on Software Reliability Engineering (ISSRE), pp. 151–170. IEEE (2010)
4. Cimatti, A., Clarke, E., Giunchiglia, F., Roveri, M.: NuSMV: a new symbolic model checker. Int. J. Softw. Tools Technol. Transf. **2**(4), 410–425 (2000)
5. Classen, A., Cordy, M., Heymans, P., Legay, A., Schobbens, P.Y.: Model checking software product lines with SNIP. Softw. Tools Technol. Transf. **14**(5), 589–612 (2012)
6. Classen, A., Heymans, P., Schobbens, P.Y., Legay, A., Raskin, J.F.: Model checking lots of systems: efficient verification of temporal properties in software product lines. In: Proceedings of the 32nd ACM/IEEE International Conference on Software Engineering (ICSE), pp. 335–344. ACM (2010)
7. Czarnecki, K., Antkiewicz, M.: Mapping features to models: a template approach based on superimposed variants. In: Glück, R., Lowry, M. (eds.) GPCE 2005. LNCS, vol. 3676, pp. 422–437. Springer, Heidelberg (2005). https://doi.org/10.1007/11561347_28
8. Czarnecki, K., Pietroszek, K.: Verifying feature-based model templates against well-formedness OCL constraints. In: Proceedings of the 5th International Conference on Generative Programming and Component Engineering (GPCE), pp. 211–220. ACM (2006)
9. Czarnecki, K., Wasowski, A.: Feature diagrams and logics: there and back again. In: Proceedings of the 11th International Conference Software Product Lines (SPLC), pp. 23–34. IEEE (2007)
10. Fantechi, A., Gnesi, S.: Formal modeling for product families engineering. In: Proceedings of the 12th International Conference on Software Product Lines (SPLC), pp. 193–202. IEEE (2008)
11. Feigenspan, J., Kästner, C., Apel, S., Liebig, J., Schulze, M., Dachselt, R., Papendieck, M., Leich, T., Saake, G.: Do background colors improve program comprehension in the #ifdef hell? Empirical Softw. Eng. **18**(4), 699–745 (2013)

12. Heidenreich, F., Kopcsek, J., Wende, C.: FeatureMapper: mapping features to models. In: Companion Volume of the 30th International Conference on Software Engineering (ICSE Companion), pp. 943–944. ACM (2008)
13. Holzmann, G.J.: The model checker SPIN. IEEE Trans. Softw. Eng. **23**(5), 279–295 (1997)
14. Jackson, D.: Software Abstractions - Logic, Language, and Analysis, Revised edn. MIT Press, Cambridge (2012)
15. Kästner, C., Apel, S., Kuhlemann, M.: Granularity in software product lines. In: Proceedings of the 30th International Conference on Software Engineering (ICSE), pp. 311–320. ACM (2008)
16. Kästner, C., Apel, S., Thüm, T., Saake, G.: Type checking annotation-based product lines. ACM Trans. Softw. Eng. Methodol. **21**(3), 14:1–14:39 (2012)
17. Macedo, N., Cunha, A., Pereira, J., Carvalho, R., Silva, R., Paiva, A.C.R., Ramalho, M.S., Silva, D.C.: Sharing and learning Alloy on the web. CoRR abs/1907.02275 (2019)
18. Plath, M., Ryan, M.: Feature integration using a feature construct. Sci. Comput. Program. **41**(1), 53–84 (2001)
19. Schaefer, I., Hähnle, R.: Formal methods in software product line engineering. IEEE Comput. **44**(2), 82–85 (2011)
20. Sree-Kumar, A., Planas, E., Clarisó, R.: Analysis of feature models using Alloy: a survey. In: Proceedings of the 7th International Workshop on Formal Methods and Analysis in Software Product Line Engineering (FMSPLE@ETAPS). EPTCS, vol. 206, pp. 46–60 (2016)

Response Time Analysis of Typed DAG Tasks for G-FP Scheduling

Xuemei Peng[1], Meiling Han[2(✉)], and Qingxu Deng[1]

[1] Northeastern University, Shenyang, China
[2] Nanjing University of Posts and Telecommunications, Nanjing, China
meilinghan@njupt.edu.cn

Abstract. With the increasing trend towards using multi-cores architecture for embedded systems, the study of parallel tasks on the heterogeneous platform becomes attractive and desirable in the literature. Although several work studying parallel task models has been proposed, the problem of precise scheduling analysis for the multiprocessor case has largely remained open. To this end, this paper concentrates on analyzing the response time for typed DAG real-time tasks scheduled on a multiprocessor platform under global fixed priority scheduling. Firstly, we use the state-of-the-art method of the single typed DAG task to bound the intra-interference. Second, we use an efficient but pessimistic way to bound the carry-in interference for a higher priority task. And we also propose a new technique based on the decomposition tree method to bound the carry-out interference. Finally, we use the classic sliding technique to bound the inter-interference of each higher priority task. Experimental evaluation validates the performance and efficiency of the proposed approach by comparing with other methods.

Keywords: Embedded real-time systems · Global fixed-priority · Multiprocessor systems · Response time analysis · Heterogeneous

1 Introduction

The multi-core is undergoing a new revolution in the form of heterogeneous hardware platforms. Examples include OMAP1/OMAP2 [18] that integrate CPU and DSP on the same chip, and the Tegra processors [19] that integrate CPU and GPU on the same chip. Heterogeneous multi-cores utilize specialized processing capabilities to handle particular computational tasks, which usually offer higher performance and energy efficiency. For example, [21] showed that a heterogeneous-ISA chip multiprocessor can outperform the best same-ISA homogeneous architecture by as much as 21% with 23% energy savings and a reduction of 32% in energy delay product.

To fully utilize the computation capacity of multi-cores, software should be properly parallelized. A representation that can model a wide range of parallel software is the DAG (directed acyclic graph) task model, where each vertex represents a piece of sequential workload and each edge represents the precedence

© Springer Nature Switzerland AG 2019
N. Guan et al. (Eds.): SETTA 2019, LNCS 11951, pp. 56–71, 2019.
https://doi.org/10.1007/978-3-030-35540-1_4

relation between two vertices. Real-time scheduling and analysis of DAG parallel task models have raised many new challenges over traditional real-time scheduling theory with sequential tasks, and have become an increasingly hot research topic in recent years. And the heterogeneous character makes it even harder.

In this paper, we consider real-time scheduling of *typed DAG tasks* on heterogeneous multi-cores, where each vertex is explicitly bound to execute on a particular type of cores. This paper aims to bound the *worst-case response time* (WCRT) for typed DAG tasks when they are scheduled under G-FP (global fixed-priority) scheduling.

To the best of our knowledge, the only known WCRT bound for the considered problem model was presented in an early work [12], which not only is grossly pessimistic, but also suffers the *non-self-sustainability* problem[1]. And the paper [10] improved the bound proposed in [12] and also solved the *non-self-sustainability* problem. But this work still only considered one typed DAG task. We call the two methods proposed in [10] as **Ty-B-1** and **Ty-B-2**, respectively. The problem to bound WCRT for typed DAG tasks under G-FP scheduling is still open.

We evaluate our proposed techniques through simulation experiments. We show the performance of our methods by evaluating the randomly generated task sets in different parameters. The results show that our method can get a safe and valid WCRT bound in reasonable analysis time.

2   Related Work

There is less work which focus on the scheduling and analysis of multiple recurring typed DAG tasks. And there is even less work for the typed DAG scheduling even for a single typed DAG task. The state-of-the-art method for the analysis of intra-task interference of single typed DAG task is proposed in [10]. This work proved the typed DAG scheduling is NP-hard and proposed an efficient method using the abstract path technique.

Yang et al. [22] studied the scheduling and analysis of multiple typed DAG tasks by decomposing each of them into a set of independent tasks with artificial release times and deadlines. After decomposition, each vertex in the DAG is scheduled and analyzed as an independent task (intra-task dependency automatically enforced by the artificial release times and the guaranteed deadlines). This method is under the G-EDF (global earliest deadline first) scheduling.

Fonseca et al. [7] studied partitioned scheduling of DAG tasks on homogeneous multi-core platforms, where the allocation of vertices to cores is assumed to be given. The execution behavior of workload partitioned to each core is modeled as a self-suspending task and the state-of-the-art analysis techniques [17] for self-suspending tasks are applied to bound the WCRT. The analysis techniques in [7] can be easily extended to typed DAG tasks on heterogeneous multi-cores (as long as each vertex has been allocated to a core of the same type).

---

[1] By a non-self-sustainable analysis method, a system decided to be schedulable may be decided to be unschedulable when the system parameters become better.

However, the work in [7] assumes the allocation of workload to cores to be already given. The problem of how to partition the workload to cores (which may greatly affect the performance) is still open.

The real-time scheduling and analysis of multiple *recurring* untyped DAG has been intensively studied in recent years, with different scheduling paradigms including federated scheduling [2–4,11,13,14] and global scheduling [1,5,16]. In their analysis, a necessary step is to bound the *intra-task* interference (based on the classical work by Graham [8,9]). But because of the typed cores, these methods can not be just used for the typed DAG tasks under global scheduling. Fonseca et al. [6] used the internal structure of each DAG to derive more accurate upper-bounds on the carry-in and carry-out interfering workloads by constructing the carry-in and carry-out workload distributions. For the carry-out job, they transformed the DAG to a NFJ-DAG (nested fork-join DAG) by removing some edges of the DAG and then use a decomposition tree to represent the NFJ-DAG. And they applied the "sliding window" technique introduced in [15] to derive the maximum total workload of carry-in and carry-out jobs.

3 Preliminaries

We consider a system $\tau = \{\tau_1, \tau_2, ..., \tau_n\}$ comprised of n typed DAG tasks which is executed on a heterogeneous multi-cores platform with different types of cores under G-FP scheduling. The tasks are sorted by the descending order of priority, which means that τ_i has higher priority than τ_j if $i < j$. Each typed DAG task τ_i is denoted by $\tau_i = (G_i, \gamma_i, c_i, T_i, D_i)$.

S is the set of core types (or *types* for short), and for each $s \in S$ there are M_s cores of this type ($M_s \geq 1$). V_i and E_i are the set of vertices and edges in G_i. Each vertex $v \in V_i$ represents a piece of code segment to be sequentially executed. Each edge $(u, v) \in E$ represents the precedence relation between vertices u and v. The *type function* $\gamma_i : V_i \times S$ defines the *type* of each vertex, i.e., $\gamma_i(v) = s$, where $s \in S$, represents vertex v must be executed on cores of type s. The *weight function* $c_i : V_i \times R_0^+$ defines the worst-case execution time (WCET) of each vertex, i.e., v executes for at most $c_i(v)$ time units (on cores of type $\gamma_i(v)$). T_i is the period (the minimum separation of any two jobs), and D_i is the relative deadline. We consider the implicit deadline tasks, i.e., $D_i = T_i$ for each task.

If there is an edge $(u, v) \in E_i$, u is a *predecessor* of v, and v is a *successor* of u. Without loss of generality, we assume G_i has a unique source vertex $v_{i,src}$ (which has no predecessor) and a unique sink vertex $v_{i,snk}$ (which has no successor)[2]. We use $\pi \in G_i$ to denote π is a path in G_i. A path $\pi = \{v_{i,1}, \cdots, v_{i,k}\}$ is a *complete path* if and only if its first vertex $v_{i,1}$ is the source vertex of G_i and last vertex $v_{i,k}$ is the sink vertex of G_i. We use $vol(G_i)$ to denote the total WCET of G_i and $vol_s(G_i)$ the total WCET of vertices of type s:

$$vol(G_i) = \sum_{u \in V_i} c_i(u), \quad vol_s(G_i) = \sum_{u \in V_i \wedge \gamma_i(u)=s} c_i(u).$$

---

[2] In case G_i has multiple source/sink vertices, one can add a dummy source/sink vertex to make it compliant with our model.

The *utilization* of a typed DAG task τ_i is $U_i = vol(G_i)/T_i$. And the *system utilization* is $U_{tot} = \sum_{i=1}^{n} U_i$. The length of a path π is denoted by $len(\pi)$ and $len(G_i)$ represents the length of the longest path in G_i:

$$len(\pi) = \sum_{u \in \pi} c_i(u), \quad len(G_i) = \max_{\pi \in G_i}\{len(\pi)\}.$$

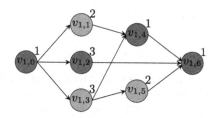

Fig. 1. A DAG task τ_1 with two types (Color figure online)

Example 1. Figure 1 illustrates a DAG with two types of vertices (type 1 marked by blue and type 2 marked by yellow). The WCET of vertex is annotated by the number next to the vertex. In Fig. 1, we can compute that $vol(G_1) = 13$, $vol_1(G_1) = 6$ and $vol_2(G_1) = 7$.

4 Rationale

The objective of this paper is to bound the WCRT of each task in a typed DAG tasks set. Without loss of generality, we take τ_k as the analyzed task in the rest of this paper. We define the path which derived WCRT of τ_k as the critical path of τ_k, which is denoted by π_k. After τ_k released, there are two kinds of interferences interfering the execution of π_k. The first is the interference generated by the vertices of task τ_k and not in π_k, and the other is the interference contributed by the tasks $\tau_{i<k}$. They are formally defined as following.

Definition 1 (Intra-Task Interference). *The intra-task interference is denoted by $I_{k,k}(\pi_k)$ and defined as the maximum cumulative time during which any vertex $v \in \pi_k$ is ready but cannot execute because access to the same core has been granted to vertices of τ_k that do not belong to π_k.*

Definition 2 (Inter-Task Interference). *The inter-task interference is denoted by $I_{i,k}(\pi_k)$ and defined as the maximum cumulative time during which any vertex $v \in \pi_k$ is ready but cannot execute because the vertices of τ_i is running on the same core.*

To achieve the objective of this paper, we should answer the following questions:

- First, how to bound the interference generated by the analyzed task itself.
- Second, how to bound the interference generated by the higher priority tasks in a problem window. This problem can be departed into two sub-problems.
  - How to bound the interference generated by a carry-in job of a higher priority task (described below).
  - How to bound the interference generated by a carry-out job of a higher priority task (described below).

4.1   Bounding Intra-interference

In this section, we solve the first problem how to bound the interference generated by task τ_k itself. Note that the interference of higher priority tasks can not effect the self-interference of τ_k. The WCRT of τ_k for a given critical path π_k can be derived by the following equation:

$$R_k = len(\pi_k) + I_{k,k}(\pi_k) + \sum_{i<k} I_{i,k}(\pi_k) \tag{1}$$

Because $len(\pi_k) + I_{k,k}(\pi_k)$ is fixed, we can directly use the method **Ty-B-2** in [10] to bound the $len(\pi_k) + I_{k,k}(\pi_k)$ which is denoted by $\widehat{R_k}$. Then the biggest problem is how to bound the inter-interference for higher priority tasks.

5   Bounding Inter-interference

In this section, we solve the problem how to bound the interference generated by higher priority tasks. The basic idea is to bound interference contributed by one higher priority task, and then get the total interference of all higher priority tasks.

For a given problem window of $[a, b)$, the interference generated by a higher priority task τ_i can be divided into three parts as following (see Fig. 2).

- *body*: body interference is such the interference contributed by all jobs with both release time and deadline in the interval.
- *carry-in*: carry-in interference is such interference contributed by the carry-in job which has release time before a and deadline in $[a, b)$ and each task at most has one such job.
- *carry-out*: carry-out interference is such interference contributed by a carry-out job which has release time in $[a, b)$ and deadline after b and each task has at most one such job.

So, the problem turns to calculate the three kinds of interference in the problem window of τ_k. According to the interference classification, the problem window of τ_k can also be divided into three continuous time intervals as following (see Fig. 2):

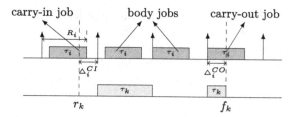

Fig. 2. Body, carry-in and carry-out jobs of τ_i in the problem window.

- Carry-in window of τ_i is defined as the time interval starts from the release time of τ_k and ends at the release time of the first body job of τ_i which is denoted as Δ_i^{CI}.
- Body window of τ_i is defined as the time interval starts at the end time of carry-in window of τ_i and ends at the start time of carry-out window of τ_i.
- Carry-out window of τ_i is defined as the time interval starts from the last release job in the problem window and ends at the end time of the problem window of τ_k which is denoted as Δ_i^{CO}.

Obviously, the problem is to maximize the total interference each higher priority tasks can generate in their corresponding interval. Clearly, the body job's interference of τ_i is easy to be bounded when the length of the problem window is given. The problem is how to bound the carry-in and carry-out interference. Let Δ_i denote total length of carry-in window and carry-out window. We have $\Delta_i = \Delta_i^{CI} + \Delta_i^{CO}$. The DAG construction makes it hard to find the worst case execution scenario of carry-in and carry-out job, so we should consider all possible combinations of the length of carry-in and carry-out windows.

We first bound the interference of carry-in job (carry-out job) for the given Δ_i^{CI} (Δ_i^{CO}). Then we use the "sliding window" technique in [15] to find the worst case scenario of carry-in and carry-out jobs.

5.1 Bounding Carry-In Interference

In this section, we solve the problem how to bound the interference of a carry-in job. To bound the carry-in interference of τ_i in the interval $[r_k, r_k + \Delta_i^{CI}]$, we should consider all possible execution scenarios of a carry-in job. Enumerating all possible execution scenarios of a carry-in job is time consuming. We should find a way to approximate the worst case execution distribution of carry-in job in the carry-in window.

This problem is even harder than the same problem for DAG tasks on homogeneous systems. First, it also suffers the same problem with the homogeneous DAG tasks. Second, it suffers the problem of types. Considering the efficiency problem, we use a simple method to bound the carry-in interference. Only when all cores are occupied by higher priority tasks, the vertices of task τ_k can not be executed. And for the type s, the interference of a higher priority task can be upper bounded by $vol_s(\tau_i)/M_s$. Then the interference contributed by the carry-in job of τ_i can be bounded by $\sum_{s\in S} vol_s(\tau_i)/M_s$.

Note that the latest finish time of the carry-in job of τ_i can not later than the time instant $r_i^{CI} + R_i$. So the actual time interval for carry-in is $\Delta_i^{CI} - (T_i - R_i)$ (see Fig. 2). Then the carry-in interference can be upper bounded by the following lemma.

Lemma 1. *In the carry-in window Δ_i^{CI}, the interference contributed by the carry-in job of a higher priority task τ_i is upper bounded by the following:*

$$I_{i,k}^{CI}(\Delta_i^{CI}) = \min\left\{\max\left\{\Delta_i^{CI} - (T_i - R_i), 0\right\}, \sum_{s\in S}\frac{vol_s(\tau_i)}{M_s}\right\} \qquad (2)$$

Proof. The total interference contributed by the carry-in job of τ_i can be bounded by $\sum_{s\in S} vol_s(\tau_i)/M_s$. Because τ_i cannot complete later than R_i, τ_i can not execute during the $T_i - R_i$ time units just before the end of the carry-in window (see Fig. 2). Therefore, τ_i executes during at most $\max\{0, \Delta_i^{CI} - (T_i - R_i)\}$ time units in the carry-in window.

5.2   Bounding Carry-Out Interference

In this section, we solve the problem how to bound the interference of a carry-out job. The theory of homogeneous multi-cores constructs a workload distribution in which the carry-out job starts executing as soon as it is released and at its highest possible concurrency level. Obviously, there are always executed the maximum workload in the carry-out window. The main challenge is how to to find the maximum parallelism which is a NP-hard problem. It uses a *decomposition tree* to get the maximum parallelism.

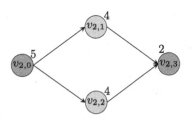

Fig. 3. A DAG task τ_2.

However, executing for the maximum parallelism may not get the worst case situation for the typed DAG task in the carry-out window, this observation can be seen in the Example 2. Note that in [6] the interference of the carry-out job is generated by the total workload using which to divide the number of cores.

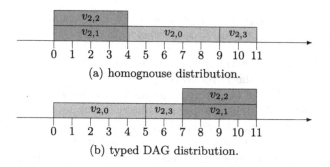

(a) homognouse distribution.

(b) typed DAG distribution.

Fig. 4. Two possible distributions of τ_2 in Fig. 3 executed on a platform with $M_1 = 1$ and $M_2 = 3$.

Example 2. For the typed DAG task shown in Fig. 3, there are two different workload distributions shown in Fig. 4. In the distribution shown in Fig. 4(a), the interference of carry-out job is $(4 + 4)/3 = 8/3$ in the interval $[0, 4]$ when it use the same distribution as homogeneous platforms. The interference generated in the distribution shown in Fig. 4(b) is $4/1 = 4$ in the same time interval. Obviously, the technique used in the homogeneous is not appropriate for the typed DAG tasks.

To achieve the worst case of the carry-out job, we should determine which vertices execute can produce the maximum interference at any point during the execution of carry-out job. To fully consider the construction of DAG and heterogeneous architecture, we define $1/M_{\gamma(v)}$ as interference parameter which is denoted as $p(v)$. And at any point during the execution of carry-out job, we choose the vertex set in which the vertices can execute in parallel and have the maximum total interference parameters. The reason can be explained by the following lemma.

Lemma 2. *At any time instant t, there are any two given eligible parallel sets denoted as PS_a and PS_b, respectively. If PS_a and PS_b hold the following condition, PS_a generates more interference than PS_b.*

$$\sum_{v \in PS_a} p(v) \geq \sum_{v \in PS_b} p(v) \tag{3}$$

Proof. We assume ϵ is a positive number which is infinitely close to 0. Therefore, at the time interval $[t, t + \epsilon)$, all the vertices in PS_a and PS_b execute for ϵ. We let I_a and I_b denote the interference produced by PS_a and PS_b, respectively. Then,

$$I_a = \sum_{v \in PS_a} \frac{\epsilon}{M_{\gamma(v)}} = \left(\sum_{v \in PS_a} \frac{1}{M_{\gamma(v)}} \right) \cdot \epsilon = \left(\sum_{v \in PS_a} p(v) \right) \cdot \epsilon$$

$$I_b = \sum_{v \in PS_b} \frac{\epsilon}{M_{\gamma(v)}} = \left(\sum_{v \in PS_b} \frac{1}{M_{\gamma(v)}} \right) \cdot \epsilon = \left(\sum_{v \in PS_a} p(v) \right) \cdot \epsilon$$

Because the total interference parameters of PS_a are more than the total interference parameters of PS_b, $I_a > I_b$. This lemma is proved.

Hence, we need to get the maximum total interference parameters for τ_i. Here, we also transform the DAG G_i into a NFJ-DAG (nested fork-join DAG) by removing some edges of G_i and then get its decomposition tree T_i (see Fig. 5) by successively applying series and parallel binary decomposition rules which are used in [6]. Note that we use Pa to label a parallel vertex and Se to label a series vertex. A vertex v labelled with Pa means that its left sub-tree can executed in parallel with its right sub-tree. A vertex v labelled with Se means that its left sub-tree and the right sub-tree must be executed in sequential.

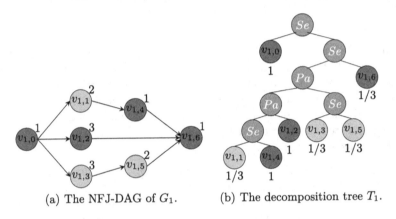

(a) The NFJ-DAG of G_1.   (b) The decomposition tree T_1.

Fig. 5. Illustration of the NFJ-DAG and decomposition tree

Example 3. We also take the DAG task shown in Fig. 1 as example. First, we remove the edge $(v_{1,3}, v_{1,4})$ from it to get a NFJ-DAG shown in Fig. 5(a). Then we decompose the NFJ-DAG shown in Fig. 5(a) to get a decomposition tree shown in Fig. 5(b).

According to the Lemma 2, we can get the set of vertices yielding the maximum total interference parameters by traversing the decomposition tree from root to the leaves. We use $P_i(v)$ to denote the set of vertices which has the maximum total interference parameters for the decomposition tree of τ_i. We also use Pa_i (Se_i) to denote the set of vertices which are labelled with $Pa(Se)$ in the decomposition tree of τ_i. $P_i^L(v)$ $(P_i^R(v))$ denotes the determined set of left(right) sub-tree when traverse to the vertex v. According to the parallel and series rules of decomposition tree, for each vertex v in a decomposition tree, one can get a set of vertices which can contribute the maximum interference parameters. The above discussion can be summarized as the following lemma.

Lemma 3. *For task τ_i's decomposition tree, v is a vertex in it. The maximum of total interference parameter vertices set can be derived by the following equation:*

$$P_i(v) = \begin{cases} P_i^L(v) \cup P_i^R(v), & if\ v \in Pa_i \\ P_i^L(v), & if\ v \in Se_i\ and \\ & \sum_{u \in P_i^L(v)} p(u) \geq \sum_{u \in P_i^R(v)} p(u) \\ P_i^R(v), & if\ v \in Se_i\ and \\ & \sum_{u \in P_i^L(v)} p(u) < \sum_{u \in P_i^R(v)} p(u) \\ \{v\}, & otherwise \end{cases} \quad (4)$$

Proof. According to the parallel and series rules of decomposition tree and Lemma 2, the proof of this lemma is obvious.

Now, we need to construct a distribution for carry-out job to derive an upper bound interference generated by it. According to Lemmas 2 and 3, we use Algorithm 1 to get the worst case distribution of carry-out job of τ_i. The intuitive of this algorithm is that to find the maximum interference parameters of vertices that can execute in parallel at each time instant of the carry-out window according to Lemma 3. First it finds the set of vertices which can get the maximum interference parameters (line 4) by traversing the decomposition tree. According to the results of Line 4, it adds a new block (line 5) to the interference distribution ID_i^{CO} with the width equal to the minimum WCET among these subtasks and height equal the sum of interference parameters. There are some vertices left workload which can not be executed in the new adding block. Updating these vertices workload in the decomposition tree (line 7). If the left workload of a vertex is 0, we remove the corresponding leaf of this vertex from the decomposition tree (line 8–9). This procedure continues until there is no leaves in the decomposition tree.

Algorithm 1. Constructing ID_i^{CO}

Require: T_i
Ensure: ID_i^{CO}
1: $ID_i^{CO} \leftarrow \emptyset$;
2: $u \leftarrow T_i.root$
3: **while** $T_i \neq \emptyset$ **do**
4:      $P \leftarrow P_i(u)$;
5:      $width \leftarrow \min\{c_i(v_p) \mid v_p \in P\}$;
6:      $ID_i^{CO} \leftarrow [ID_i^{CO}, (width, \sum_{v_p \in P} p(v_p))]$;
7:      $\forall v_p \in P : c_i(v_p) \leftarrow c_i(v_p) - width$;
8:      $\forall v \in T_i$ such that $c_i(v) = 0$: remove v from T_i;
9: **end while**
10: **return** ID_i^{CO};

Example 4. Figure 6 gives the interference distribution ID_1^{CO} of τ_1 shown in Fig. 1.

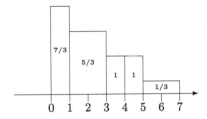

Fig. 6. The interference distribution ID_1^{CO} of τ_1 in Fig. 1.

Algorithm 1 gives a distribution which combines the types and workload together. To derive the maximum interference, the carry-out job must start executing as soon as it is released. So we align the start of ID_i^{CO} with the start of carry-out window. There are $|ID_i^{CO}|$ blocks in the distribution ID_i^{CO}. For the bth, the height of it is denoted by h_b and the width of it is denoted by w_b. Note that the last block may execute part of it in the carry-out window. Hence, the actually width of the bth block is $\min\{w_b, \max\{\Delta_i^{CO} - \sum_{j=1}^{b-1} w_j, 0\}\}$. Obviously, for the length of Δ_i^{CO} the maximum interference of carry-out job is bounded by the following lemma.

Lemma 4. *Assume the length of the carry-out window of τ_i is Δ_i^{CO}, the interference of it is upper bounded by the following:*

$$I_{i,k}^{CO}(\Delta_i^{CO}) = \sum_{b=1}^{|ID_i^{CO}|} h_b \times \min\left\{w_b, \max\{\Delta_i^{CO} - \sum_{j=1}^{b-1} w_j, 0\}\right\} \quad (5)$$

Proof. According to the Lemmas 2 and 3, this lemma is obviously true.

6   Schedulability Analysis

We have derived upper-bounds on the interference generated by the carry-in and carry-out jobs of τ_i as a function of Δ_i^{CI} and Δ_i^{CO}, respectively. Then, we need to balance Δ_i^{CI} and Δ_i^{CO} such that the interference in the problem window of length X is maximum. The value of Δ_i can be computed based on [6]:

$$\Delta_i = X - \max\{0, \left\lfloor \frac{X - len(G_i)}{T_i} \right\rfloor\} \times T_i \quad (6)$$

Let $I_{i,k}^C(\Delta_i)$ be the maximum interference produced by the carry-in and carry-out jobs of τ_i over Δ_i. Hence, an upper-bound on the total interference generated by τ_i in a time interval of length X is given by

$$I_{i,k}(X) = I_{i,k}^C(\Delta_i) + \max\{0, \left\lfloor \frac{X - \Delta_i}{T_i} \right\rfloor\} \times \sum_{s \in S} \frac{vol_s(G_i)}{M_s} \quad (7)$$

Therefore, we need to get the $I_{i,k}^C(\Delta_i)$. Here, we formulate it as the maximization of $I_{i,k}^{CI}(x_1) + I_{i,k}^{CO}(x_2)$ subject to $\Delta_i = x_1 + x_2$. We use the technique named "sliding window" introduced in [15] to solve this problem.

So far, we get the upper bound intra-interference and the inter-interference. Hence, the WCRT of τ_k can be derived by the following theorem.

Theorem 1. *For any task τ_k in a task set τ, the R_k can be derived by the following iterative Equation with the beginning $R_k = \widehat{R_k}$:*

$$R_k = \widehat{R_k} + \sum_{i<k} I_{i,k}(R_k) \tag{8}$$

Proof. By the above discussion, this theorem is clearly true.

7   Evaluation

The analysis presented in this paper has been simulated by Python 3.7. The DAG structure of the task is randomly generated by the technique in [16]. The procedure is as follows:

- It initially generates the source and sink vertices and then recursively add the source and sink vertices for its sub-DAGs.
- Each vertex has two probabilities p_{par} and p_{term} to generate a parallel branch and a terminal vertex, respectively. Note that $p_{par} + p_{term} = 1$. The numbers of parallel branches are uniformly chosen within $[2, Br]$, where Br is the maximum number of branches. And the *depth* determines the maximum recursion depth for the generation of the task graphs.
- Finally, the series-parallel graph is transformed into a general DAG by randomly adding an edge between pairs of vertices that can be connected. The probability of adding an edge between two nodes is given by P_{add}.

We first define a default parameter setting, and then tune different parameters to evaluate the performance of the methods regarding different parameter changing trends. The default parameter setting as follows:

- In the case of homogeneous multi-cores, the considered platform is implicitly determined by the number of cores. Whereas for the heterogeneous multi-cores, it is determined by not only the number of cores but also the number of types. So there is no way to systematically choose platforms to evaluate. Here, we set the number of types $|S|$ to be uniformly chosen in $[2, 5]$. And for M_s, we uniformly choose it in $[1, 4]$ and $[5, 8]$, respectively.
- For the generation of each DAG task, we set $p_{par} = 0.7$, $p_{term} = 0.3$, $Br = 3$, $depth = 3$ and $P_{add} = 0.2$. These settings lead to a rich variety of internal DAG structures: we observed different degrees of parallelism and sequential segments in each task set.
- The WCET of each vertex in the DAG is uniformly chosen in the interval $[1, 100]$. The task length $len(G_i)$ and the workload $vol(G_i)$ of τ_i are computed based on the internal structure of the DAG and the WCET of its nodes.

- We let M denote the total number of all the cores in the system, i.e., $M = \sum_{s \in S} M_s$. A vertex is assigned to the type s by the probability $P_s = M_s/M$.
- If the number of tasks n is fixed, we set $U_{tot} = 0.2M$. Then We use UUnifast to derive individual task utilization U_i for a fixed value of n and then get the minimum inter-arrival time T_i by $T_i = vol(G_i)/U_i$. If n is not fixed, we uniformly choose the minimum inter-arrival time T_i of τ_i in the interval $[len(G_i), vol(G_i)/\beta]$, where β is used to define the minimum utilization of all the tasks, until the total utilization reach the U_{tot}. We set β to be randomly chosen in $(0, 0.5]$.
- For each point of each experiment, we randomly generate 500 DAG task sets.
- Priorities are assigned following the Rate Monotonic policy.

To our knowledge, there is no solution of such problem that we consider. Therefore, we compared our method (referred to as NRTA-FP) with the most pessimistic method (referred to as WRTA-FP) in the following:

$$I_{i,k}(X) = \left(\left\lceil \frac{X}{T_i} \right\rceil + 1\right) \times \sum_{s \in S} \frac{vol_s(\tau_i)}{M_s}$$

We compared them by the *acceptance ratio* for the same task sets. The acceptance ratio is defined as the ratio between the number of tasks which can be scheduled by a particular method and the total number of tasks which we tested.

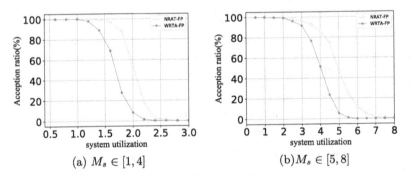

(a) $M_s \in [1, 4]$ (b) $M_s \in [5, 8]$

Fig. 7. The acceptance ratios by NRAT-FP and WRTA-FP when varying U_{tot}.

Figure 7(a)–(b) show the acceptance ratio when varying U_{tot}. In all these figures, NRAT-FP performs much better than WRTA-FP. In addition, we can see that the acceptance ratios of NRAT-FP and WRTA-FP all decrease when U_{tot} increases. This is because a task becomes more difficult to be schedulable when its utilization is larger. Comparing Fig. 7(a) and (b), the acceptance ratio increases when M_s is larger, simply because a task set is easier to be scheduled when more cores are used.

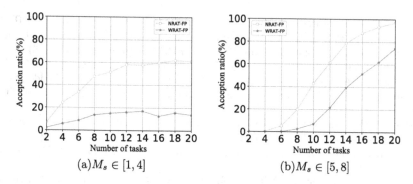

(a)$M_s \in [1,4]$ (b)$M_s \in [5,8]$

Fig. 8. The acceptance ratios by NRAT-FP and WRTA-FP when varying n.

Figure 8(a)–(b) shows the acceptance ratio when varying n. In all these figures, We can see that NRAT-FP performs much better than WRTA-FP. The acceptance ratio increases basically as n increases. This is because when n increases, the utilization of each task decreases.

8 Conclusion

In this paper, we extended the state-of-the-art response time analysis method for single typed DAG task to a typed DAG task set under G-FP scheduling. First, we achieved the upper bound of the intra-interference. And then we discussed the worst case scenario of carry-in and carry-out window. Due to the DAG structure and typed platform, the analysis is much harder. We took a deep look to the typed DAG tasks and proposed a method to bound the carry-in interference which is still pessimistic. We proposed a technique to find the worst case interference distribution of carry-out job based on the decomposition tree. Finally, we used the classic sliding technique to get the upper bound of the inter-interference of each task. Finally, we conducted simulation tests to validate the performance of our methods in terms of both accuracy and efficiency with randomly generated typed DAG task sets. But the results are still pessimistic, we can not find a more precise way to analysis the carry-in interference which will be our future work.

References

1. Baruah, S.: Improved multiprocessor global schedulability analysis of sporadic DAG task systems. In: 26th Euromicro Conference on Real-Time Systems, ECRTS 2014, Madrid, Spain, 8–11 July 2014, pp. 97–105. IEEE Computer Society (2014)
2. Baruah, S.: The federated scheduling of constrained-deadline sporadic DAG task systems. In: Nebel, W., Atienza, D. (eds.) Proceedings of the 2015 Design, Automation & Test in Europe Conference & Exhibition, DATE 2015, Grenoble, France, 9–13 March 2015, pp. 1323–1328. ACM (2015)

3. Baruah, S.: Federated scheduling of sporadic DAG task systems. In: 2015 IEEE International Parallel and Distributed Processing Symposium, IPDPS 2015, Hyderabad, India, 25–29 May 2015, pp. 179–186. IEEE Computer Society (2015)

4. Baruah, S.: The federated scheduling of systems of conditional sporadic DAG tasks. In: Girault, A., Guan, N. (eds.) 2015 International Conference on Embedded Software, EMSOFT 2015, Amsterdam, Netherlands, 4–9 October 2015, pp. 1–10 IEEE (2015)

5. Bonifaci, V., Marchetti-Spaccamela, A., Stiller, S., Wiese, A.: Feasibility analysis in the sporadic DAG task model. In: 25th Euromicro Conference on Real-Time Systems, ECRTS 2013, Paris, France, 9–12 July 2013, pp. 225–233. IEEE Computer Society (2013)

6. Fonseca, J., Nelissen, G., Nélis, V.: Improved response time analysis of sporadic DAG tasks for global FP scheduling. In: Proceedings of the 25th International Conference on Real-Time Networks and Systems - RTNS. ACM Press (2017)

7. Fonseca, J.C., Nelissen, G., Nélis, V., Pinho, L.M.: Response time analysis of sporadic DAG tasks under partitioned scheduling. In: 11th IEEE Symposium on Industrial Embedded Systems, SIES 2016, Krakow, Poland, 23–25 May 2016, pp. 290–299. IEEE (2016)

8. Graham, R.L.: Bounds for certain multiprocessing anomalies. Bell Syst. Tech. J. **45**, 1563–1581 (1966)

9. Graham, R.L.: Bounds on multiprocessing timing anomalies. SIAM J. Appl. Math. **17**, 416–429 (1969)

10. Han, M., Guan, N., Sun, J., He, Q., Deng, Q., Liu, W.: Response time bounds for typed dag parallel tasks on heterogeneous multi-cores. IEEE Trans. Parallel Distrib. Syst. **30**, 1–17 (2019)

11. Han, M., Zhang, T., Deng, Q.: Bounding carry-in interference for synchronous parallel tasks under global fixed-priority scheduling. J. Syst. Arch. **90**(2018), 34–43 (2018)

12. Jaffe, J.M.: Bounds on the scheduling of typed task systems. SIAM J. Comput. **9**(3), 541–551 (1980)

13. Li, J., Chen, J.-J., Agrawal, K., Lu, C., Gill, C., Saifullah, A.: Analysis of federated and global scheduling for parallel real-time tasks. In: 26th Euromicro Conference on Real-Time Systems, ECRTS 2014, Madrid, Spain, 8–11 July 2014, pp. 85–96. IEEE Computer Society (2014)

14. Li, J., Ferry, D., Ahuja, S., Agrawal, K., Gill, C.D., Chenyang, L.: Mixed-criticality federated scheduling for parallel real-time tasks. Real-Time Syst. **53**(5), 760–811 (2017)

15. Maia, C., Bertogna, M., Nogueira, L., Pinho, L.M.: Response-time analysis of synchronous parallel tasks in multiprocessor systems. In: Proceedings of the 22nd International Conference on Real-Time Networks and Systems - RTNS. ACM Press (2014)

16. Melani, A., Bertogna, M., Bonifaci, V., Marchetti-Spaccamela, A., Buttazzo, G.C.: Response-time analysis of conditional DAG tasks in multiprocessor systems. In: 27th Euromicro Conference on Real-Time Systems, ECRTS 2015, Lund, Sweden, 8–10 July 2015, pp. 211–221. IEEE Computer Society (2015)

17. Nelissen, G., Fonseca, J., Raravi, G., Nelis, V.: Timing analysis of fixed priority self-suspending sporadic tasks (2015)

18. OMAP (2018). https://en.wikipedia.org/wiki/OMAP

19. Tegra Processors (2018). https://www.nvidia.com/object/tegra.html

20. Zynq-7000 SoC (2018). https://www.xilinx.com/products/silicon-devices/soc/zynq-7000.html

21. Venkat, A., Tullsen, D.M.: Harnessing ISA diversity: design of a heterogeneous-ISA chip multiprocessor. In ACM/IEEE 41st International Symposium on Computer Architecture, ISCA 2014, Minneapolis, MN, USA, 14–18 June 2014, pp. 121–132. IEEE Computer Society (2014)
22. Yang, K., Yang, M., Anderson, J.H.: Reducing response-time bounds for DAG-based task systems on heterogeneous multicore platforms. In: Plantec, A., Singhoff, F., Faucou, S., Pinho, L.M. (eds.) Proceedings of the 24th International Conference on Real-Time Networks and Systems, RTNS 2016, Brest, France, 19–21 October 2016, pp. 349–358. ACM (2016)

A Formal Modeling and Verification Framework for Flash Translation Layer Algorithms

Lei Qiao[1,4(✉)], Shaofeng Li[3], Hua Yang[1], and Mengfei Yang[2]

[1] Beijing Institute of Control Engineering, Beijing 100089, China
fly2moon@aliyun.com
[2] Chinese Academy of Space Technology, Beijing 100094, China
[3] School of Computer Science and Technology,
Xidian University, Xian 710071, China
[4] The State Key Laboratory of Computer Science, Institute of Software,
Chinese Academy of Sciences, Beijing 100094, China

Abstract. Flash translation layer (FTL) is a part of software running on the NAND flash memory, which is ubiquitous in various devices. FTL algorithm hides the complexity of NAND flash characteristics and provides a simple and standard interface like magnetic disks. In this paper, we present a general and abstract formal model for FTL algorithms, define their functional correctness as refinement, and propose a verification framework. We demonstrate its use by verifying a classic FTL algorithm BAST. Our entire development has been formalized in the proof assistant Coq.

Keywords: NAND flash · FTL · Formal verification

1 Introduction

NAND flash memory has been deployed in various computer systems from embedded devices to laptops, desktops, and data centers. It promises enormous performance gains and power savings relative to traditional magnetic disks while being much denser. Although flash offers a huge performance improvement, making it as easy and efficient to use as traditional magnetic disk drives presents a challenge.

The storage system accessing NAND flash directly must be aware of the complexities involved in doing so, in particular, the inability to update data in place. In other words, if the system wants to overwrite the old data at a memory cell, it has to erase the entire *block*, which contains the cell and is possibly

Foundation item: National Natural Science Foundation of China (61632005, 61502031); The State Key Laboratory of Computer Science, Institute of Software, Chinese Academy of Sciences Open Project Fund (SYSKF1804).

N. Guan et al. (Eds.): SETTA 2019, LNCS 11951, pp. 72–88, 2019.
https://doi.org/10.1007/978-3-030-35540-1_5

hundreds of KBs. One approach to utilizing flash is through the use of flash-based file systems, such as JFFS3, Yaffs2, UBIFS which however, requires an extensive rework of the storage system's existing infrastructure and file system. Another more popular approach is to package NAND flash as a device (e.g., SSD, SDCard, USB drive) that provides a standard disk interface (e.g., IDE, SATA, SAS). As flash memory does not support overwriting data in place, flash devices require a translation layer to map logical blocks to their locations within physical flash memory. This layer is called the flash translation layer (FTL) [13–16]. To hide the limitation of erase-before-write, FTL redirects each write request to an empty location in NAND flash memory that has been erased in advance, and manages an internal mapping table to record the mapping information from the logical address to the physical location.

NAND flash has been suffering from the following inferent hardware issues [9–11]: bit-error-rate, data retention, wear endurance, etc., which are becoming worse with the rapid development of hardware. The growing hardware unreliability makes the FTL software much more complicated nowadays than what it was ten years ago. However, the FTL software is not as reliable as we thought according to a study done recently [17]. A large recall of Macbook Air laptops conducted by Apple Inc. in Oct. 2013 was due to serious SSD firmware bugs [3], technically, bugs from the FTL.

On the one hand, much work has been done about verifying file systems in the past decade, however, their research results assume that the devices underlying are functionally correct and reliable. On the other hand, few work can be found about modeling or verifying the FTL bridging NAND flash and file systems. With the FTL software (or firmware) growing rapidly, it is definitely worth doing research to improve the reliability of NAND flash based devices.

In this paper, we propose a verification framework to prove the correctness of the FTL algorithms: the FTL software with NAND flash hardware *emulates* a virtual standard disk device. The correctness suggests that if there are a hard disk and a flash device, when we send the same sequence of read/write commands to the two devices simultaneously, we expect to get exactly the same data from them. We also show how to verify a classical FTL algorithm, BAST [13], in our framework. All of the definitions and the proofs we present in this paper are developed in a proof assistant Coq [2]. The code can be downloaded online [1].

We make the following main contributions:

– As far as we know, our work is the first attempt to formalize the semantic model of an FTL. We give the formal specifications and the definition of the correctness property for FTLs, providing a solid basis for develop reliable file systems at the upper layer.
– We propose a framework to prove the correctness of FTLs by using invariant-based proof techniques. We show that if an FTL algorithm defined in the framework satisfies five hypotheses, we can have the conclusion that the FTL is correct. The approach is general and can be adapted to verify various FTL algorithms.

– We prove the functional correctness of a classic FTL algorithm BAST. All of
the definitions and proofs are implemented in Coq.

2   Informal Development

In this section, we informally explain our basic ideas about modeling FTL algorithms, the correctness requirement, and how we prove it.

2.1   Modeling FTL Algorithms

An FTL is working like a driver in conjunction with an existing operating system
to make linear flash memory appear to be a disk drive. The main challenge of
modeling FTL algorithms is due to the innate characteristics of NAND flash.

A NAND flash chip consists of multiple *blocks* [8]. Each block is further
divided into multiple (32, 64, or 128) *pages*, the minimum unit of data transfer.
The data capacity of each page may vary from 512 B to 8 KB. In addition to
the data cells, each page also contains additional cells in the spare area, also
known as *Out of Band* (OOB) cells. The primary purpose of OOB cells is to
store the error correcting code and the meta-data of FTLs. Compared with
traditional magnetic storage media, NAND flash has certain characteristics [8,12]
that impose restrictions on how to use it.

(1) A page, once written, cannot be rewritten unless it is erased;
(2) An erase can only be done for an entire block;
(3) A block has a limited number of erasure operations before it becomes unusable.
(4) The erase operation is fairly slow, 2 ms typically, while a read operation
costs only about 25 us;
(5) All pages within one block must be programmed in order, otherwise, bits in
the page will more likely be corrupted by *program disturb* [12].

Traditional magnetic disk devices perform input and output upon structured
pieces called "sectors", supporting *update in place*. Flash devices intend to provide the same functionality, but the underlying NAND flash doesn't support
page-overwriting. The problem is solved by adding an FTL on NAND flash.
Users access the flash devices through *logical* addresses, which are mapped by
the FTL to the physical flash pages. The mapping information is stored as *metadata* which is maintained by the FTL. When users intend to overwrite a logical
address, the FTL will write the data in different areas of the flash, and then
update the mapping. Therefore, most popular file systems designed for magnetic disks (e.g., FAT16/32, EXT2/3) can directly be reused for NAND flash
with the FTL.

Formally, an FTL algorithm can be defined as a quadruple:

$$\mathcal{A} \triangleq \langle f_\mathcal{A}, ftl\_init_\mathcal{A}(), ftl\_read_\mathcal{A}(), ftl\_write_\mathcal{A}() \rangle$$

where $f_\mathcal{A}$ is the configuration of meta-data maintained by the FTL, the rest of
three functions are the common FTL operations for initialization, read, write.

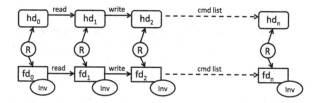

Fig. 1. The invariant and simulation

2.2 Correctness Requirement of FTL Algorithms

Another challenging work of this paper is how to specify the correctness of FTL algorithms, which is able to convince users that a NAND flash device will work well. We specify the correctness requirement of FTLs in terms of the abstract interface provided to users. The abstract view of a NAND flash device running an FTL should be the same with the view of a magnetic disk device. The latter is a sequence of sectors supporting update-in-place, in the sense that if we write a value v to a sector, we can read v out of the sector immediately. If we continue to update the sector with a new value v', we will read v' out.

Suppose we now have two empty (initialized) devices, a disk device hd, and a virtual device fd composed of NAND flash with an FTL. We may send read/write commands to them and receive the data read out. We say the flash device is implemented correctly if: we can read exact the same sequence of data from the two devices if we send the same sequence of commands to them simultaneously. In other words, the flash device emulates a virtual disk device.

The correctness can be specified in terms of refinement. We establish a relation $\sqsubseteq$ between a flash device (concrete view) fd and a more abstract disk device hd. The refinement, $fd \sqsubseteq hd$, requires that fd have no more observable behaviors than hd. The refinement guarantees that we could safely replace a disk device with a flash device in any system.

2.3 Our Proof Technique Based on Invariant

The basic idea of proving refinement is shown in Fig. 1. We use the invariant-based simulation proof technique to prove the refinement that the two devices have same behaviors w.r.t. the same commands. The refinement can be proved in the framework for any FTL algorithm $\mathcal{A}$, as long as the algorithm $\mathcal{A}$ can satisfies five hypotheses, which we will explain later.

To establish the simulation relation, we first use a relation, R, that relates the two devices and is maintained forever. The relation R ensures that the data read from the both sides are equal. To prove the preservation of the relation, we need to find a global invariant, $inv_{\mathcal{A}}$, which reflects the design of the FTL in the flash device. More accurately, the invariant specifies the consistency of the meta-data of the FTL algorithm, and the consistency between the FTL meta-data in RAM and the data stored in the flash. We then can prove that if two devices satisfy R and the flash device satisfies inv_A, then the relation R will be preserved after the two devices both go one step forward. Suppose the two devices process one command and become hd' and fd', respectively. We can prove the following lemma:

$$R(hd, fd) \wedge Inv_A(fd) \Rightarrow R(hd', fd')$$

Now we need to prove a lemma that the invariant Inv_A will be preserved after the flash device goes one step. This lemma can be reduced to the following lemma:

$$\textbf{Hyp1}(A, Inv_A) \wedge \textbf{Hyp2}(A, Inv_A) \wedge \textbf{Hyp3}(A, Inv_A) \wedge \textbf{Hyp4}(A, Inv_A) \wedge \textbf{Hyp5}(A, Inv_A)$$
$$\Rightarrow Inv_A(fd) \Rightarrow Inv_A(fd')$$

where **Hyp1−5** are five hypotheses describing the intuitive facts about a correct FTL algorithm. They are about the relationship between three FTL operations, $ftl\_init()$, $ftl\_read()$, $ftl\_write()$. The hypothesis **Hyp1** says any empty flash device satisfies the invariant Inv_A. **Hyp2** says any data read from an empty flash device is always zero. **Hyp3** says if we write a value to the flash device, we can read the value out from the same address in the next step. **Hyp4** says if we write a value to the page in flash device, other pages won't be changed. **Hyp5** says that any read operation from a valid address won't fail. The formal definitions of them can be found in Sect. 4.

3   Modeling FTL and Its Functional Correctness

3.1   Disk Device

A disk device (hd) can simply be viewed as a list of units, which are generally called "sectors" (See Fig. 2). The number of sectors is denoted by a parameter, max_sec. A sector (sec), the minimal data unit of r/w, is defined as a data chunk of 512 bytes. The r/w address is thus equal to a sector number $read(lsn)$. Disk devices support two commands: $read(lsn)$ is to read data from a sector with the logical sector number (lsn); $write(d, lsn)$ is to write data (d) into a sector with the number (lsn). A data chunk (d) is 512 bytes by default. Each command generates an event that is able to be observed by users. An event (ev) can be a successful read event ($data(d)$), a successful write event ($void$), or an error event ($error$). The behavior of a device (B) is defined as a list of events. The notation $cmds$ specifies a sequence of commands.

There are three operations on disk devices, $hd\_init()$ $hd\_read()$ and $hd\_write()$, defined as functions in the monadic style, which allows us to define imperative computations in a pure functional programming language in Coq. Here we give the definitions of two important operations. The definition of $hd\_init()$ can be found in the Coq code.

```
hd_read(hd, lsn):                    hd_write(hd, lsn, d):
    test lsn < max_sec;                  test lsn < max_sec;
    do    d ← list_get(hd, lsn);         do    hd' ← list_get(hd, lsn, d);
    ret   d                              ret   hd'
```

$$
\begin{array}{llll}
(Disk) & hd ::= sec_0, \ldots, sec_{(max\_sec-1)} & (FlashDev) & fd ::= (c, f_A) \\
(Sec) & sec ::= d[512] & (NANDchip) & c ::= b_0, b_1, \ldots, b_{(max\_blk-1)} \\
(Addr) & lsn ::= naturalnumber & (Block) & b ::= (p[pages\_blk - 1], np, ec) \\
(Cmd) & cmd ::= read(lsn) \mid write(d, lsn) & (PageList) & p[n] ::= [p_0, \ldots, p_n] \\
(Event) & ev ::= data(d) \mid void \mid error & (Erase-count) & ec ::= n \quad n \in integer \\
(Behav) & B ::= \varepsilon \mid ev \cdot B & (Page) & p ::= (d[512], d[8], ps) \\
(Cmd-list)\ cmds ::= \cdot \mid cmd; cmds & & (Page-state) & ps ::= free \mid programmed
\end{array}
$$

Fig. 2. Definition of disk device and flash device

A monadic function is defined by a sequence of steps, as a procedure is in any imperative programming language like C, or functional languages like Haskell. A "do" step in the function either outputs a value, or fails. If any step fails, the function will fail immediately. Otherwise, the output value will be passed to the next step. A "test" step doesn't output any value, and it succeeds if and only if the condition followed is checked to be true. The final step of a monadic function is always a "ret" step, i.e., returning the result of the function to the caller. The operational semantics of disk devices are defined in the form of:

$$
hd[cmd] \mapsto hd' \downarrow ev,
$$

specifying that a disk device hd gets a command cmd and steps to a new configuration hd', with an event ev output.

3.2 Flash Device and FTL

A configuration of a NAND flash device fd consists of two parts, software and hardware. The hardware part is a configuration of a NAND flash chip (c), which is defined as a list of blocks. Each block (b) is a triple of a list of pages ($p[n]$), an offset of next unprogrammed page (np), and an erase-counter (ec)). A page (p) is a triple of normal data, OOB data and page status (ps). We use small block NAND flash in which page size is 512 bytes, resembling the capacity of a sector in traditional disk drives. A page status value is either free (unprogrammed) or programmed. The software part of (fd) is a configuration of the FTL (f_A), which comes from an FTL algorithm $\mathcal{A}$ and is abstract here. The parameter max_blk is the number of all physical blocks, and the parameter max_pages is the number of pages in one block.

The operations of NAND flash chips are defined as monadic functions also. The function nand_read(c, pbn, ppo) takes three arguments: a flash chip c, a block number pbn, and an offset (ppo) of the page to read; and returns two chunks of data, normal data and OOB data. The function nand_write(c, pbn, ppo, d_1, d_2) writes two chunks of data d_1 and d_2 to the page with the offset ppo in the block pbn. The function nand_read() returns an nand chip filled with junk data. The function nand_erase(c, pbn) is defined below. It erases the block of pbn, by replacing the old block with a empty block, specified by an auxiliary function make_block($\cdots$). After an erase operation, the erase count of the block will increase by one. The auxiliary functions can be found in the Coq code.

nand_erase(c, phn):
  test ($pbn < max\_blk$);
  do $b \leftarrow chip\_get\_block(c, pbn)$;
  do $ec \leftarrow block\_get\_erase\_count(b)$;
  do $b' \leftarrow make\_block(empty\_pages(), 0, ec + 1)$;
  do $c' \leftarrow chip\_set\_block(c, pbn, b')$;
  ret c'

For the flash device, the operations, fld_read() and fld_write() and fld_init(), are defined upon the interface of the FTL $\mathcal{A}$. The first two are defined below:

fld_read(fd, lsn):
  do $(c, f) \leftarrow fd$;
  do $(lbn, lpo) \leftarrow addr\_decode(lsn)$;
  do $d \leftarrow ftl\_read_{\mathcal{A}}(c, f, lbn, lpo)$;
  ret d;

fld_write(fd, lsn, d):
  do $(c, f) \leftarrow fd$;
  do $(lbn, lpo) \leftarrow addr\_decode(lsn)$;
  do $(c', f') \leftarrow ftl\_write_{\mathcal{A}}(c, f, lbn, lpo, d)$;
  ret d;

Here $ftl\_read()_{\mathcal{A}}$ and $ftl\_write()_{\mathcal{A}}$ are abstract in the framework. The operational semantics of flash devices are defined in the form of

$$fd[cmd] \mapsto fd' \downarrow ev.$$

We use the notation $fd[cmds] \mapsto^* fd' \downarrow B$ to specify that a flash device runs multiple steps and has the behavior B.

3.3   The Correctness Definition of FTL

We here give the definition of the correctness property:

Definition 1 (Correctness). *For any empty disk device hd_0 and any flash device fd_0, if hd_0 processes a list of commands successfully and generates a behavior B, then the device fd_0 can generate the same behavior after processing the same command list.*

$$Correctness(\mathcal{A}) \triangleq \forall hd_0, fld_0, cmds, B (hd_0 = hd\_init()) \land (fd_0 = fld\_init())$$
$$\Rightarrow hd_0[cmds] \mapsto^* hd' \downarrow B$$
$$\Rightarrow \exists fd' fd_0[cmds] \mapsto^* fd' \downarrow B$$

The correctness of an FTL algorithm $\mathcal{A}$ states that the process of an empty flash device refines that of an empty disk device.

4   Verification Framework

In this section, we show how to prove the correctness property of an FTL algorithm $\mathcal{A}$. As we explained in Sect. 2, we prove the simulation relation between a disk device and a flash device by using a global invariant and five hypotheses about the FTL.

$\textbf{Hyp1}(\mathcal{A}, Inv_{\mathcal{A}}) \triangleq Inv_{\mathcal{A}}(nand\_init(), ftl\_init_{\mathcal{A}})$

$\textbf{Hyp2}(\mathcal{A}, Inv_{\mathcal{A}}) \triangleq \forall lbn, lpo.(lbn * pages\_blk < max\_sec \bigwedge lpo < pages\_blk)$
$\qquad\qquad\qquad \Rightarrow ftl\_read(nand\_init(), ftl\_init(), lbn, lpo) = 0$

$\textbf{Hyp3}(\mathcal{A}, Inv_{\mathcal{A}}) \triangleq \forall c, f_{\mathcal{A}}, lbn, lpo, d, c', f'_{\mathcal{A}}.$
$\qquad\qquad\qquad Inv_{\mathcal{A}} \Rightarrow (ftl\_write(c, f_{\mathcal{A}}, lbn, lpo, d) = (c', f'_{\mathcal{A}}))$
$\qquad\qquad\qquad \Rightarrow ftl\_read(c', f_{\mathcal{A}}, lbn, lpo) = d$

$\textbf{Hyp4}(\mathcal{A}, Inv_{\mathcal{A}}) \triangleq \forall c, f_{\mathcal{A}}, lbn, lpo, d, c', f'_{\mathcal{A}}.$
$\qquad\qquad\qquad Inv_{\mathcal{A}} \Rightarrow (ftl\_read(c, f_{\mathcal{A}}, lbn, lpo, d) = (c', f'_{\mathcal{A}}))$
$\qquad\qquad\qquad \Rightarrow (\forall lbn', lpo'.(lbn' \neq lbn \bigvee lpo' \neq lpo)$
$\qquad\qquad\qquad \Rightarrow (ftl\_read(c', f'_{\mathcal{A}}, lbn', lpo') = ftl\_read(c, f_{\mathcal{A}}lbn, lpo)))$

$\textbf{Hyp5}(\mathcal{A}, Inv_{\mathcal{A}} \triangleq \forall c, f_{\mathcal{A}}, lbn, lpo, d, c', f'_{\mathcal{A}}.(lbn * pages\_blk < max\_sec \bigwedge lpo < pages\_blk)$
$\qquad\qquad\qquad \Rightarrow Inv_{\mathcal{A}}(c, f_{\mathcal{A}})$
$\qquad\qquad\qquad \Rightarrow \exists c', f'_{\mathcal{A}}.Inv_{\mathcal{A}}(c', f'_{\mathcal{A}}) \bigwedge ftl\_write(c, f_{\mathcal{A}}, lbn, lpo) = (c', f'_{\mathcal{A}})$

Fig. 3. Hypotheses of FTL algorithm

Global Invariant. Any FTL needs to maintain the information about the organization of user's data on the flash memory. To guarantee the correctness of the FTL, we have to make sure that the internal meta-data manipulated by the FTL algorithm are well-formed or consistent. This can be done by a global invariant $Inv_{\mathcal{A}}(c, f_{\mathcal{A}})$, which relates the data on the flash memory c and the meta-data $f_{\mathcal{A}}$. The invariant should hold before every command is received by a flash device, and also hold after the command is processed by the device.

The global invariant varies from FTL to FTL and is abstract in the framework. Generally speaking, what $Inv_{\mathcal{A}}$ specifies are about: (1) the nand flash chip is in a good state, (2) the internal state and data stored in the chip are consistent to the meta-data maintained in RAM, and (3) the meta-data themselves are consistent. The well-formedness ensures that the device could step forward as expected.

Five Hypotheses. The FTL operations, like ftl_init(), ftl_read() and ftl_write are abstract in the framework, and they have to follow five hypotheses in order to ensure they are defined correctly. The hypotheses are defined in Fig. 3. The first hypothesis **Hyp1** says that a flash device satisfies the invariant $Inv_{\mathcal{A}}$. The second hypothesis **Hyp2** is that any data read from an empty flash device is always zero. The hypothesis **Hyp3** says that for any flash device $(c, f_{\mathcal{A}})$ which satisfies $Inv_{\mathcal{A}}$, if we write data d to the address (lbn, lpo) and get a new device (c', f'), then we can read the data from the same address in fd' and the data will be equal to the data d just written. The hypothesis **Hyp4** says that for any flash device $(c, f_{\mathcal{A}})$ which satisfies $Inv_{\mathcal{A}}$, if we write data d to the address (lbn, lpo) and get a new device (c', f'), then any data read from a different address (lbn', lpo') in (c', f') will be equal to the data read from (lbn', lpo') in the device before writing. The last hypothesis **Hyp5** says that for any flash device $(c, f_{\mathcal{A}})$ satisfying $Inv_{\mathcal{A}}$, if the address (lbn, lpo) is valid, then we can write data d to the flash device at the address (lbn, lpo). Then after the writing, the new device (c', f') will still satisfy Inv.

Simulation Relation. A disk device needs to be associated with a flash device by a binary relation R that is supposed to be preserved after a sequence of commands which is processed by the two devices. The main purpose of the relation is to guarantee that the two devices are "equal": a disk device and a flash device satisfy the relation R if and only if the data read from the same address of the two devices are equal.

$$R(hd, fd) \triangleq \forall lsn.hd\_read(hd, lsn) = fld\_read(fd, lsn)$$

The final correctness theorem of an FTL algorithm $\mathcal{A}$ is shown below:

Theorem 1 (Correctness). *For any FTL algorithm $\mathcal{A}$, if it satisfies the five hypotheses with a global invariant $Inv_\mathcal{A}$, then it is correct.*

$$\forall \mathcal{A}.\forall Inv_\mathcal{A}.\textbf{Hyp1}(\mathcal{A}, Inv_\mathcal{A}) \bigwedge \textbf{Hyp2}(\mathcal{A}, Inv_\mathcal{A}) \bigwedge \textbf{Hyp3}(\mathcal{A}, Inv_\mathcal{A}) \bigwedge \textbf{Hyp4}(\mathcal{A}, Inv_\mathcal{A})$$
$$\bigwedge \textbf{Hyp5}(\mathcal{A}, Inv_\mathcal{A}) \Rightarrow Correctness(\mathcal{A})$$

We can prove the theorem by induction simply. Firstly, we prove the base case that empty devices satisfy the relation R:

Lemma 1. *For any empty disk device hd and any empty flash device fd, they satisfy R:*

$$R(hd\_init(), fld\_init()).$$

Proof. By **Hyp1** and **Hyp2**.   □

There are two lemmas for the inductive case. One is that any two devices satisfying the relation R will still satisfy the relation after processing one command; another is that if the disk device is able to step forward, the flash device is able to do so as well.

Lemma 2 (R Preservation). *For any hd and fd satisfying R, if they get a command cmd and step to hd' and fd', and output ev and ev' respectively, then the two events will be equal and the new devices will still satisfy the relation R:*

$$\forall hd, fd, cmd, ev, ev', hd', fd'.R(hd, fd) \bigwedge Inv_\mathcal{A}(fd)$$
$$\Rightarrow (hd[cmd] \mapsto hd' \downarrow ev) \Rightarrow (fd[cmd] \mapsto fd' \downarrow ev')$$
$$\Rightarrow (ev = ev') \bigwedge R(hd', fd')$$

Proof. By case analysis on the command cmd. If cmd is read, we have the conclusion by the definition of R; if cmd is write, we can prove the subgoals by **Hyp3** and **Hyp4**.   □

Lemma 3 (R Progress). *For any hd and fd satisfying R, if hd processes a command cmd successfully, then there will exist a new flash device fd' such that the device fd is also able to process the same command and step to fd' successfully.*

$$\forall hd, fd, cmd, ev, ev', hd', fd'.R(hd, fd) \bigwedge Inv_\mathcal{A}(fd)$$
$$\Rightarrow hd[cmd] \mapsto hd' \downarrow ev$$
$$\Rightarrow \exists fd'.fd[cmd] \mapsto fd' \downarrow ev$$

$$
\begin{aligned}
(FTL) \qquad & f \ ::= (bit, bmt, fbq) \\
(BlockMapTbl) \ & bmt ::= \{lbn \rightsquigarrow mr\}^* \\
(BMTEntry) \ & bmr ::= (\cdot, \cdot) \mid (pbn, \cdot) \mid (\cdot, pbn) \mid (pbn, pbn) \\
(BlockInfoTbl.) \ & bit \ ::= \{pbn \rightsquigarrow bi\}^* \\
(BlockInfo) \ & bi \ ::= (bs, up, ec) \\
(BlockState) \ & bs \ ::= invalid \mid erased \mid fatblk(lbn) \mid logblk(pmt, lbn) \\
(PageMapTbl) \ & pmt ::= \{lpo \rightsquigarrow ppo\}^* \\
(BlockQueue) \ & fbq ::= pbn \mid pbn; fbq
\end{aligned}
$$

Fig. 4. Definition of BAST meta-data

Proof. By case analysis on the command *cmd*. If *cmd* is read, we can easily have the conclusion; if *cmd* is write, we can prove the subgoals by **Hyp3**, **Hyp4** and **Hyp5**. □

5   Case Study: Verifying an FTL Algorithm BAST

In this section, we illustrate an FTL algorithm–BAST [13,15] that has widely been used in NAND flash based devices.

5.1   Overview of BAST

As mentioned in Sect. 2, an FTL algorithm $\mathcal{A}$ is defined as:

$$
\mathcal{A}_{bast} \triangleq \langle f, ftl\_init(), ftl\_read(), ftl\_write() \rangle.
$$

Below we explain how BAST initiates these components.

BAST Meta-data f. The meta-data of BAST f consists of three main structures: (1) a block mapping table *bmt*, (2) a block info table *bit*, and (3) a free block queue *fbq*, as shown in Fig. 4. The block mapping table is used for address translation. The block info table records the status of every physical block.

(1) Block mapping table. BAST is a block-mapped FTL, which divides a logical sector number into a logical block number and a logical page offset *lbn, lpo*. The logical block number is translated into a physical block number with the help of a block mapping table *bmt*. The logical page offset *lpo* helps find the target page within the physical block located. We model a block mapping table *bmt* by a finite map from logical block numbers *lbn* to mapping entries *mr*. An entry is a pair that contains two physical block numbers. The first is the number of a data block and the other is the number of a log block. A data block is used to store user data, and the capacity of data blocks is equal to that of effective storage space provided by the FTL. A log block is managed by the FTL to handle the erase-before-write characteristic of NAND flash. If the FTL receives

a write request to one page in a data block that is already programmed, FTL will write the new data into an unprogrammed page in the corresponding log block, invalidating the old data. If a log block becomes full, the FTL will merge the data from the data block and the log block, into a fresh block, which will be served as the new data block for that logical block number. Meanwhile, the old data block and the old log block will be recycled as free blocks for future use.

(2) Block info table and page mapping table. The block info table is also a finite map from physical block numbers bpn to records of block information, denoted by bi. A record of block information consists of a field of block state bs, the number of programmed pages in the block and a counter specifying how many times this block has been erased. A block may be marked as one of four states:invalid, erased, used as a data block, and used as a log block. In the block info table, a data block carries a logical block number, which is used as a backward pointer, to back trace to which logical block this physical block is associated with. Besides the logical block number, a log block carries a *page-mapping table*, a finite map from physical page numbers ppo to logical page offset lpo. The logical page offsets are maintained in the RAM and stored into the spare area of every page, allowing for rebuilding the page-mapping table after reboot.

(3) Free block queue. All free blocks are organized into a queue, so as to do dynamic allocation. The free block queue fbq is simply modeled as a non-empty list, consisting of physical block numbers. The FTL may allocate fresh blocks from the queue and recycle the unused blocks back into it. The FTL needs to evenly distribute program/erase cycles over all blocks to extend flash devices' lifetime by an allocation algorithm providing blocks with less erase counts. The erase counts information of physical blocks are maintained both in the block info table in RAM and in the OOB area of each block.

BAST Operations. Figure 5 shows how ftl_read works. Suppose we read the data from the logical address lsn_x that is able to be divided into a pair of (lbn, lpo), where $lbn = 1$. From the block mapping table, we know that the data and log block are $pbn_d (= 103)$ and $pbn_l (= 44)$. The FTL then looks up the page-mapping table in the log block at first to see if there are logs about the page lpo. Assume that $lpo = 2$, we can find two logs in the page-mapping table of the log block and the newest log is d_7. If we assume that $lpo = 3$, we will find no log in the log block and then find d_3 from the data block at the offset 3.

We here give the definition of ftl_write of BAST in Fig. 6. The function takes five arguments: (1) a NAND flash chip c, a configuration of the FTL f, a logical block number lbn, a logical page offset lpo, the data that will be written d. It firstly check if the logical offset is out of boundary, then gets the block mapping table, the block info table and the free blocks queue from the FTL configuration. The code followed (ln: 6–38) differs by checking the block mapping entry mr at lbn in the block mapping table. If there is a log block number at lbn in the table (ln: 8–25), the code will check if the log block is full or not. If the block is full already (ln: 11–21), the code will call the merge function merge_block() and

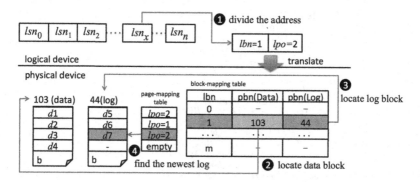

Fig. 5. The address translation of BAST

allocation function alloc_block(), then write the data into the newly allocated block, and at last update the block mapping table and the block info table. If the log block at *lbn* is not full (ln: 23–25), the code will just write the data into it by calling write_log_block(), and update the block info table only. If there is no log block at *lbn* (ln: 27–37), the code will allocate one fresh block to write the data, and update the block mapping table and the block info table. The function ftl_write() will return an updated chip and FTL. Other definitions can be seen in the Coq code.

5.2   The Global Invariant for BAST

As we stated in Sect. 2, the key to the correctness of algorithm is to find a global invariant that holds forever from the very beginning. We decompose the global invariant into a set of individual invariants, each of which clearly depicts one aspect of the well-formedness of the FTL meta-data:

$$Inv_{bast}(c, f) \triangleq \mathbf{Inv0} \wedge \mathbf{Inv1}(f) \wedge \mathbf{Inv3}(f) \wedge \mathbf{Inv4}(f) \wedge \mathbf{Inv5}(f)$$
$$\wedge \mathbf{Inv6}(f) \wedge \mathbf{Inv7}(f) \wedge \mathbf{Inv8}(f) \wedge \mathbf{Inv9}(f) \wedge \mathbf{Inv10}(c, f)$$

Inv0: The number of physical blocks is greater than the double of the greatest logical block number. Since every logical block number may consume at most two physical blocks at the worst case, the parameters of the framework must follow the equation:

$$max\_blk \geq min\_free\_blocks + 2 * max\_sec$$

where min_free_block is the minimum blocks required to do block merging for one time. The following ten invariants are about the meta-data:

Inv1: Every valid pbn has an entry in the bit, and every pbn appearing in bit is valid.
Inv2: Every pbn appearing in the BMT is valid.

```
0.  ftl_write(c, f, lbn, lpo, d):
1.  test   (lpo < pages_blk);
2.  do     bit ← ftl_get_bit(f);
3.  do     bmt ← ftl_get_bmt(f);
4.  do     fbq ← ftl_get_fbq(f);
5.  do     mr ← bmt_get(bmt, lbn);
6.  match mr with
7.    | (−, pbn_l) ⇒
8.      do  bi_l ← bit_get(bit, pbn_l);
9.      if  (check_log_block_is_full(bi_l))
10.     then
11.       do  (c', f') ← merge_block(c, f, lbn);
12.       do  (pbn_n, c'', f'') ← alloc_block(c', f');
13.       do  bit'' ← ftl_get_bit(f'');
14.       do  bmt'' ← ftl_get_bmt(f'');
15.       do  fbq'' ← ftl_get_fbq(f'');
16.       do  bi_n ← bit_get(bit'', pbn_n);
17.       do  bi'_n ← bi_set_state(bi_n, logblk(pmt_init(), lbn));
18.       do  (c_r, bi''_n) ← write_log_block(c'', bi'_n, pbn_n, lpo, d);
19.       do  bmt_r ← bmt_update_log(bmt'', lbn, pbn_l);
20.       do  bit_r ← bit_update(bit'', pbn_l, bi''_n);
21.       ret (c_r, (bit_r, bmt_r, fbq''))
22.     else
23.       do  (c_r, bi'_l) ← write_log_block(c, bi_l, pbn_l, lpo, d);
24.       do  bit_r ← bit_update(bit, pbn_l, bi'_l);
25.       ret (c_r, (bit_r, bmt, fbq))
26.     eif
27.   | | (−, ·) ⇒
28.       do  (pbn_l, c', f') ← alloc_block(c, f);
29.       do  bit' ← ftl_get_bit(f');
30.       do  bmt' ← ftl_get_bmt(f');
31.       dp  fbq' ← ftl_get_fbq(f');
32.       do  bi_l ← bit_get(bit', pbn_l);
33.       do  bi'_l ← bi_set_state(bi_l, logblk(textpmt_init(), lbn));
34.       do  (c_r, bi''_l) ← write_log_block(c', bi'_l, pbn_l, lpo, d) ;
35.       do  bmt_r ← bmt_update_log(bmt', lbn, pbn_l);
36.       do  bit_r ← bit_update(bit', pbn_l, bi''_l);
37.       ret (c_r, (bit_r, bmt_r, fbq'))
38. end
```

Fig. 6. Definition of ftl_write in BAST

Inv3: Every pbn appearing in the free block queue is valid.

Inv4: Every pbn appearing in the free block queue is in the state of "invalid" or "erased".

Inv5: Every pbn appearing in the BMT is in the state of "data" or "log".

Inv6: Every valid pbn should either appear in the BMT or in the free block queue, but not appear in the both places.

Inv7: Every two pbns in the BMT are not equal.

Inv8: Every two pbns in the free block queue are not equal.

Inv9: Every valid lbn has an entry in the BMT, and vice versa.

Inv10: Every block info entry in the BIT is consistent to the status of the corresponding physical block in the flash.

Last invariant is the only one associating the meta-data in RAM with the actual data stored in the flash. It says that every entry in the BIT describes the state of the corresponding physical block. The descriptions and the physical states should be consistent. For instance, if an entry says the block is erased, the physical block should be in the state that every page in that block is unprogrammed. If an entry says the block is used as a log block with a page-level mapping table, the pages of logs in the physical block should be consistent with the page-level mapping table. The last

With the global invariants, we can prove that the FTL operations satisfy the five hypotheses defined in Sect. 4. Finally by Theorem 1, we can have the conclusion that the FTL algorithm BAST is correct.

Table 1. The Coq proof

	Layer (Module)	Proof (LOC)	Definitions	Lemmas & Theorems
8	Correctness proof	293	1	10
7	Lemmas of FTL hypotheses	350	0	5
6	Lemmas of FTL operations	3807	0	18
5	Global invariant	3060	33	75
4	Framework	321	35	3
3	FTL model	1943	72	70
2	NAND flash model	456	25	9
1	Basic data types	1872	19	74
	Total	12,102	185	264

5.3 Mechanized Proof and Experience

All of the proof for the final theorem of refinement is structured into layers, resembling the structure of the storage model (See Table 1). From the bottom up, the proof at the lowest layer is a set of libraries about basic data types, such as lists, natural number and mapping, which form the basis of the whole framework. The second lowest layer is for the NAND flash model and the proof of its properties. The most important lemmas proved at this layer are about the semantics of nand_erase() and nand_write(). Next is the layer of the FTL algorithm. Most of the proof at this layer are for auxiliary functions, such as bit_get(), bit_update(), bmt_update(), and meta-data-related lemmas. The verification framework is defined at the 4th layer, including the devices, data format, monads, and parameters. The 5th layer is for invariants. At this layer there are three types of lemmas: (1) how these invariants are related to each other; (2) the intro- and elim-lemmas of the invariants; (3) how the invariants can be preserved after the modification of meta-data. The most difficult part of the proof is the 6th layer, where we prove the semantics of the FTL operations, as well as important functions like merge_block(). The five hypotheses of the FTL are proved at the 7th layer. The proof is relatively easy with the help of lemmas provided by the 6th layer. The correctness theorem is proved at the 8th layer.

The entire proof cost about 2 months of one person to complete. The models of NAND, FTL and the definitions of our framework had been done by the end of first week. Except for the first layer, the proof was developed from top down. Before the proving phase, we defined a few auxiliary functions to help us test the Coq definitions and find a few bugs that might possibly have increased the proof burden. However, testing cannot cover every corner. There were two bugs that were so subtle that we didn't find them by testing until we dived into the very depth of the formal proving.

Considering that the invariants were too strong would dramatically increase the proof efforts, we selected a small set of invariants apparently sound, which unfortunately turned out to be incomplete and inconsistent. Redefining the invariants, which in one respect invalidated a large amount of lemmas, in the other respect, made us reorganize the proof such that it would not be susceptible to the modification of invariants. Before the proof of the 6th layer had been done, some invariants were found derivable from a smaller basic set, and then a number of lemmas were cut off. The most difficult part of the proof is to find the loop invariants for the code with while loops.

As we estimated, about 60% of the proof might be automated with the help of a SMT solver that can output explicit proof objects. We might also have developed tactics in Coq to accelerate the proving, for the fact that many proof patterns scattered in the lemmas are very similar. The rest of the proof, however, requiring domain-specific knowledge of NAND model or the algorithm, would not be easy to be done by an automated solver for general purpose.

6   Related Work and Conclusion

Kang and Jackson used Alloy to model and analyze the design of a flash-based filesystem [5]. They modeled the NAND flash hardware in a way similar to ours. Their filesystem is simple but has realistic features, such as wear-leveling and power fault tolerance, that we have yet to tackle in our first step. Their verification relies on the Alloy, using a SAT solver to do the analysis job. But our work provide the mechanized proof that can grow to prove algorithms with more features, without suffering from the exponential nature of SAT problem.

Maric and Sprenger verified an industrially deployed persistent memory manager [6]. They used another popular proof assistant Isabelle/HOL as the basis to develop the formal proof. They also used state monad to define the functions of the software like us.

Butterfield et al. formalized NAND flash memory in Z [7], according to an open specification of NAND flash hardware interface–ONFI. They modeled realistic NAND geographic organization.

Our approach is quite similar to the well-known seL4 [4] project except that we don't use haskell as the prototype language. Instead, we directly define the algorithm in Coq, which is a logic language.

7 Conclusion

In this paper, we presented a verification framework for FTL algorithms. We also showed how to verify a classic FTL algorithm in the framework by global invariants. Our work provides a solid basis for verifying the functional correctness of various FTLs.

References

1. Guo, Y.: The Coq Implementation of a Simple FTL Algorithm and the Functional Correctness Proof (2014)
2. Coq Development Team, INRIA: The Coq Proof Assistant Reference Manual (2012)
3. Apple Inc.: MacBook Air Flash Storage Drive Replacement Program (2013)
4. Klein, G., Elphinstone, K., Heiser, G.: seL4: formal verification of an OS kernel. In: Proceedings of SOSP 2009, pp. 207–220, October 2009
5. Kang, E., Jackson, D.: Formal modeling and analysis of a flash filesystem in alloy. In: Börger, E., Butler, M., Bowen, J.P., Boca, P. (eds.) ABZ 2008. LNCS, vol. 5238, pp. 294–308. Springer, Heidelberg (2008). https://doi.org/10.1007/978-3-540-87603-8_23
6. Marić, O., Sprenger, C.: Verification of a transactional memory manager under hardware failures and restarts. In: Jones, C., Pihlajasaari, P., Sun, J. (eds.) FM 2014. LNCS, vol. 8442, pp. 449–464. Springer, Cham (2014). https://doi.org/10.1007/978-3-319-06410-9_31
7. Butterfield, A., Woodcock, J.: Formalising flash memory: first steps. In: IEEE International Conference on Engineering of Complex Computer Systems, pp. 251–260 (2007)
8. Semiconductor, Hynix and others: Open NAND flash interface specification (2006)
9. Cooke, J.: The inconvenient truths of NAND flash memory. In: Micron MEMCON, 7 (2005)
10. Thatcher, J., Coughlin, T., Handy, J., Ekker, N.: NAND flash solid state storage for the enterprise: an in-depth look at reliability. Solid State Storage Initiative (SNIA) (2009)
11. Grupp, L.M., Davis, J.D., Swanson, S.: The bleak future of NAND flash memory. In: Proceedings of the 10th USENIX Conference on File and Storage Technologies, p. 2 (2012)
12. Grupp, L.M., Caulfield, A.M., Coburn, J., Swanson, S., Yaakobi, Ei., Siegel, P.H., Wolf, J.K.: Characterizing flash memory: anomalies, observations, and applications. In: 42nd Annual IEEE/ACM International Symposium on Microarchitecture, MICRO-42, pp. 24–33. ACM (2009)
13. Kim, J., Kim, J.M., Noh, S.H., Min, S.L., Cho, Y.: A space-efficient flash translation layer for CompactFlash systems. IEEE Trans. Consum. Electron. 48, 366–375 (2002)
14. Lee, S.-W., Park, D.: A log buffer-based flash translation layer using fully-associative sector translation. ACM Trans. Embed. Comput. Syst. (TECS) 6, 18 (2007)
15. Kim, S.-Y., Jung, S.-I.: A log-based flash translation layer for large NAND flash memory. In: The 8th International Conference Advanced Communication Technology, ICACT 2006, vol. 3, pp. 1641–1644. IEEE (2006)

16. Gupta, A., Kim, Y., Urgaonkar, B.: DFTL: a flash translation layer employing demand-based selective caching of page-level address mappings. In: Proceedinngs of ASPLOS 2009, pp. 229–240. ACM (2009)
17. Zheng, M., Tucek, J., Qin, F., Lillibridge, M.: Understanding the robustness of SSDS under power fault. In: FAST, pp. 271–284 (2013)
18. Lu, L., Arpaci-Dusseau, A.C., Arpaci-Dusseau, R.H., Lu, S.: A study of Linux file system evolution. ACM Trans. Storage (TOS) **10**, 3 (2014)

Mixed Criticality Scheduling
of Probabilistic Real-Time Systems

Jasdeep Singh[1(✉)], Luca Santinelli[1(✉)], Federico Reghenzani[2(✉)],
Konstantinos Bletsas[3(✉)], David Doose[1], and Zhishan Guo[4(✉)]

[1] ONERA-DTIS Toulouse, Toulouse, France
{jasdeep.singh,luca.santinelli,david.doose}@onera.fr
[2] DEIB-Politecnico di Milano, Milan, Italy
federico.reghenzani@polimi.it
[3] CISTER Research Centre and ISEP/IPP, Porto, Portugal
koble@isep.ipp.pt
[4] University of Central Florida, Orlando, USA
zhishan.guo@ucf.edu

Abstract. In this paper we approach the problem of Mixed Criticality
(MC) for probabilistic real-time systems where tasks execution times are
described with probabilistic distributions. In our analysis, the task enters
high criticality mode if its response time exceeds a certain threshold,
which is a slight deviation from a more classical approach in MC. We
do this to obtain an application oriented MC system in which criticality
mode changes depend on actual scheduled execution. This is in contrast
to classical approaches which use task execution time to make criticality
mode decisions, because execution time is not affected by scheduling
while the response time is. We use a graph-based approach to seek for an
optimal MC schedule by exploring every possible MC schedule the task
set can have. The schedule we obtain minimizes the probability of the
system entering high criticality mode. In turn, this aims at maximizing
the resource efficiency by the means of scheduling without compromising
the execution of the high criticality tasks and minimizing the loss of lower
criticality functionality. The proposed approach is applied to test cases
for validation purposes.

1 Introduction

Real-time applications demand timing guarantees at all of their execution scenarios. Classical approaches apply Worst Case Execution Times (WCET) in order
to have safe/pessimistic models of task executions. The actual task execution
time may vary but will always lie below the WCET because the instances when
the actual execution time is equal to WCET are unlikely [15,17]. Predictability is
assured with schedulability analysis that applies worst-case models like WCETs.

This work is also a result of the CISTER Research Unit (UID/CEC/04234), supported
by FCT/MCTES (Portuguese Foundation for Science and Technology).

N. Guan et al. (Eds.): SETTA 2019, LNCS 11951, pp. 89–105, 2019.
https://doi.org/10.1007/978-3-030-35540-1_6

A recent approach to timing analysis involves defining execution times using a probabilistic Worst Case Execution Time (pWCET). The pWCET is a probabilistic distribution which upper bounds all the possible execution times of a task [7]. The pWCET generalizes the notion of WCET with multiple worst-case execution time values, each with the associated worst case probability of being exceeded. The flexibility from pWCET representations allow for probabilistic quantification of pessimism in the WCET deterministic models. Moreover, the probabilistic models are less pessimistic because they are close approximation to the actual task execution. They contain more information about execution time than single-valued deterministic WCET.

The probabilistic schedulability analysis like [4, 12, 18, 19] applies on top of probabilistic models like pWCETs. The results obtained thereafter are also probabilistic as worst-case response time distributions. The probabilistic schedulability analysis exploits the flexibility of probabilistic representations, aiming at reducing the pessimism. There is always an associated cost of complexity when dealing with probabilistic distributions. Operations like convolution add to this complexity. The probabilistic models deal with more information given in the probability distribution than models using WCET. All the possible scenarios of execution of tasks, given by the pWCET as well as schedule, have to be taken into account.

In addition, today's safety critical applications are being approached through the Mixed Criticality (MC) perspective [5]. MC systems operate by switching between various criticality modes depending on the resource requirements by the executing tasks. Whenever there is a higher requirement of resources, the system switches to a mode of higher criticality in order to guarantee the most critical tasks in the least. In this mode, only the safety critical tasks are executed and more resource for their execution is provisioned [22].

The MC problem is supported by the Vestal's model [22] in which a tuple of WCETs describe the task execution behaviour. The WCETs in the tuple are less pessimistic at lower criticalities, and are more pessimistic at higher ones in order to upper bound more execution conditions. The system mode change to higher criticality is classically means that all task in lower criticalities are discarded. This does not take into account if there is room for allowing execution of low criticality tasks in system high mode. Obtaining a solution for applied MC scheduling which is ensured safe as well as resource efficient is a complex problem.

Both MC and probabilistic schedulability analysis tend to have a common characteristic, that is to quantify the existing pessimism and utilize it to maximize resource usage by making intelligent scheduling decisions. This also originates from the fact that safety standards e.g., stemming from the IEC6150, ISO26262 or DO-178C standards, demand a probability or frequency of the system failing at run-time. These standards also extend to mixed criticality systems. Some works are extending the Vestal's model to the probabilistic case [8, 14, 16]. Works involving probabilities in MC systems [1, 2, 8, 14] can be found among the citations in the MC survey [5]. Scheduling approaches in [10, 13] and [3] focus on assigning safe and feasible task priorities.

1.1   Problem Discussion and Contribution

In this work, we look for a probabilistic MC scheduling analysis which provides a reliable probabilistic picture of the system, and safe timing guarantees, especially for high criticality tasks, or low probability of occurrence of critical events. In addition, it must be able to exploit the common objective of the MC and probabilistic approaches, which is leveraging probabilities into maximizing resource usage and minimizing pessimism.

Given a MC periodic non-preemptive task set known beforehand to be executed on a uniprocessor machine, with each task described with a pWCET, instead of a WCET, and given a maximum probability of deadline miss for the tasks, how do we find a schedule such that the probability of the system entering high criticality mode is minimum?

We aim for a minimization of the probability of system entering high criticality because there are certain predefined actions that are taken when the system does enter high criticality. Usually, these actions involve discarding the lower criticality tasks. With our approach, we make such actions least likely. With this objective in mind, we propose a graph-based task execution model. We begin constructing a graph based model to represent the possible job orderings. The possible schedules are then represented in exploration trees. These trees are explored to obtain a resource efficient schedule. Using graphs allows us explore all the possible combinations of job scheduling. Only by exploring all the combinations, we can confidently conclude for a schedule with the least probability of the system switching mode to high criticality among all the possibilities. Using the graph and other structures to model task executions, we are able to extract crucial schedulability information like pWCRT and the probabilities associated. There exist some approaches like [9, 20] which use graphs to express for task execution, but they do so in a non-probabilistic and non-MC domain.

Our approach mainly consists of an offline analysis to obtain a schedule for the jobs. The schedule obtained is a sequence of jobs which are ensured to contain all the high criticality jobs. In addition, the schedule results in the minimum probability that the system enters high criticality mode. The exploration process has exponential complexity. It originates from the complexity of the probabilistic models in addition to the complexity of the MC approaches. However, the relatively high offline complexity is a trade-off we make at the moment where we gain a new application oriented MC approach through the advantages of probabilistic models. The complexity of this exploration is somewhat reduced in parallel of the offline construction of the schedule by discarding unfeasible schedules. The complexity will be further improved in the future works.

The online part of the schedule consists of execution of jobs in the sequence given from the offline analysis. It simply executes the jobs given in the scheduling order. The online complexity is drastically reduced through our method as the schedule is a simple list to follow.

As in most works on MC scheduling, we assume a system with tasks of two criticalities and modes. However, our work can easily extend to multi-criticality system. Moreover, contrary to classical MC we use probabilistic Worst Case

Response Time (pWCRT) to make criticality decisions. Any increased resource demand from a jobs occurs at run-time. The criticality mode change for a job is a reflection of this increased demand. This run-time execution information is represented by the response time and not execution time. With this, we also leverage probabilities into scheduling decisions in order to maximize the resource usage. This is because the pWCRT is affected by the schedule and the schedule defines the resource assignment to the jobs.

Outline of the Paper. The paper is divided as follows: Sect. 1 introduces the context and states the problems which we answer in this paper. Section 2 gives the reader the necessary background to understand this paper as well as the assumptions made. Section 3 presents the graph-based model and the exploration trees. Section 4 details the schedulability analysis from graph and tree representations, together with the offline and online strategies developed. The paper is concluded in the Sect. 5.

2 Notations and Definitions

In this work we consider pWCETs to define task execution which is probability distribution.

For a discrete random variable C, the Probability Mass Function (PMF) $f_C(x)$ of C gives the probability that x takes a certain value in C, $f_C(x) \overset{def}{=} \mathcal{P}(x = C)$ with the condition $\Sigma_{-\infty}^{\infty} \mathcal{P}(x) = 1$. Alternative representations of C are the discrete Cumulative Distribution Function (CDF) $F_C(x) \overset{def}{=} \Sigma f_C(c)$, and the discrete Inverse Cumulative Distribution Function (ICDF) $\overline{F}_C(x) \overset{def}{=} 1 - F_C(x)$. In the rest of the paper, calligraphic letters are for random variables, while non-calligraphic letters are for deterministic variables. Figures 1 shows an example of a certain distribution in PMF, discrete CDF and discrete ICDF forms. The discrete cumulative forms show probability increment or decrement in a step-wise fashion.

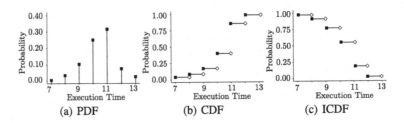

(a) PDF   (b) CDF   (c) ICDF

Fig. 1. Example of PDF, discrete CDF and discrete CCDF representations of a certain distribution.

The task pWCET is a discrete random variable C taking task execution values where PMF $f_C(x)$ represents the probability that the task takes a certain

WCET. In its representation with CDF, $F_C(x)$ is the cumulative probability that the task respects WCET x while executing; in the ICDF representation, $\overline{F}_C(x)$ is the probability that the task overcomes WCET x. The deterministic WCET C from $\mathcal{C}$ is the maximum value of $\mathcal{C}$; for it $F_C(C) = 1$, and $\overline{F}_C(C) = 0$. Figure 2 shows a discrete form of a pWCET with its maximum value as WCET.

The convolution of two PMFs $f_X(x)$ and $g_Y(y)$, denoted by $\otimes$, refers to the summation of the random variables X and Y, given as: $f \otimes g(u) = \Sigma_{v=-\infty}^{\infty} f(v)g(u-v)$.

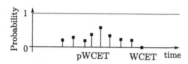

Fig. 2. pWCET PMF with each worst case execution time having a worst case probability.

2.1 Computational Model

We assume a fixed set of periodic tasks executing in a system with each instance of a task called a *job*. All the tasks are known beforehand. We focus our analysis on the jobs. A MC job J_i is represented with a tuple of parameters:

$$J_i = (\mathcal{C}_i, a_i, d_i, L_i, l_i); \tag{1}$$

$\mathcal{C}_i$ is the job pWCET probability distribution; the job arrives at time a_i; has the deadline d_i; and l_i is the criticality execution time threshold. The arrival time and the deadline are deterministic variables. The criticality level of the job is L_i. We assume that the arrival of the first job of each task is always at time zero. The tasks are scheduled periodically and non-preemptively on a uniprocessor machine in which execution of jobs are suspended at their respective deadlines.

For the jobs, we consider pWCET described with discrete distributions, although our method applies to both, continuous and discrete distributions. We analyze the jobs in the hyperperiod because the schedule repeats each hyperperiod. Since the jobs are suspended at the deadline, the execution order does not change across the hyperperiods. The sequence of the jobs remain the same and the execution room for each job is sufficiently given within the hyperperiod. The execution behaviour of the jobs across the hyperperiods can be different and our approach takes that into account. The hyperperiod is defined as the least common multiple of the periods of all the tasks.

Definition 1. *For a probabilistic job J_i as defined in Eq. (1), its probabilistic Worst Case Response Time pWCRT is the PMF $f_{\mathcal{R}_i}(x)$ which gives the probability that J_i will take certain time $\mathcal{R}_i$, to end execution after its release. The CDF is $F_{\mathcal{R}_i}(x) = \Sigma f_{\mathcal{R}_i}(c)$, and the ICDF is $\overline{F}_{\mathcal{R}_i}(x) = 1 - F_{\mathcal{R}_i}$.*

Because the response time is a probability distribution, which in turn comes from pWCET of the jobs, the deadline miss also has an associated probability. This is easily extracted from the response time. We assume a certain allowed maximum probability of deadline miss for any job $\mathcal{P}_{dm}^{max}$ is given. A job J_i is said to have missed its deadline if $1 - \Sigma_{x=0}^{d_i} f_{\mathcal{R}_i}(x) > \mathcal{P}_{dm}^{max}$.

Criticality Levels. We consider two level criticality case, HI and LO, with HI having higher importance than LO. The high criticality job can execute in HI or LO mode, the low criticality job executes only in LO mode. After its release, the high criticality job executes in LO criticality mode until the response time threshold l_i. A job execution exceeding this threshold is said to execute in the high criticality mode. Evidently, l_i is a deterministic single-valued parameter. The job criticality is given by L_i which is its relative importance over others. L_i can take values HI or LO.

Definition 2. *A job J_i is said to have entered* HI *criticality if its response time exceeds a threshold l_i, $f_{\mathcal{R}_i}(x) > l_i$.*

We explain criticality using the response time because we can make scheduling decisions based on actual job execution. This implies, criticality decision takes into account the affect of other job executions as well. Figure 3 shows an example of a job pWCET and pWCRT. It shows both the distributions with criticality thresholds. The criticality obtained from threshold applied on response time contains more run-time information than that obtained from pWCET.

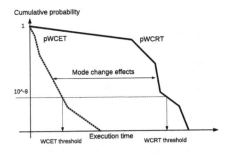

Fig. 3. pWCET and pWCRT representation for criticality mode change using thresholds on pWCET and pWCRT distributions.

In the hyperperiod there are n jobs, and the set of jobs is Λ. There are n^{HI} high criticality jobs in Λ, and n^{LO} low criticality jobs in Λ; Λ^{HI} represents the set of high criticality jobs, and Λ^{LO} represents the set of low criticality jobs; $\Lambda = \Lambda^{HI} \cup \Lambda^{LO}$, and $n = n^{LO} + n^{HI}$.

Worst-Case Independence. The pWCETs are assumed to be independent [6]; this is because the pWCET represents the worst case execution scenario of the job. Independence implies that the execution of one job does not inherently affect the execution of another (dependence in this case would be in the cases like shared resources by the two jobs). Any dependencies on execution and criticality mode changes due to scheduling of the jobs is not assumed and is taken into account. Any execution delays which are caused apart from the scheduling must already be included in the pWCET distribution.

3   Probabilistic Scheduling Model

We propose an exploration of graph models for possible job execution combinations. We find a schedule which ensures the schedulability all the jobs. Then, it ensures that the probability that the system enters high criticality is minimum. This is when the job criticality is computed from its response time. We begin by defining the graph model. We follow by elaborating the graph model into exploration tree.

3.1   Graph Model

The graph represents the possible job combinations as schedules of the system in each hyperperiod. It uses nodes to represent the jobs and arcs to represent the possible ordering of execution among them. A *directed graph* is defined as a tuple $G = \{V(G), E(G)\}$, where $V(G)$ is a finite set of elements called nodes and $E(G)$ is the finite set of ordered pairs of elements of $V(G)$ called arcs. The graph is acyclic because the schedule repeats each hyperperiod. Since there is no passing of information across the hyperperiods, it is not required to be represented through cyclic graph.

Nodes. Each node $J_i \in V(G)$ represents the execution of a job $J_i \in \Lambda$. Since the elements of $V(G)$ are one-to-one mapped to the elements of Λ, i.e. it represents the jobs, we directly use J_i to represent the node.

The system can begin execution with any of the jobs which arrive at time zero, i.e. first jobs of the tasks. The nodes representing these first jobs are called the *early nodes*. The *early nodes set* $S(G)$ is a subset of the node set $V(G)$, $S(G) \subseteq V(G)$ such that $\forall J_i \in S(G) : a_i = 0$. The system can potentially begin execution by any of the jobs in this set. Graphically, we identify the early nodes set $S(G)$ with extra arcs entering in $J_i \in S(G)$ without the source node, see Fig. 5 for an example. These arcs are not considered part of the $E(G)$ set.

Arcs. An arc $\{J_i, J_j\} \in E(G)$ represents a possible ordering of jobs, in particular, that the job J_j executes after the execution of the task J_i. Formally, for $\{J_i, J_j\} \in V(G)$:

$$\{J_i, J_j\} \in E(G) \text{ if } \begin{cases} a_i < d_j & \text{if } i \neq j \\ a_j = a_i + T_i & \text{if } i = j. \end{cases} \tag{2}$$

An arc only exists when the deadline of the next job is greater than the arrival time of the executing job (previous job). This is enforced to prevent the scheduling of a job which has already passed its deadline. Also, in order to prevent

scheduling the same job more than once, no self loop (arcs connecting themselves) exist, $\nexists \{J_i, J_i\} \in E(G)$. It should be noted that, since the graph is
directed, $\{J_i, J_j\}$ is not the same as $\{J_j, J_i\}$. Also, the arcs do not represent the
time of execution of the jobs, they simply direct to the next job to execute J_j
once the executing job J_i finishes. For $\{J_i, J_j\}$, we define a *successor node* as
$succ(J_i) = J_j$ and a *predecessor node* $pred(J_j) = J_i$.

3.2   Scheduling Tree

In order to search for a schedule, the graph is unfolded into trees defined as
follows.

Definition 3 (Exploration Tree). *The* exploration tree $T_s(G)$ *of a graph G
with an early node* $J_s \in S(G)$ *is defined as* $T_s(G) = \{V(T_s(G)), E(T_s(G))\}$:
$1 - \Sigma_{x=0}^{d_i} f_{\mathcal{R}_i}(x) > \mathcal{P}_{dm}^{max} \forall J_i \in V(T_s(G))$, *where* $V(T_s(G))$ *is the set of nodes of*
$T_s(G)$ *and* $E(T_s(G))$ *is the set of arcs of* $T_s(G)$ *such that* $E(T_s(G)) \exists E(G)$ *and*
$V(T_s(G)) \exists V(G)$.

The *exploration tree* is constructed from the graph beginning with a root
node of the graph as the first job to execute in the schedule. Each node of the
tree is labelled with the job J_i it represents. A node is only added to the tree if
it does not miss its deadline and a corresponding arc exists in the graph, given
that the corresponding node exists the graph. At each time it is added to the
tree, the deadline miss is checked for by the condition $1 - \Sigma_{x=0}^{d_i} f_{\mathcal{R}_i}(x) > \mathcal{P}_{dm}^{max}$
for a job J_i. If there is a deadline miss, the node/job is not added because the
system should never be scheduled beyond this job.

To relax the notation, from now on we simply write $V(T)$ and $E(T)$ to
represent nodes/jobs and arcs respectively of the tree. In particular, since the
tree is a rooted tree, its root is defined as the unique node with the label J_s.
Because the system can begin with one of the jobs arriving at time zero, there
are different possible roots of a tree; this implies the number of possible trees is
equal to the number of tasks because each task has a first job arriving at time
zero. These trees are collectively called a *forest*.

The set of all *exploration trees* is called the *exploration forest*: $F =
\{T_{s_1}(G), T_{s_2}(G), ...T_{s_k}(G)\}$, where $s_1, ..., s_k$ are the indices of early jobs in $S(G)$.
The trees represent possible orderings or sequences of jobs beginning with an
early job at the root. A *leaf node* in the tree is a node with no outgoing transitions, J_n is a leaf node if $succ(J_n)$ does not exist. Thus, a schedule is a path
taken through the tree from a node to a leaf node defined as follows.

Definition 4 (Path).   *A path in the T-th tree* $path_T(J_i, J_n)$ *is a unique
sequence of connected arcs starting from a node* J_i *to a leaf node* J_n:
$path_T(J_i, J_n) = \{\{J_i, J_j\}, \{J_j, J_k\}, ..., \{J_l, J_n\}\}$ *with* $\{J_x, J_y\} \in E(T)$ *for any*
$x, y, i \neq j \neq k \cdots \neq n$.

Whenever we refer to the notation $path_T(J_i, J_n)$, we always refer to a unique
path with a node J_i and leaf node J_n. Two paths are same if their elements,

which are the sequences of arcs, are the same. We specify this because there are many possible paths from the root node to a leaf node notated by the same job. Also, a path can begin at any node and it ends at a leaf node.

For any node in the tree, there must not exist a same node in the path between itself and the root node This is done to prevent scheduling the same job more than once, we enforce the following definition. Formally, a node J_i is not added to the tree if it already exists between the root and the desired point of addition:

$$J_j = succ(J_n) \text{ if } \nexists J_j \in path_T(J_s, J_n) : J_n \text{ is leaf node}, J_s \in S(G). \quad (3)$$

Example 1. We use a set of jobs Λ_1 shown in Fig. 4 to explain our method. It consists of five jobs (from two periodic tasks) in the hyperperiod of 30 time units. The jobs are shown with their pWCET PMF in the figure to visualize a probabilistic execution and not deterministic execution, the exact values of PMFs are not yet important. The jobs of task τ_1 ((J_1, J_4)), are HI criticality and those of task τ_2 ((J_2, J_3, J_5)) are LO criticality.

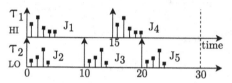

Fig. 4. Jobs of the set Λ_1.

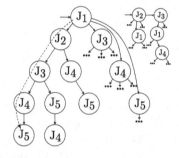

Fig. 6. Graph unfolded into a tree for jobs of Λ_1.

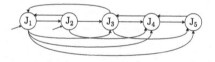

Fig. 5. The graph of the jobs in Λ_1.

The graph is a direct representation of all the possible ordering of the jobs in the system, see Fig. 5. There are nodes J_1, J_2, etc. for each job which are interconnected by uni-directed arcs which refer to the order of executions; e.g., if J_3 is executing, then it can be followed by the jobs J_1, J_4 or J_5. The system can begin execution with J_1 or J_2. This set of early nodes of the jobs J_1 and J_2 are represented by the extra arcs entering those nodes. In order to explore this graph to look for a schedule, it is unfolded into a forest of trees.

For Λ_1, a portion of the tree is represented in the Fig. 6. The tree begins with a root J_1 followed by possible jobs which can execute, namely, J_2, J_3, J_4, J_5. This goes on until the leaf nodes where any more addition of nodes will mean a repetition of the same job in the schedule on the path. For the tree job set Λ_1 the Fig. 6, one possible path is shown by a dotted line. The dotted line represents a path J_1, J_2, J_4, J_3, J_5. It also shows another possible tree with just its root J_2.

With the construction of the exploration model complete, we now proceed extracting certain metrics from the exploration trees in order to decide for a MC schedule.

4   Evaluation

We first the define the metrics necessary for system criticality and then apply them to our model. We begin with obtaining a non-preemptive pWCRT for a job.

Classically, the pWCETs of the jobs are simply convoluted in order to obtain the pWCRT. The convolution operation does not take different arrival times into account. Thus, performing a convolution contains a hidden assumption that all the jobs arrive at the same time, i.e. at a critical instant. This results in a pessimistic pWCRT. Our approach to obtain the pWCRT involves handling the discrete distributions in a piece-wise manner. To do so, we first define a tail PMF as follows.

Definition 5 (Tail Probability Mass Function). *A tail distribution of the response time* $f_{R_i}(x)$ *of a job* J_i *with Worst Case Execution Time* $WCET_i$ *for some time* $a_j(0 < a_j < WCET_i)$, *is a PMF* $f_{tail_i}^{[a_j, WCET_i]}(x)$ *given as:*

$$f_{tail_i}^{[a_j, WCET_i]}(x) = \begin{cases} f_{R_i}(x + a_j) & \text{if } 0 < x \leq WCET_i \\ \Sigma_{y=0}^{a_j} f_{R_i}(y) & \text{if } x = 0. \end{cases} \quad (4)$$

The tail distribution represents a complete PMF which probabilistically delays the execution of the next job in the schedule where the next job arrives at time a_j. The probability accumulated at the instant a_j ($x = 0$ in the function) in the tail PMF represents the probability that the job J_i has finished execution by then. As in Fig. 7, the tail distribution of job J_1 (from Λ_1 in Example 1) accumulates $0.1 + 0.15 + 0.15 + 0.2 = 0.6$ time zero. By doing so we prevent any loss of information in the distribution. We use this to obtain the pWCRT of the delayed job.

In order to obtain the response time of the jobs, we present the following theorem. The approach we propose is similar to the ones used by [12,14] but applied to every job with respect to their arrival times. It is not same as the classical convolution because convolution does not take the relative arrival times and the deadlines of the jobs into account. Classical convolution between the pWCETs of two jobs contains a hidden assumption that the jobs arrive at the same time. This is easily seen as the tail distribution approaches full pWCET when the arrival times are equal. Since this is not always the case, convolution results in a pessimistic response time distribution.

Theorem 1 (Non-Preemptive Probabilistic Worst Case Response Time). *The pWCRT of a job without preemption is represented by convolution between its pWCET and the Tail PMF of the job executing immediately before.*

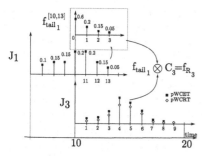
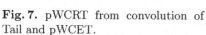
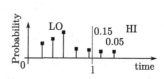

Fig. 7. pWCRT from convolution of Tail and pWCET.

Fig. 8. High criticality from a threshold l_1 on pWCRT of a job J_1 of Λ_1.

Proof. Consider two jobs, J_i arriving at time a_i and J_j arriving at time a_j, $a_i \leq a_j$. A representative example is shown in Fig. 7 as J_1 and J_3 for the jobs in Λ_1 of Example 1. Probabilistically, J_i can continue to execute after the arrival time of J_j. That means, there exists a probabilistic delay to the execution of the job J_j due to the execution of the job J_i. However, the probabilistic delay only exists due to J_i executing between time a_j and its $WCET$ (which is the maximum value of its pWCET). Thus, the state space which affects the execution of J_j is $[a_j, WCET]$. This state space contains the tail of the pWCRT of J_i. In order for the state space to be complete it must respect the property that sum of all the probabilities in the state space is equal to one. This implies, the tail of pWCRT of J_i must be a PMF on its own. This distribution is given by the function $f_{tail_i}^{[a_j, WCET]}(x)$.

The probability that J_j ends execution at time a_j depends on the probability that J_j finishes at time a_j and J_i finishes at time a_j OR J_i finishes at time $a_j + 1$ OR at time $a_j + 2$ OR ... and so on. Similarly, J_j ends execution at time $a_j + 1$ depends on the probability that J_j finishes at time a_j and J_i finishes at time $a_j + 1$ OR at time $a_j + 2$ OR ... and so on. This way we approach the classical convolution operation between the pWCET $f_{C_j}(x)$ of J_j and the tail function $f_{tail_i}^{[a_j, WCET]}(x)$, given as:

$$f_{R_j}(x) = f_{C_j}(x) \otimes f_{tail_i}^{[a_j, WCET_i]}(x).$$

$\square$

Our approach to obtain the pWCRT separates the part of the pWCRT PMF which affects the execution of the next job. We do not lose any information in the distribution as the probabilities before the time a_j are accumulated[1]. Moreover, we retain the information within the time intervals in the distribution.

Using the pWCRT we apply the job criticality Definition 2 on the paths through the exploration tree.

---

[1] The distribution function accumulates the probabilities in the intervals of discretization at the worst case, e.g. probabilities at execution times $0.2, 0.5, 0.7$, etc. are accumulated the time 1.

Definition 6 (Job Criticality). *A job J_j in a path $path_T(J_i, J_n)$ is said to have entered high criticality if its response time crosses the threshold l_j, $f_{\mathcal{R}_j}(x) > l_j$, the probability of which is given as:*

$$\mathcal{P}_j^{HI}(path_T(J_i, J_n)) = 1 - \Sigma_{x=0}^{l_j} f_{\mathcal{R}_j}(x), \tag{5}$$

where $l_j < d_j$ and J_n is a leaf node.

Example 2. Figure 7 shows a scenario where job J_3 executes after J_1 from the jobs in Λ_1 in Example 1; for explanation, a pWCET PMF is assumed for J_1. The Tail PMF for the same is shown in the box. To obtain the pWCRT of J_3, this PMF is then convoluted with the pWCET of the job J_3.

A pWCRT of the job J_1 with its threshold is shown in Fig. 8. The threshold is shown by the dotted line labelled $l_i = 12$. From the Figure, the probability that this job enters HI-criticality mode is $0.15 + 0.05 = 0.20$.

From the job criticality defined using its pWCRT, we define the probability of the system entering high criticality as follows.

Definition 7 (System Criticality). *The system enters high criticality mode if at least one high criticality job enters high criticality mode.*

To elaborate the above definition, system enters high criticality if the first high criticality job enters high criticality OR the second high criticality job enters high criticality OR the third..., and so on. This represents a summation of probabilities. However, the probability that a job enters high criticality is given from its pWCRT which has its own sample space. In order to sum the probabilities of all the high criticality jobs involved, we also need to sum the sample space. This is clear from the fact that the summation of probabilities without considering the sample space can result in a probability greater than one[2]. For each job entering high criticality, the probability adjusted for state space is $\Sigma \mathcal{P}_i^{HI}(path_T)/$(number of high criticality jobs). We use the law $\mathcal{P}(A \cup B) = \mathcal{P}(A) + \mathcal{P}(B) - \mathcal{P}(A \cap B)$ for any two events A and B with $\mathcal{P}()$ giving their probability of occurrence [21]. Therefore, the probability that the system enters high criticality is given as the summation of probability of each high criticality job entering high criticality minus their product.

We apply these definitions to the graph and tree model. In our model, the schedule is represented as paths. Because the paths represent the schedule, the probability that the system enters high criticality is also a function of paths. However, not all the paths in the exploration tree are available for scheduling because not all paths contain all the high criticality jobs. The set of available paths are defined as follows.

---

[2] Same reasoning also applies to multiplication of probabilities, however the denominator 1 gets multiplied too.

Definition 8 (Available paths). *Available paths is a set of all possible paths in a T-th tree from the root node $J_s \in S(G)$ to a leaf node J_n, $P_{avail} = \{path_T(J_s, J_n)\}$ such that*

$$\forall k : J_k = \Lambda \implies \exists J_k \in path_T(J_s, J_n); \tag{6}$$

and

$$\forall J_k \in path_T(J_s, J_n) \implies 1 - \Sigma_{x=0}^{d_k} f_{R_k}(x) < P_{dm}^{max}$$

P_{avail} is a set of possible schedules of the jobs in MC through the trees as the available paths. The available paths are the paths in which contain all the jobs in it and all those jobs meet their respective deadlines. In our context, the set of available paths represent the possible candidates to find a schedule. It should be noted that the criteria of all jobs meeting their deadlines is already met while constructing exploration tree. A node is not added to the tree if it misses its deadline. To quantify the probability of these paths we apply the definition of system criticality on the available paths as follows.

Definition 9 (Probability of system entering high criticality). *For an available path $path_T(J_s, J_n) \in P_{avail}$, the probability $\mathcal{P}_{sys}(path_T(J_s, J_n))$ that the system enters high criticality by taking this path is given as:*

$$\mathcal{P}_{sys}(path_T(J_s, J_n)) = \Sigma_j \frac{\mathcal{P}_j^{HI}}{n^{HI}} - \Pi\mathcal{P}_j^{HI}, \forall J_j \in path_T(J_s, J_n), \forall J_j \in \Lambda^{HI}; \tag{7}$$

$$path_T(J_s, J_n) \in P_{avail}.$$

Using the available paths and the system criticality metric defined above, we finally obtain a *mixed criticality (MC) schedule* as follows.

Definition 10 (Mixed Criticality Schedule). *A path $P_{MC} = path_T(J_s, J_n)$ is the mixed criticality schedule if $\mathcal{P}_{sys}(path_T(J_s, J_n))$ is the minimum among all possible $path_T(J_s, J_n) \in P_{avail}$ $\forall i, \exists J_i \in path_T(J_s, J_n)$, and $\forall i \exists J_i \in \Lambda$ where $J_s \in S(G)$.*

The MC schedule is a path P_{MC} through the exploration tree which contains all the jobs, no job misses its deadline and the probability of the system entering high criticality is minimum. It represents the schedule that should be taken by the system as the ordered sequence of execution of the jobs. To recall, the probability is minimum given the criticality is defined using the response time. Thus, we have found a solution to our problem which is a schedule represented by the path P_{MC}. The path P_{MC} by definition is from root node to a leaf node, thus we do not need to notate them (unlike jobs J_s and J_n in $path_T(J_s, J_n)$). Since this method is based on complete exploration, the schedule is guaranteed to be the optimal by minimizing the probability of system entering high criticality. Any impossible schedule is the one in which a job does not meet its timing constraints. These impossible schedules are already excluded while building the tree as we calculate response time in parallel.

Offline Schedule. As we see, the offline analysis results in a schedule P_{MC} such that the probability of system entering high criticality is minimum. The schedule ensures that no job missed its deadline. It uses an exploration of tree based on a graph representation of job executions. Because it is an exhaustive exploration, the minimum probability is ensured.

Online Schedule. The online part of our method is straightforward. It takes the schedule P_{MC} obtained in the offline analysis and executes the jobs as given in the sequence. The minimization of the probability of system entering high criticality has already been performed in the offline and is not required to be done in the online. The jobs are suspended if they reach their deadline and the sequence of jobs repeat each hyperperiod.

Example 3. We analyze the set of jobs Λ_2 shown in Table 1 which consists of 4 periodic tasks and 15 jobs with pWCET and implicit deadline as shown. There are 6 high criticality jobs from task τ_1 and 11 low criticality jobs from the rest of the tasks. To recall, the job set is to be scheduled non-preemptively on a uniprocessor system and the jobs are suspended at their deadlines. The threshold for the high criticality jobs of task τ_1 is set at 4 time units. The maximum allowed probability of deadline miss P_{dm}^{max} for any job is set at $1E-03$.

Table 1. Job set Λ_2.

Task	Deadline	pWCET						Criticality
τ_1	10	1 2 3 4 5 8 0.1 0.3 0.5 0.094 0.005 0.001						HI
τ_2	20	1 2 3 4 0.1 0.4 0.4 0.1						LO
τ_3	15	1 2 3 4 0.1 0.4 0.3 0.2						LO
τ_4	30	1 2 3 0.1 0.7 0.2						LO

The proposed schedule P_{MC} is: $J_{11}, J_{41}, J_{31}, J_{32}, J_{21}, J_{12}, J_{13}, J_{42}, J_{33}, J_{22}, J_{14}, J_{15}, J_{34}, J_{23}, J_{16}$. The probability that the system enters high criticality is $0.0.00509$. The pWCRT of some of the jobs is shown in Fig. 9. The pWCRT jobs of the high criticality task τ_1 remains unchanged as their pWCET as shown in Fig. 9(a). The pWCRTs of jobs which have been affected by probabilistic delay in execution are $J_{21}, J_{22}, J_{23}, J_{31}, J_{33}, J_{34}$ and J_{41} whose pWCRTs are shown in Figs. 9(b), (c), (d), (e), (f) and (g), respectively.

We obtain this result along with other possible schedules in which there is no deadline miss but the probability of the system entering high criticality is higher. For example, another possible schedule is: $J_{11}, J_{21}, J_{12}, J_{31}, J_{41}, J_{32}, J_{13}, J_{14}, J_{22}, J_{42}, J_{15}, J_{33}, J_{34}, J_{23}, J_{16}$. In this case the probability of system entering high criticality is 0.00605.

On computation, the tree for the job set Λ_2 contains $716, 132$ nodes.

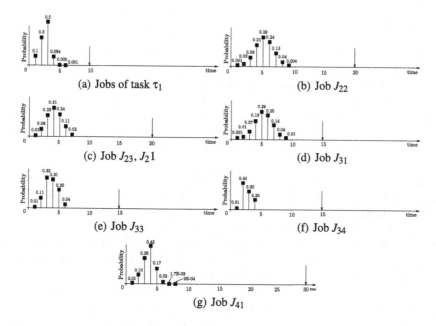

Fig. 9. pWCRT PMF of various jobs in Λ_2.

Overall, we observe that we can quantify the probability of something occurring in the system, like deadline miss or entering high criticality. This gives us a global picture of the MC system with pWCETs in terms of risk involved of system entering high criticality when applying such a system. In addition, we can control it through observing the pWCRTs and making the scheduling decisions accordingly.

Complexity. In general, MC problem lies beyond NP and PSPACE complexity and it is NP in uniprocessor case [11]. The complexity of our approach depends on the number of jobs n. The maximum complexity of building the graph is $O(n!)$. However, this might not always be the case because the tree is not built in the direction of a node which missed its deadline. Thus, the complexity also depends on the maximum allowed probability of deadline miss. The complexity of analyzing the tree and finding the paths is linear to the number of leaf nodes in the tree. In addition to this, there exists computational complexity of the convolution operation, which in turn depends on the possible values a random variable can take. Assuming that all jobs release at one critical instant, the convolution complexity is $O(n^n)$.

Actual complexity of the offline process is much less. Firstly, it is rarely the case that all the jobs are release at the same time since they belong to periodic tasks in the hyperperiod. Second, some combinations of sequences of jobs will result in a deadline miss. This means that the exploration tree is not built in that direction.

5   Conclusion

We have utilized a graph base exploratory method to obtain a non-preemptive schedule for MC probabilistic real-time system on uniprocessor machine, where task executions are suspended at the deadline. The task criticalities are defined using the pWCRT. We do this to make criticality decisions based on tasks demanding more resource at run-time. The obtained schedule minimizes the probability of system entering high criticality mode. This way, the actions needed to perform to cope with system high criticality are made less likely for the application.

At the current state of the work, the complexity of searching through enumerations is high. This work is one of the first steps to formalize the mixed criticality domain through response time. At the cost of complexity, we gain an application oriented perspective of the mixed criticality approach by using the response time. We adapt the schedule to the application itself and minimize the probabilities accordingly. We intend to reduce the complexity through methods like ordered searches and merging common and similar paths.

We intend to perform comparisons with real benchmarks in the future once the complexity is feasible for very large task sets. In future work we will extend this model to optimize the decisions when the system does enter high criticality. This future step is a hybrid approach where offline probability minimization has been performed. The online step of the hybrid approach will take care of the real-time response of the tasks and adjust the schedule accordingly to safer scenarios without jeopardizing the system critical functionality. We also aim to perform a sensitivity analysis on the criticality definition using the task response times.

References

1. Alahmad, B., Gopalakrishnan, S.: A risk-constrained Markov decision process approachto scheduling mixed-criticality job sets. In: Workshop on Mixed-Criticality Systems (2016)
2. Alahmad, B., Gopalakrishnan, S.: Risk-aware scheduling of dual criticality job systems using demand distributions. LITES **5**(1), 01:1–01:30 (2018). https://doi.org/10.4230/LITES-v005-i001-a001
3. Baruah, S., Easwaran, A., Guo, Z.: Mc-fluid: Simplified and optimally quantified. In: 2015 IEEE Real-Time Systems Symposium, pp. 327–337, December 2015
4. Bucci, G., Carnevali, L., Ridi, L., Vicario, E.: Oris: a tool for modeling, verification and evaluation of real-time systems. Int. J. Softw. Tools Technol. Transf. **12**(5), 391–403 (2010)
5. Burns, A., Davis, R.: Mixed criticality systems - a review, 12th edn. Technical report, Department of CS, U. of York, UK, March 2019
6. Cucu-Grosjean, L.: Independence - a misunderstood property of and for (probabilistic) real-time systems. In: Real-Time Systems: the Past, the Present and the Future (2013)
7. Davis, R.I., Burns, A., Griffin, D.: On the meaning of pWCET distributions and their use in schedulability analysis. In: In Proceedings Real-Time Scheduling Open Problems Seminar at ECRTS (2017)

8. Guo, Z., Santinelli, L., Yang, K.: EDF schedulability analysis on mixed-criticality systems with permitted failure probability. In: Proceedings of the RTCSA (2015)
9. Huang, H., Gill, C., Lu, C.: Mcflow: a real-time multi-core aware middleware for dependent task graphs. In: 2012 IEEE International Conference on Embedded and Real-Time Computing Systems and Applications, pp. 104–113, August 2012
10. Huang, S., Zhu, Y., Duan, J.: A new scheduling approach for mix-criticality real-time system. In: 2013 Fourth International Conference on Intelligent Control and Information Processing (ICICIP), pp. 43–46, June 2013
11. Kahil, R., Socci, D., Poplavko, P., Bensalem, S.: Algorithmic complexity of correctness testing in MC-scheduling. In: Proceedings of the 26th International Conference on Real-Time Networks and Systems, RTNS 2018, Chasseneuil-du-Poitou, France, 10–12 October 2018, pp. 180–190. ACM (2018)
12. Kim, K., Diaz, J., Lo Bello, L., Lopez, J., Lee, C.G., Min, S.L.: An exact stochastic analysis of priority-driven periodic real-time systems and its approximations. IEEE Trans. Comput. **54**(11), 1460–1466 (2005)
13. Li, H., Baruah, S.: An algorithm for scheduling certifiable mixed-criticality sporadic task systems. In: Proceedings of the 2010 31st IEEE Real-Time Systems Symposium, RTSS 2010, pp. 183–192. IEEE Computer Society, Washington, DC (2010). https://doi.org/10.1109/RTSS.2010.18
14. Maxim, D., Davis, R.I., Cucu-Grosjean, L., Easwaran, A.: Probabilistic analysis for mixed criticality systems using fixed priority preemptive scheduling. In: Proceedings of the 25th International Conference on Real-Time Networks and Systems, RTNS 2017, pp. 237–246. ACM, New York (2017). http://doi.acm.org/10.1145/3139258.3139276
15. Nélis, V., Yomsi, P.M., Pinho, L.M., Fonseca, J., Bertogna, M., Quiñones, E., Vargas, R., Marongiu, A.: The challenge of time-predictability in modern many-core architectures. In: 14th International Workshop on Worst-Case Execution Time Analysis (2014)
16. Santinelli, L., George, L.: Probabilities and mixed-criticalities: the probabilistic C-space. In: 3rd International Workshop on Mixed Criticality Systems WMC at RTSS (2016)
17. Santinelli, L., Guet, F., Morio, J.: Revising measurement-based probabilistic timing analysis. In: 2017 IEEE Real-Time and Embedded Technology and Applications Symposium, RTAS 2017, Pittsburg, PA, USA, 18–21 April 2017, pp. 199–208 (2017)
18. Santinelli, L., Meumeu Yomsy, P., Maxim, D., Cucu-Grosjean, L.: A component-based framework for modeling and analysing probabilistic real-time systems. In: 16th IEEE International Conference on Emerging Technologies and Factory Automation (2011)
19. Singh, J., Santinelli, L., Infantes, G., Doose, D., Brunel, J.: Mixed criticality probabilistic real-time systems analysis using discrete time Markov chain. In: 6th International Workshop on Mixed Criticality Systems (WMC) (2018)
20. Stigge, M., Ekberg, P., Guan, N., Yi, W.: The digraph real-time task model. In: Proceedings of the 2011 17th IEEE Real-Time and Embedded Technology and Applications Symposium, RTAS 2011, pp. 71–80. IEEE Computer Society, Washington, DC (2011). https://doi.org/10.1109/RTAS.2011.15
21. Soong, T.: Fundamentals of probability and statistics for engineers, p. 391, January 2004. ISBN 9780470868157
22. Vestal, S.: Preemptive scheduling of multi-criticality systems with varying degrees of execution time assurance. In: Proceedings of the 28th IEEE International Real-Time Systems Symposium (RTSS), pp. 239–243. IEEE Computer Society (2007)

Improving the Analysis of GPC
in Real-Time Calculus

Yue Tang[1], Yuming Jiang[2]($\boxtimes$), and Nan Guan[1]

[1] The Hong Kong Polytechnic University, Kowloon, Hong Kong
csyuetang@comp.polyu.edu.hk, nan.guan@polyu.edu.hk
[2] Norwegian University of Science and Technology, Trondheim, Norway
yuming.jiang@ntnu.no

Abstract. Real-Time Calculus (RTC) is a framework for modeling and performance analysis of real-time networked systems. In RTC, workload and resources are modeled as arrival and service curves, and processing semantics are modeled by abstract components. Greedy Processing Component (GPC) is one of the fundamental abstract components in RTC, which processes incoming events in a greedy fashion as long as there are available resources. The relations between inputs and outputs of GPC have been established, which are consistent with its behaviors. In this paper, we first revise the original proof of calculating output curves in GPC, and then propose a new method to obtain tighter output arrival curves. Experiment results show that the precision of output arrival curves can be improved by our method compared with the original calculation and existing work.

Keywords: RTC · GPC · Output arrival curves

1 Introduction

Real-Time Calculus (RTC), originated in Network Calculus, is a framework for modeling and performance analysis of real-time networked embedded systems. RTC uses arrival and service curves to model workload and resource, and the performance analysis is mainly based on min-plus and max-plus algebra. Compared with the traditional real-time scheduling theory, RTC is more expressive and can model a much wider range of realistic systems due to usage of much more general workload and resource models. At the same time, the models and analysis techniques of RTC generate closed-form analytical results, thus having higher analysis efficiency, compared to state-based modeling and analysis techniques such as model checking [2,7]. All these advantages make RTC draw much attention from both real-time community and industry.

Greedy Processing Component (GPC) is one of the fundamental abstract components in RTC, which processes input events in a greedy fashion in FIFO order, as long as there are available resources. GPCs can be connected into networks to model the behaviors of real-time systems, and one of the typical

© Springer Nature Switzerland AG 2019
N. Guan et al. (Eds.): SETTA 2019, LNCS 11951, pp. 106–121, 2019.
https://doi.org/10.1007/978-3-030-35540-1_7

scenarios is fixed-priority scheduling, where the remaining resource of one GPC related to a higher-priority task is used as input resource of the GPC related to a lower-priority task.

The analysis of GPC has been consistently studied and improved since it was proposed in [1,5,6]. The improvement involves two aspects: efficiency and precision. For efficiency, [9] proved that the output curves can be calculated with a finite length of input curves, thus greatly shortening the computation time for output curves. This work was further generalized in [10], which eliminates the dependency of Finitary RTC on the semantics of GPC and applied Finitary RTC to the level of RTC-operators. For precision, [8] proposed to reduce the unused resource from total resource before calculating the output arrival curves, which improves the precision of output arrival curves.

Contributions. In this work, we improve the analysis of GPC in two aspects. First, we revise the proof of output curves in GPC and complement the missing deduction steps, which further clarifies the correctness of the original results. Second, we propose a new method for calculating output arrival curves, which generates more precise results based on the connection between output arrival curves and the number of accumulated events, rather than focusing on the interaction of between arrival and service curves as in [8].

2   RTC Basics

2.1   Arrival and Service Curves

RTC uses arrival curves and service curves to describe timing properties of event streams and available resource.

Definition 1 (Arrival Curve). *Let $R[s, t)$ denote the total number of arrived events in time interval $[s, t)$[1], where s and t are two arbitrary non-negative real numbers. Then, the corresponding upper and lower arrival curves are denoted as α^u and α^l, respectively, and satisfy:*

$$\forall s < t, \quad \alpha^l(t - s) \leq R[s, t) \leq \alpha^u(t - s),$$

where $\alpha^u(0) = \alpha^l(0) = 0$.

Generally we assume that α^u is concave satisfying $\alpha^u(t) + \alpha^u(s) \geq \alpha^u(t+s)$.

Definition 2 (Service Curve). *Let $C[s, t)$ denote the total available resource in time interval $[s, t)$[2]. Then, the corresponding upper and lower service curves are denoted as β^u and β^l, respectively, and satisfy:*

$$\forall s < t, \quad \beta^l(t - s) \leq C[s, t) \leq \beta^u(t - s),$$

where $\beta^u(0) = \beta^l(0) = 0$.

---

[1] $R[s, t) = -R[t, s), R[s, s) = 0$.
[2] $C[s, t) = -C[t, s), C[s, s) = 0$.

In our work, we adopt the PJD workload model for arrival curve and TDMA model for service curve in [4] for easy understanding. In detail, the input arrival curves are characterized by (p, j, d), where p denotes the period, j the jitter, and d the minimum inter-arrival distance of events in the modeled stream:

$$\alpha^u(\Delta) = \min\left(\left\lceil\frac{\Delta+j}{p}\right\rceil, \left\lceil\frac{\Delta}{d}\right\rceil\right), \quad \alpha^l(\Delta) = \left\lfloor\frac{\Delta-j}{p}\right\rfloor.$$

The service curves are characterized by (s, c, b):

$$\beta^u(\Delta) = \left(\left\lfloor\frac{\Delta}{c}\right\rfloor \cdot s + \min(\Delta \bmod c, s)\right) \cdot b, \beta^l(\Delta) = \left(\left\lfloor\frac{\Delta'}{c}\right\rfloor \cdot s + \min(\Delta' \bmod c, s)\right) \cdot b,$$

where $\Delta' = \max(\Delta - c + s, 0)$.

Figure 1(a) shows an example of arrival curve with $p = 10, j = 2, d = 0$ and service curve $s = 1, c = 5, b = 1$, and Fig. 1(b) shows a possible sequence of workload and TDMA resource corresponding to Fig. 1(a).

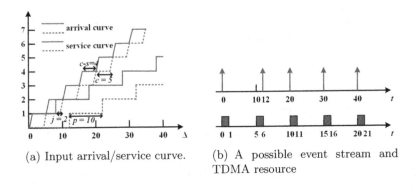

(a) Input arrival/service curve.   (b) A possible event stream and TDMA resource

Fig. 1. An example for inputs

2.2   Greedy Processing Component (GPC)

In this paper, we focus on one of the widely used abstract components in RTC called Greedy Processing Component (GPC). A GPC processes events from the input event stream in a greedy fashion, as long as it complies with the availability of resource. If we use $R'[s,t]$ and $C'[s,t]$ to describe the accumulated number of processed events and remaining resources during the time interval $[s,t)$, then it satisfies

$$R'[s,t] = C[s,t] - C'[s,t]$$
$$C'[s,t] = \sup_{s \le u \le t} \{C[s,u) - R[s,u) - B(s), 0\}$$

The output event stream produced by GPC is described by arrival curve α'^u, α'^l, and the remaining resource is described by service curve β'^u, β'^l.

$$\alpha'^u = \min((\alpha^u \otimes \beta^u) \oslash \beta^l, \beta^u),$$
$$\alpha'^l = \min((\alpha^l \oslash \beta^u) \otimes \beta^l, \beta^l),$$
$$\beta'^u = (\beta^u - \alpha^l)\overline{\oslash}0,$$
$$\beta'^l = (\beta^l - \alpha^u)\overline{\otimes}0,$$

where

$$(f \otimes g)(\Delta) = \inf_{0 \le \lambda \le \Delta}\{f(\Delta - \lambda) + g(\lambda)\},$$
$$(f\overline{\otimes}g)(\Delta) = \sup_{0 \le \lambda \le \Delta}\{f(\Delta - \lambda) + g(\lambda)\},$$
$$(f \oslash g)(\Delta) = \sup_{\lambda \ge 0}\{f(\Delta + \lambda) - g(\lambda)\},$$
$$(f\overline{\oslash}g)(\Delta) = \inf_{\lambda \ge 0}\{f(\Delta + \lambda) - g(\lambda)\}.$$

The maximum delay d_{max} experienced by any event on the event stream and the amount of events in the input buffer b_{max}, i.e., the backlog, are respectively bounded by

$$d_{max} \le \sup_{\lambda \ge 0}\left\{\inf\{\delta \ge 0 : \alpha^u(\lambda) \le \beta^l(\lambda + \delta)\}\right\} = Del(\alpha^u, \beta^l)$$
$$b_{max} \le \sup_{\lambda \ge 0}\{\alpha^u(\lambda) - \beta^l(\lambda)\} = Buf(\alpha^u, \beta^l)$$

GPCs can be connected together to model systems with various scheduling and arbitration policies. One of the typical scenarios is to model fixed-priority scheduling, where the resource allocation for tasks with different priorities is described by the resource stream direction.

An Example. Suppose two event streams S_1, S_2 are processed on two successive processors. S_1 has higher priority than S_2 and the execution of S_2 will be preempted by S_1 as long as an event of S_1 arrives on each processor. Such a system (Fig. 2(a)) can be modeled by a GPC network (Fig. 2(b)). The processing of each stream on each processor is modeled as a GPC component. The output arrival curves of G_1 are the input arrival curves of G_2, corresponding to the system behavior that the events of S_1 completing execution on P_1 are further processed on P_2. And the remaining service curve of $G_1(G_2)$ is the input service curve $G_3(G_4)$, since S_1 has higher priority on both processors.

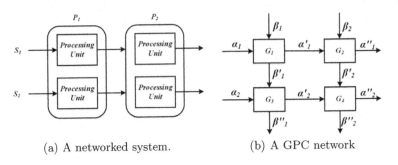

(a) A networked system.   (b) A GPC network

Fig. 2. An example for GPC network.

3   Revised Proof of Output Curves

Although how to calculate bounds for output curves in GPC has been proved
in [4], some important deduction steps are missing. In detail, the process of
specifying the numerical relations between some critical parameters is too simple
to be convincing. In this section, we add these missing deduction parts and give
revised proof of calculating output curves in GPC.

Theorem 1. *Given a GPC with arrival curve α^u, α^l and service curve β^u, β^l,
then its remaining service curves are bounded by*

$$\beta'^u = ((\beta^u - \alpha^l)\overline{\oslash}0)^+$$
$$\beta'^l = (\beta^l - \alpha^u)\overline{\otimes}0$$

where for a function $f(\Delta)$, $(f(\Delta))^+ = max(f(\Delta), 0)$.

Proof. (1) We first prove β'^l.

   Suppose p is an arbitrarily small time such that the backlog satisfies $B(p) = 0$.
Then for all $p \leq s \leq t$,

$$
\begin{aligned}
&C'[s,t]\\
&= C'[p,t] - C'[p,s]\\
&= \sup_{p \leq a \leq t} \{C[p,a) - R[p,a)\}^+ - \sup_{p \leq b \leq s} \{C[p,b) - R[p,b)\}^+
\end{aligned}
$$

Since $C[p,p) = R[p,p) = C[p,p) - R[p,p) = 0$, the suprema are nonnegative
and we have

$$
\begin{aligned}
&C'[s,t]\\
&= \sup_{p \leq a \leq t} \{C[p,a) - R[p,a)\} - \sup_{p \leq b \leq s} \{C[p,b) - R[p,b)\}\\
&= \inf_{p \leq b \leq s} \{ \sup_{p \leq a \leq t} \{C[b,a) - R[b,a)\}\}\\
&= \inf_{p \leq b \leq s} \{max\{ \sup_{b \leq a \leq t} \{C[b,a) - R[b,a)\}, \sup_{p \leq a \leq b} \{C[b,a) - R[b,a)\}\}\}
\end{aligned}
$$

Let $\chi_1(b) = \sup\limits_{b \le a \le t} \{C[b,a] - R[b,a]\} = max\{C[b,b] - R[b,b], C[b,b+1] - R[b,b+1], ..., C[b,t] - R[b,t]\} \ge 0^3$,

$\chi_2(b) = \sup\limits_{p \le a \le b} \{C[b,a] - R[b,a]\} = max\{C[b,p] - R[b,p], C[b,p+1] - R[b,p+1), ..., C[b,b-1] - R[b,b-1], C[b,b] - R[b,b]\} \ge 0$.

Next we prove that[4]

$C'[s,t] = \inf\limits_{p \le b \le s} \{max\{\chi_1(b), \chi_2(b)\}\} = \inf\limits_{p \le b \le s} \{\chi_1(b)\}$.

We consider two cases:

(1) For any $i \in [p,s]$, $\chi_1(i) \ge \chi_2(i)$, then

$C'[s,t] = \inf\limits_{p \le b \le s} \{max\{\chi_1(b), \chi_2(b)\} = \inf\limits_{p \le b \le s} \{\chi_1(b)\}$,

then $C'[s,t] = \inf\limits_{p \le b \le s} \{\chi_1(b)\}$.

(2) There exists at least one $i \in [p,s]$ that $\chi_1(i) < \chi_2(i)$, that is, there exists one $x \in [p,i]$ that

$C[b,a] - R[b,a] = C[i,x] - R[i,x] = max\{\chi_1(i), \chi_2(i)\} = max\{C[i,p] - R[i,p], ..., C[i,x-1] - R[i,x-1], ..., C[i,x+1] - R[i,x+1], ..., C[i,t] - R[i,t]\}$

Then we have

$$R[x,i] - C[x,i] \ge R[p,i] - C[p,i] \Rightarrow C[p,x] \ge R[p,x]$$

$$R[x,i] - C[x,i] \ge R[p+1,i] - C[p+1,i] \Rightarrow C[p+1,x] \ge R[p+1,x]$$

$$...$$

$$R[x,i] - C[x,i] \ge R[x-1,i] - C[x-1,i] \Rightarrow C[x-1,x] \ge R[x-1,x]$$

$$R[x,i] - C[x,i] \ge R[x+1,i] - C[x+1,i] \Rightarrow R[x,x+1] \ge C[x,x+1]$$

$$R[x,i] - C[x,i] \ge C[i,i+1] - R[i,i+1] \Rightarrow R[x,i+1] \ge C[x,i+1]$$

$$R[x,i] - C[x,i] \ge C[i,t] - R[i,t] \Rightarrow R[x,t] \ge C[x,t]$$

Then when $b = x$, we have

$\chi_1(x) = max\{C[x,x] - R[x,x], C[x,x+1] - R[x,x+1], ..., C[x,t] - R[x,t]\} = 0$,

$\chi_2(x) = max\{C[x,p] - R[x,p], C[x,p+1] - R[x,p+1), ..., C[x,b-1] - R[x,b-1], C[x,x] - R[x,x]\} = 0$.

So $max\{\chi_1(x), \chi_2(x)\} = 0$.

Then

$C'[s,t] = \inf\limits_{p \le b \le s} \{max\{\chi_1(b), \chi_2(b)\}\} = max\{\chi_1(x), \chi_2(x)\} = 0$ (since $C'[s,t] \ge 0$).

On the other hand,

$\inf\limits_{p \le b \le s} \{\chi_1(b)\} = min\{\chi_1(p), \chi_1(p+1), ..., \chi_1(x), ..., \chi_1(s)\} = 0$, then we have

$C'[s,t] = \inf\limits_{p \le b \le s} \{\chi_1(b)\} = 0$.

---

[3] For ease of presentation we assume s, t, a, b, p to be integer in following proofs.

[4] This part is just briefly explained as $'a \ge b$ since $t \ge s'$ in the existing proof [4].

So in both cases, $C'[s,t] = \inf\limits_{p\leq b\leq s}\{\chi_1(b)\}$, which implies that removing the cases when $a < b$ does not influence the final result. Note that $a \geq b$ is a consequence of above deduction, but not simply a direct result of $s \leq t$ as implied in [4].

Then we continue to lower bound $C'[s,t]$.

$$
\begin{aligned}
&C'[s,t]\\
&= \inf_{p\leq b\leq s}\{\sup_{b\leq a\leq t}\{C[b,a) - R[b,a)\}\\
&= \inf_{p\leq b\leq s}\{\sup_{0\leq a-b\leq t-b}\{C[b,a) - R[b,a)\}\\
&\geq \inf_{p\leq b\leq s}\{\sup_{0\leq\lambda\leq t-b}\{\beta^l(\lambda) - \alpha^u(\lambda)\}\\
&\geq \sup_{0\leq\lambda\leq t-s}\{\beta^l(\lambda) - \alpha^u(\lambda)\}\\
&= (\beta^l - \alpha^u)\overline{\otimes}0
\end{aligned}
$$

(2) Next we prove β'^u.

$$
\begin{aligned}
&C'[s,t]\\
&= C'[p,t) - C'[p,s)\\
&= \sup_{p\leq a\leq t}\{\inf_{p\leq b\leq s}\{C[b,a) - R[b,a)\}\}\\
&= max\{\sup_{p\leq a\leq s}\{\inf_{p\leq b\leq s}\{C[b,a) - R[b,a)\}\}, \sup_{s\leq a\leq t}\{\inf_{p\leq b\leq s}\{C[b,a) - R[b,a)\}\}\}\\
&= max\{\sup_{p\leq a\leq s}\{min\{\inf_{a\leq b\leq s}\{C[b,a) - R[b,a)\}, \inf_{b\leq a\leq s}\{C[b,a) - R[b,a)\}\}\},\\
&\quad \sup_{s\leq a\leq t}\{\inf_{p\leq b\leq s}\{C[b,a) - R[b,a)\}\}\}
\end{aligned}
$$

Similar as above, we define $\psi = \sup\limits_{p\leq a\leq s}\{\inf\limits_{p\leq b\leq s}\{C[b,a) - R[b,a)\}\}$, $\psi_1(a) = \inf\limits_{a\leq b\leq s}\{C[b,a) - R[b,a)\}$, and $\psi_2(a) = \inf\limits_{b\leq a\leq s}\{C[b,a) - R[b,a)\}$. Next we prove $\psi \leq 0$.

For any $a \in [p,s]$, we consider three cases:

(1) $\psi_1(a) = \psi_2(a)$. Then there must exist $b_{inf} = a$ such that $C[b_{inf},a) - R[b_{inf},a) = 0 = min\{\psi_1(a), \psi_2(a)\}$.
(2) $\psi_1(a) > \psi_2(a)$. Then there must exist $b_{inf} < a$ such that $C[b_{inf},a) - R[b_{inf},a) = min\{\psi_1(a), \psi_2(a)\} < \psi_1(a) \leq 0$.
(3) $\psi_1(a) < \psi_2(a)$. Then there must exist $b_{inf} > a$ such that $C[b_{inf},a) - R[b_{inf},a) = min\{\psi_1(a), \psi_2(a)\} < \psi_2(a) \leq 0$.

Then combining the above three cases, for each $a \in [p,s]$, $min\{\psi_1(a), \psi_2(a)\} \leq 0$, so $\psi \leq 0$.

By now we have

$$C'[s, t)$$
$$= \sup_{p \leq a \leq t} \{ \inf_{p \leq b \leq s} \{ C[b, a) - R[b, a) \} \}$$
$$= \sup_{s \leq a \leq t} \{ \inf_{p \leq b \leq s} \{ C[b, a) - R[b, a) \} \}^+$$
$$= \sup_{s \leq a \leq t} \{ \inf_{a-s \leq a-b \leq a-p} \{ C[b, a) - R[b, a) \} \}^+$$

Note that $a \geq b$ is a consequence of $a \geq s$, but not a direct result of $s \leq t$. Then with substitution λ we have

$$C'[s, t) \leq \sup_{s \leq a \leq t} \{ \inf_{a-s \leq a-b \leq a-p} \{ \beta^u(\lambda) - \alpha^l(\lambda) \} \}^+$$
$$\leq \sup_{s \leq a \leq t} \{ \inf_{t-s \leq a-b \leq p} \{ \beta^u(\lambda) - \alpha^l(\lambda) \} \}^+$$
$$= \inf_{t-s \leq \lambda \leq p} \{ \beta^u(\lambda) - \alpha^l(\lambda) \} \}^+$$
$$= \inf_{t-s \leq \lambda} \{ \beta^u(\lambda) - \alpha^l(\lambda) \} \}^+$$
$$= ((\beta^u - \alpha^l) \overline{\oslash} 0)^+$$

□

Theorem 2. *Given a GPC with arrival curve α^u, α^l and service curve β^u, β^l, then its output arrival curves are bounded by*

$$\alpha'^u = \min((\alpha^u \otimes \beta^u) \oslash \beta^l, \beta^u)$$
$$\alpha'^l = \min((\alpha^l \oslash \beta^u) \otimes \beta^l, \beta^l)$$

Proof. The proofs are presented in the Appendix.   □

An example. We take the calculation of β'^l as an example to show $C'[s, t) = \inf_{p \leq b \leq s} \{ \chi_1(b) \}$. Let $p = 0$, $s = 3$, $t = 5$. Then the value of $C'[s, t)$ with different values of a, b is shown in Table 1.

Table 1. An example for part of Theorem 1.

	$b = 0$	$b = 1$	$b = 2$	$b = 3$
$a = 0$	0	$R[0, 1) - C[0, 1)$	$R[0, 2) - C[0, 2)$	$R[0, 3) - C[0, 3)$
$a = 1$	$C[0, 1) - R[0, 1)$	0	$R[1, 2) - C[1, 2)$	$R[1, 3) - C[1, 3)$
$a = 2$	$C[0, 2) - R[0, 2)$	$C[1, 2) - R[1, 2)$	0	$R[2, 3) - C[2, 3)$
$a = 3$	$C[0, 3) - R[0, 3)$	$C[1, 3) - R[1, 3)$	$C[2, 3) - R[2, 3)$	0
$a = 4$	$C[0, 4) - C[0, 4)$	$C[1, 4) - R[1, 4)$	$C[2, 4) - R[2, 4)$	$C[3, 4) - R[3, 4)$
$a = 5$	$C[0, 5) - R[0, 5)$	$C[1, 5) - R[1, 5)$	$C[2, 5) - R[2, 5)$	$C[3, 5) - R[3, 5)$

Assume that when $b = 2$, $\chi_1(2) < \chi_2(2)$ and $\chi_2(2) = R[1,2] - C[1,2]$. Then we have

$$R[1,2] - C[1,2] \geq R[0,2] - C[0,2] \Rightarrow C[0,1] \geq R[0,1]$$

$$R[1,2] - C[1,2] \geq C[2,3] - R[2,3] \Rightarrow R[1,3] \geq C[1,3]$$

$$R[1,2] - C[1,2] \geq C[2,4] - R[2,4] \Rightarrow R[1,4] \geq C[1,4]$$

$$R[1,2] - C[1,2] \geq C[2,5] - R[2,5] \Rightarrow R[1,5] \geq C[1,5]$$

Then when $b = 1$, $max\{\chi_1(1), \chi_2(1)\} = \chi_1(1) = 0$, and
$C'[0,3] = \inf_{0 \leq b \leq 3}\{max\{\chi_1(b), \chi_2(b)\}\} = 0 = min\{\chi_1(0), \chi_1(1), \chi_1(2),$
$\chi_1(3)\} = \inf_{0 \leq b \leq 3}\{\chi_1(b)\}$.

4   Improving Output Arrival Curves

In this section, we adopt the idea in [3] and derive a new upper bound for output arrival curves, which combined with the original result in [4] generates a tighter upper bound, as shown in Sect. 5.

Lemma 1. *Given an event stream with input function $R(t)$, output function $R'(t)$, arrival curve α^u, α^l, service curve β^u, β^l, the output arrival curve of a GPC is upper bounded by $\alpha'^u(\Delta) = \alpha^u(\Delta) + Buf(\alpha^u, \beta^l) - \alpha^u(0^+)$.*

Proof. We use $B(s)$ to denote the backlog at time s. For all $s \leq t$, we have

$$B(t) - B(s) = R[s,t] - R'[s,t]$$

Suppose p is an arbitrarily small time satisfying $B(p) = 0$, then substituting t with p gives

$$B(s) = R[p,s] - R'[p,s]$$

Based on the behaviors of GPC, it holds that

$$C'[p,s] = \sup_{p \leq u \leq s}\{C[p,u] - R[p,u] - B(p), 0\}$$

Then

$$R'[p,s] = C[p,s] - C'[p,s] = C[p,s] - \sup_{p \leq u \leq s}\{C[p,u] - R[p,u] - B(p), 0\}$$

Since $B(p) = 0$ and $C[p,p] - R[p,p] = 0$, we have

$$R'[p,s] = C[p,s] - C'[p,s] = C[p,s] - \sup_{p \leq u \leq s}\{C[p,u] - R[p,u]\}$$

Since $\alpha^u(\Delta)$ is concave, there exists $\widetilde{\alpha^u}(\Delta)$ satisfying that for any $\Delta > 0$, $\alpha^u(\Delta) = \widetilde{\alpha^u}(\Delta) + \alpha^u(0^+)$. Then

$$
\begin{aligned}
R'[s,t] &= R[s,t] + B(s) - B(t) \\
&\leq R[s,t] + B(s) \\
&= R[p,t] - R[p,s] + R[p,s] - \{C[p,s] - \sup_{p \leq u \leq s} \{C[p,u] - R[p,u]\}\} \\
&= R[p,t] - C[p,s] + \sup_{p \leq u \leq s} \{C[p,u] - R[p,u]\} \\
&= \sup_{p \leq u \leq s} \{R[u,t] - C[u,s]\} \\
&\leq \sup_{p \leq u \leq s} \{\alpha^u(t-u) - \beta^l(s-u)\} \\
&= \sup_{p \leq u \leq s} \{\widetilde{\alpha^u}(t-u) + \alpha^u(0^+) - \beta^l(s-u)\} \\
&\leq \sup_{p \leq u \leq s} \{\widetilde{\alpha^u}(s-u) + \widetilde{\alpha^u}(t-s) + \alpha^u(0^+) - \beta^l(s-u)\} \\
&= \widetilde{\alpha^u}(t-s) + \sup_{p \leq u \leq s} \{\alpha^u(s-u) - \beta^l(s-u)\} \\
&\leq \widetilde{\alpha^u}(t-s) + Buf(\alpha^u, \beta^l) \\
&= \alpha^u(t-s) + Buf(\alpha^u, \beta^l) - \alpha^u(0^+)
\end{aligned}
$$

Then the lemma is proved. $\qquad\qquad\qquad\qquad\qquad\qquad\qquad\qquad\qquad\qquad\square$

Theorem 3. *Given a GPC with input arrival curves α^u, α^l and service curves β^u, β^l, the output events can be upper bounded by:*
$$\alpha'^u = ((\alpha^u \otimes \beta^u) \oslash \beta^l) \wedge \beta^u \wedge (\alpha^u + Buf(\alpha^u, \beta^l) - \alpha^u(0^+)),$$
where $f \wedge g = min(f, g)$.

An Example. Suppose a GPC has arrival curves and service curves as in Fig. 1, then the output arrival curves calculated by Theorem 3 (blue dashed lines) and the original result (blue full lines) are shown in Fig. 3(a). Next we show the influence of j, s to the results calculated with these two methods, where the result of original method is denoted with full lines, and that of our new method (Theorem 3) is denoted with dashed lines.

Figure 3(a) shows the influence of j with 4 different sets of inputs. All these 4 inputs are generated with $p = 10, d = 0, s = 1, c = 5, b = 1$, and they differ in j which equals $2, 4, 5, 6$ respectively. Comparing the cases when $j = 2, 4, 5$ and that when $j = 6$, it implies when $p - j > c - s$, the new method is more possible to outperform the original one[5]. Focusing on the cases when $j = 2, 4, 5$, it is observed that the new method performs better when j is smaller.

Figure 3(b) shows the influence of s with 3 different sets of inputs. All these 4 inputs are generated with $p = 10, j = 6, d = 0, c = 5, b = 1$, and they differ in s which equals $1, 2, 3$ respectively. Our method outperforms the original one

---

[5] Note that this is not applicable to all task sets.

when $s = 2, 3$ with $p - j > c - s$, which is consistent with the trend in Fig. 3(a). Considering the inputs with $s = 2, 3$, the difference between our method and the original one grows larger when s is smaller.

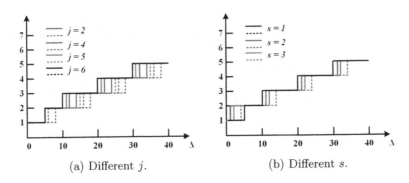

(a) Different j.   (b) Different s.

Fig. 3. Intuitive observations about the influence of j and s. (Color figure online)

5   Experiments

We implement our new theoretical results in RTC Toolbox [11] and conduct experiments to evaluate their performance. The new proposed method (denoted by *new*) is compared with the original GPC (denoted by *org*), and the existing work in [8] (denoted by *ext*). Task sets of two different parameter settings are generated, under which both single GPC and GPC network are considered . For single GPC, the comparison is conducted with regards to two aspects:

(1) Percentage, denoted by $p(method_1, method_2)$, describes the ratio between the number of task sets where $method_1$ generates more precise upper output arrival curves than $method_2$ and the total number of generated task sets.
(2) Average distance, denoted by $d(method_1, method_2)$, shows the average numerical distance between upper output arrival curves calculated with $method_1$ and $method_2$ in each setting. The distance of two curves f and g is defined as follows, and n is fixed to be 500.

$$dist(f, g) = \frac{\sum_{\Delta=1}^{n} |(f(\Delta) - g(\Delta))|}{n}.$$

For GPC network, we compare the delay bound calculated by different methods.

5.1   Parameter Setting I

Under this parameter setting, arrival curves and service curves are generated as: $p \in [20, 100]$, $j \in [1, x]$, $d \in [1, 20]$, $s = y$, $c = 50$, $b = 1$ (x and y to be specified in the following)[6]. For each setting, we generate 200 task sets.

---

[6] Note that p and c are relatively small since larger values will cause computation exception with larger-scale GPC networks.

Single GPC. Figure 4(a) shows the results with different s (X-axis) with $x = 100$. Figure 4 (b)(c)(d) shows the results with different jitter range (X-axis) with $y = 20, 30, 40$ respectively. The number of task sets where our new method generates more precise results than the original calculation and existing work increases with larger s and smaller jitter range.

GPC Network. In Fig. 5, we generate $3 \times 3, 4 \times 4, 5 \times 5$ GPC networks and evaluate the normalized quality, which is the ratio between delay bound calculated with two different methods. The parameters are the same as Fig. 4 (b)(c)(d). The improvement of our method is more obvious when the network scale is larger.

5.2 Parameter Setting II

Under this parameter setting, arrival curves and service curves are generated as: $p \in [20, 50]$, $j \in [10, 100]$, $d \in [1, 10]$, $c = 60$, $b = 1$, and s varies for different groups of experiments (corresponding to the X-axis). With each s value, we generate 200 task sets.

Single GPC. Figure 6(a) shows the results with s from 2 to 6. Under this parameter setting, the percentage of task sets where the new proposed method outperforms the original calculation grows with increasing s, while it does not perform better than the method in existing work [8].

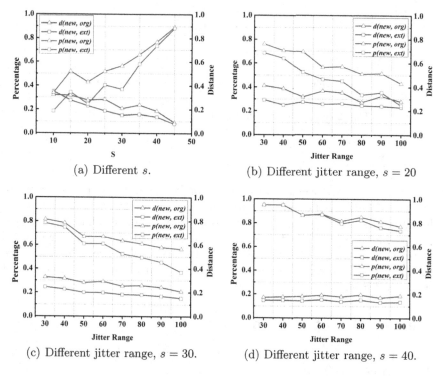

(a) Different s.

(b) Different jitter range, $s = 20$

(c) Different jitter range, $s = 30$.

(d) Different jitter range, $s = 40$.

Fig. 4. Experiment results for single GPC under parameter setting I.

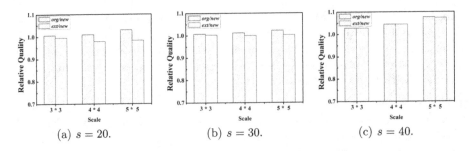

(a) $s = 20$.   (b) $s = 30$.   (c) $s = 40$.

Fig. 5. Experiment results for GPC network under parameter setting I.

GPC Network. As shown in Fig. 6(b), we generate $3 \times 3, 4 \times 4, 5 \times 5$ GPC networks and evaluate the normalized quality. s is fixed to be 20. The method in existing work [8] has better performance than the new proposed method with regards to delay bound.

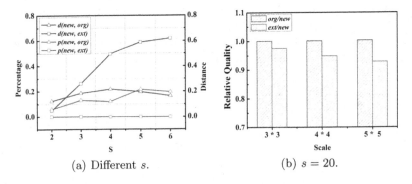

(a) Different s.   (b) $s = 20$.

Fig. 6. Experiment results under parameter setting II.

6   Conclusion

In this work, the improvement of GPC is conducted in two aspects. First, we revise the existing proof of output curves in GPC. Specially, we add the missing deduction parts about the numerical relations between critical parameters. Second, we propose a new method to calculate output arrival curves, which generates more precise results than original methods. In future work, we tend to explore other fundamental abstract components in RTC and improve the precision of related calculation.

Appendix : Proof of Theorem 2

(1) We first prove α'^u. Suppose p is an arbitrarily small time such that the backlog satisfies $B(p) = 0$.

Then for all $p \leq s \leq t$,

$R'[s,t)$

$= R'[p,t) - R'[p,s)$

$= \sup_{p \leq b \leq s} \{C[p,b) - R[p,b)\}^+ - \sup_{p \leq a \leq t} \{C[p,a) - R[p,a)\}^+ + C[p,t) - C[p,s)$

Since $C[p,p) = R[p,p) = C[p,p) - R[p,p) = 0$, the suprema are nonnegative and we have

$R'[s,t)$

$= \sup_{p \leq b \leq s} \{C[p,b) - R[p,b)\} - \sup_{p \leq a \leq t} \{C[p,a) - R[p,a)\} + C[p,t) - C[p,s)$

$= \sup_{p \leq b \leq s} \{ \inf_{p \leq a \leq t} \{R[b,a) + C[a,t) - C[b,s)\}\}$

$= \sup_{p \leq b \leq s} \{ \inf_{p \leq a \leq t} \{C[s,t) + C[a,b) - R[a,b)\}\}$

$= C[s,t) + \sup_{p \leq b \leq s} \{ \inf_{p \leq a \leq t} \{C[a,b) - R[a,b)\}\}$

$= C[s,t) + \sup_{p \leq b \leq s} \{min\{ \inf_{b \leq a \leq t} \{C[a,b) - R[a,b)\}, \inf_{p \leq a \leq b} \{C[a,b) - R[a,b)\}\}\}$

Let $\chi = \sup_{p \leq b \leq s} \{min\{ \inf_{b \leq a \leq t} \{C[a,b) - R[a,b)\}, \inf_{p \leq a \leq b} \{C[a,b) - R[a,b)\}\}\}$,

$\chi_1(b) = \inf_{b \leq a \leq t} \{C[a,b) - R[a,b)\} = min\{C[b,b) - R[b,b), C[b+1,b) - R[b+1,b), ..., C[t,b) - R[t,b)\} \leq 0$,

$\chi_2(b) = \inf_{p \leq a \leq b} \{C[a,b) - R[a,b)\} = min\{C[p,b) - R[p,b), C[p+1,b) - R[p+1,b), ..., C[b-1,b) - R[b-1,b), C[b,b) - R[b,b)\} \leq 0$.

Next we prove $\chi = \sup_{p \leq b \leq s} \{\chi_1(b)\}$[7].

We consider two cases:

(1) For any $i \in [p,s]$, $\chi_1(i) \leq \chi_2(i)$, then $\chi = \sup_{p \leq b \leq s} \{\chi_1(b)\}$.

(2) There exists at least one $i \in [p,s]$ satisfying $\chi_1(i) > \chi_2(i)$, then $min\{\chi_1(i), \chi_2(i)\} = \chi_2(i) < 0$,

Similar as the proof for β'', there exists $x \in [p,s]$ such that $min\{\chi_1(x), \chi_2(x)\} = \chi_1(x) = \chi_2(x) = 0$.

Then

$\chi = \sup_{p \leq b \leq s} \{min\{\chi_1(b), \chi_2(b)\}\}$

$= max\{min\{\chi_1(p), \chi_2(p)\}, ..., min\{\chi_1(x), \chi_2(x)\}, ..., min\{\chi_1(s), \chi_2(s)\}\}$

$= \sup_{b \in \phi}\{min\{\chi_1(b), \chi_2(b)\}\} = \sup_{b \in \phi}\{\chi_1(b)\}$

---

[7] This is not detailed in [4].

where ψ is the set of values in $[p, s]$ which satisfy for any $b \in \phi$, $\chi_1(b) \leq \chi_2(b)$.

On the other hand, $\sup\limits_{p \leq b \leq s} \{\chi_1(b)\} = \sup\limits_{b \in \psi}\{\chi_1(b)\}$, since when $b \in ([p, s] - \psi)$, $\chi_1(b) < 0$. Then we have $\chi = \sup\limits_{p \leq b \leq s} \{\chi_1(b)\}$.

So in both two cases we have $\chi = \sup\limits_{p \leq b \leq s} \{\chi_1(b)\}$.

Then

$$
\begin{aligned}
R'[s,t] \\
&= C[s,t] + \sup_{p \leq b \leq s} \{ \inf_{p \leq a \leq t} \{C[a,b] - R[a,b)\}\} \\
&= C[s,t] + \sup_{p \leq b \leq s} \{ \inf_{b \leq a \leq t} \{C[a,b] - R[a,b)\}\} \\
&= \sup_{p \leq b \leq s} \{ \inf_{b \leq a \leq t} \{C[s,t] + C[a,b] - R[a,b)\}\} \\
&= \sup_{p \leq b \leq s} \{ \inf_{b \leq a \leq t} \{R[b,a) + C[a,t] - C[b,s)\}\}
\end{aligned}
$$

Then with $\lambda = s - b$ and $\mu = a + \lambda - s$, we have

$$
\begin{aligned}
R'[s,t] \\
&= \sup_{p \leq b \leq s} \{ \inf_{b \leq a \leq t} \{R[b,a) + C[a,t] - C[b,s)\}\} \\
&= \sup_{0 \leq \lambda \leq s-p} \{ \inf_{0 \leq \mu \leq \lambda+(t-s)} \{R[s-\lambda, \mu - \lambda + s) + C[\mu - \lambda + s, t] - C[s - \lambda, s)\}\} \\
&\leq \sup_{0 \leq \lambda \leq s-p} \{ \inf_{0 \leq \mu \leq \lambda+(t-s)} \{\alpha^u(\mu) + \beta^u(\lambda + (t - s) - \mu) - \beta^l(\lambda)\}\} \\
&\leq \sup_{0 \leq \lambda} \{ \inf_{0 \leq \mu \leq \lambda+(t-s)} \{\alpha^u(\mu) + \beta^u(\lambda + (t - s) - \mu) - \beta^l(\lambda)\}\} \\
&= (\alpha^u \otimes \beta^u) \oslash \beta^l
\end{aligned}
$$

Since the number of processed events can not be larger than the available resource, $R'[s,t] \leq \beta^u(t - s)$, then we have $R'[s,t] \leq \min((\alpha^u \otimes \beta^u) \oslash \beta^l, \beta^u)$.

(2) The results for α''^l can be proved as with a combination of β'^u and α''^u .

References

1. Thiele, L., Chakraborty, S., Gries, M., Kunzli, S.: Design space exploration of network processor architectures. Netw. Processor Des. : Issues Pract. **1**, 1–12 (2002)
2. Fersman, E., Mokrushin, L., Pettersson, P., Yi, W.: Schedulability analysis of fixed-priority systems using timed automata. Theor. Comput. Sci. - Tools Algorithms Constr. Anal. Syst. **354**(2), 301–317 (2006)
3. Bondorf, S., Schmitt, J.: Improving cross-trac bounds in feed-forward networks there is a job for everyone. In: Remke, A., Haverkort, B.R. (eds.) Measurement, Modeling and Evaluation of Dependable Computer and Communication Systems. Lecture Notes in Computer Science, vol. 9629, pp. 9–24. Springer, Cham (2016). https://doi.org/10.1007/978-3-319-31559-1_3

4. Wandeler, E.: Modular performance analysis and interface-based design for embedded real-time systems. Ph.D. Thesis, Publisher, Swiss federal institute of technology Zurich (2006)
5. Chakraborty, S., Knzli, S., Thiele, L.: A general framework for analysing system properties in platform-based embedded system designs. In: DATE, pp. 1–6. IEEE, Munich, Germany, Germany (2003)
6. Thiele, L., Chakraborty, S., Gries, M., Kunzli, S.: A framework for evaluating design tradeoffs in packet processing architectures. In: DAC, pp. 880–885. IEEE, New Orleans, Louisiana, USA (2002)
7. Chakraborty, S., Phan, L.T.X., Thiagarajan, P.S.: Event count automata: a state-based model for stream processing systems. In: RTSS, pp. 87–98. IEEE, Miami, FL, USA (2005)
8. Tang, Y., Guan, N., Liu, W.C., Phan, L.T.X., Yi, W.: Revisiting GPC and AND connector in real-time calculus. In: RTSS, pp. 1–10. IEEE, Paris, France (2017)
9. Guan. N., Yi, W.: Finitary real-time calculus: efficient performance analysis of distributed embedded systems. In: RTSS, pp. 1–10. Vancouver, BC, Canada (2013)
10. Lampka, K., Bondorf S., Schmitt, J.B., Guan N., Yi, W.: Generalized finitary real-time calculus. In: INFOCOM, pp. 1–9. Atlanta, GA, USA (2017)
11. RTC Toolbox Homepage. https://www.mpa.ethz.ch/static/html/Navigation.html

A Verified Specification of TLSF Memory Management Allocator Using State Monads

Yu Zhang[1], Yongwang Zhao[1(⊠)], David Sanan[2], Lei Qiao[3], and Jinkun Zhang[3]

[1] School of Computer Science and Engineering, Beihang University, Beijing, China
zhaoyw@buaa.edu.cn
[2] School of Computer Science and Engineering, Nanyang Technology University, Singapore, Singapore
[3] Beijing Institute of Control Engineering, Beijing, China

Abstract. Formal verification of real-time services is important because they are usually associated with safety-critical systems. In this paper, we present a verified Two-Level Segregated Fit (TLSF) memory management model. TLSF is a dynamic memory allocator and is designed for real-time operating systems. We formalize the specification of TLSF algorithm based on the client requirements. The specification contains both functional correctness of allocation and free services and invariants and constraints of the global memory state. Then we implement an abstract TLSF memory allocator using state monads in Isabelle/HOL. The allocator model is built from a high-level view and the details of data structures are simplified but it covers all the behavioral principles and procedures of a concrete TLSF implementation. Finally, we verify that our TLSF model is correct w.r.t. the specification using a verification condition generator (VCG) and verification tools in Isabelle/HOL.

Keywords: Formal verification · Memory management · Isabelle/HOL

1 Introduction

Operating system kernels and hypervisors form the backbone of safety-critical software systems in the world. Formal verification can play an important role in addressing the issue of software safety and reliability. Using formal methods and theorem proving techniques, software systems can be formally proved bug-free with respect to their specification. Remarkable examples include seL4 [15] and CertikOS [14], which are both verified trustworthy operating systems.

In recent years, there has been an increasing interest in real-time operating systems (RTOS) due to the increasing amount of real-time applications. They are frequently deployed on critical systems, making formal verification of RTOS

This work has been supported in part by the National Natural Science Foundation of China (NSFC) under the Grant No. 61872016.

N. Guan et al. (Eds.): SETTA 2019, LNCS 11951, pp. 122–138, 2019.
https://doi.org/10.1007/978-3-030-35540-1_8

necessary to ensure their reliability. As an important module in RTOS, the memory management provides clients with an allocation function to request a portion of memory and a deallocation function to free that part of memory if it is no longer in use. Since these systems are often running infinitely, without rebooting, it is important to ensure the absence of memory leakages. Thus, we start investigating formal verification on RTOS by studying the TLSF algorithm, which has been applied in many OSs [1,2].

TLSF is a dynamic memory management algorithm and it organizes free memory blocks using two-level segregated lists. The main challenges of verifying TLSF algorithm come from complex data structures and algorithm to satisfy the strict requirements of real time systems. To achieve bounded response time and fast response time, the TLSF allocator deploys a nested bitmap structure, represents bitmaps in integers and manipulates them using bit-wise operations. Thus, explicit search for blocks using loops can be avoided. However, additional data structures increase the complexity in the modeling and verification work. The complexity of data structures and algorithms imply as well complex invariants and properties. The invariants have to guarantee the well-shaped bitmaps and their consistency to segregated lists. To prevent memory leaks and block overlapping, a precise reasoning will keep track of both numerical and shape properties.

Our model is concerned with the TLSF allocator from a high level and we cover all the functional behaviours of memory allocation and deallocation abstractly. The data structures and simple functions are specified using the logic that Isabelle/HOL provides. The model for the function malloc and free is defined using state monads. State monads allow the computation with side effects and we store the relative information in the states. Moreover, using state monads, we can present the computational procedures like in imperative programming languages, which is more natural. We reason about functions represented in state monads using the verification condition generator (VCG) within the framework of Hoare Logic. Later on, as future work, we plan to extend our verification to a lower level implementation and by using the state monads and a refinement framework based on simulation to conduct top-down verification.

The overall structure of our verification work is organized in two layers. The first layer is the abstract specification of the memory management module. At this level, we consider the memory management as a component in the entire operating system model and the interaction between other modules and memory management should depend on the abstraction instead of a concrete implementation. Because our model does not consider interruptions, the execution of programs can be interpreted as a state transition relation. The abstraction mainly concerns the state flow, including invariants and pre- and post-conditions. Therefore, in this layer, we formalize the data structures, state invariants, and functional specification of function malloc and free without any insight on their behaviours.

In the second layer, we developed a TLSF algorithm model that captures the behaviour of function malloc and free. This model is built from a high-level view, hiding part of the implementation details. A state is maintained in the process of the two functions using the non-deterministic monads that allow multiple possible state flow paths. We verify that the model implements the abstraction in the first layer by proving that the monadic models of the allocation and free services preserve the invariants and fulfills the pre- and post-conditions. The verification work is done in the theorem prover Isabelle/HOL.

More layers can be developed and formalized below the first two layers. A concrete implementation can be proved correct by verifying a refinement relation with reference to the layer above. The C code level implementation is the bottom layer and contains the fine-grained data structure and well optimized calculation procedure. By this means, we could disentangle the complex problem layer by layer finally.

Our main contribution includes: (1) We formalized the abstract specification of the memory management module in the context of a real-time operating system. The formalization specifies invariants and constraints of the global state and functional correctness of allocation and deallocation functions; (2) We present a TLSF model in Isabelle/HOL framework, where the model captures the behaviours of the memory allocation and deallocation from a high-level view; (3) We formally verify the model with respect to the specification. In the verification, we spot a flaw in the design of TLSF algorithm. The formal specification and proofs in Isabelle/HOL are available at https://lvpgroup.github.io/tlsf_spec/.

2   Background and Related Work

2.1   TLSF Algorithm

TLSF (Two-Level Segregated Fit) is a dynamic memory allocator specifically designed to meet real-time requirements.

Segregated List. In TLSF algorithm, free blocks are organized in segregated lists and each segregated list only contains the free blocks within a specific size interval. Moreover, as shown in Fig. 1, segregated lists have a two-level structure. The first level splits sizes in power of 2 ranges, e.g. [32, 63], [64, 127], [128, 255], etc. The second level sub-divides each first level range linearly, e.g. [64, 71], [72, 79], [80, 87], etc. The two-level structure composes a free list matrix where each element is a list of free blocks within a specific size interval and the size interval is related to the matrix indices.

Bitmap. Also as shown in Fig. 1, segregated lists are associated with bitmaps. Each bit in the bitmaps is set means there is at least one free block whose size lies in the interval the bit corresponds to. The length of the bitmap are determined by the parameters in the system configuration.

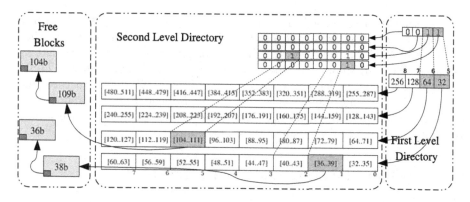

Fig. 1. Segregated list structure [3]

Blocks. Information needs to be stored in the block itself. To keep track of the physical neighbours, the size and the pointer to the previous block are stored in the overhead. The next block is located at the address of the block itself plus its size. For a free block, it is necessary to store the pointers to its neighbours in a doubly-linked list. The information about the free list can be removed when a block is allocated so it is stored in a buffer and can be used by users.

Malloc. Function malloc is provided for memory allocation and it takes the requested size as a parameter. Firstly, it searches for a safe list which means that the blocks in the list are all larger than the requested size. If such a list does not exist, the allocation failed. Secondly, it takes the head element from the safe free list. Finally, if its size minus the requested size is enough to construct a complete block, it is split and the remaining part is inserted back to the segregated list. Otherwise, the block is simply returned to the user.

Free. Function free is provided for memory deallocation and it accepts the address of the block to be deallocated as a parameter. Before inserting the block back into the free list, the function checks whether its adjacent blocks are free. If it has free neighbours, they are merged immediately to obtain a larger free block and the new block is inserted to the free list.

Further implementation details about TLSF implementation and analysis can be found in [3].

2.2 Related Work

Memory models [6] provide the necessary abstraction to separate the behaviour of a program from the behaviour of the memory it reads and writes. There are many formalizations of memory models in the literature, e.g., [8–12]. Some of them create abstract specification of memory allocation and release [10–12]. Formal verification of OS memory management has been studied in CertiKOS

[13,14], seL4 [15,16], Verisoft [17], and in some hypervisors [18,19]. Algorithms and implementations of dynamic memory allocation have been formally specified and verified [7,20–24]. However, the TLSF algorithm was only studied in [20,23] using the Event-B approach. Compared to the Event-B modelling of TLSF, our work follows an imperative representation of the TLSF data structures and algorithm by state monads. Moreover, using the Isabelle/HOL theorem prover, our specification and proof of TLSF are able to be directly reused in formal verification of the TLSF implementation in the future.

3   The Data Structure and Configuration

3.1   System Configuration

The TLSF memory management allocator runs on different operating systems and its performance is closely related to the system configurations. In our model, we parameterize the system configurations and propose several constraints to keep it flexible but not arbitrarily defined. We use an Isabelle/HOL record to store parameters and a specification to constrain these parameters. The Isabelle/HOL specification command allows to constrain a data type with a number of requirements that they data type must hold.

record *Sys-Config* =
  sli   :: *nat*
  sm   :: *nat*
  min-block :: *nat*
  overhead :: *nat*
  mem-size :: *nat*

specification(*conf*)
  sm-ge-sli   : *sm conf* $\geq$ *sli conf*
  min-gt-0   : *min-block conf* > 0
  total-mem-gt-0: *mem-size conf* > 0

- *sli* represents the logarithm to the base 2 (the default base if not explicitly mentioned) of the length of second level bitmap. As a consequence, we define the length of second level bitmap in this system configuration as $sl\ cfg = 2^{sli\ cfg}$, where *cfg* is an instance of the configuration record, *sl* is a function from a configuration to a natural number and *sli* reads the corresponding field from the *cfg* which is of type *Sys_Config*. Therefore, one of the validity constraints of second level index is to be smaller than *sl cfg*.
- *sm* represents the logarithm of the threshold for the size of blocks. We refer to blocks with sizes smaller than 2^{sm} as small blocks. Small free blocks belong to the segregated lists with a first level index 0. That is, for a block with size r, if $0 \leq r < 2^{sm}$, its first level index in the bitmap matrix is 0; otherwise, for r such that $2^{sm\ +\ i\ -\ 1} \leq r < 2^{sm\ +\ i}$, its corresponding first level index is i.
- *over_head* represents the size of the overhead part that related information resides in. Overhead of a block is described in Sect. 2.1.
- *min_block* represents the minimum possible size of a valid block. Note that in the source code, *min_block* is defined as a macro equal to the size of the

temporary buffer that every block contains. As mentioned above, for users the buffer is simply a normal piece of memory that they have access to write while the allocator uses it to store pointers that connect the block itself to the double linked free block list. However, we do not maintain such pointers for the sake of simplicity in our logical model. Therefore, the parameter min_block does not equal to a specific value and it remains abstract.

– mem_size represents the total size of the memory pool.

These five parameters are adequate for the system configuration. Note that the length of the second level bitmap is among the five parameters while the first level one is not. This is because the length of the first level bitmap is fixed given the total memory size and the threshold for small blocks. In fact, the following equation holds implicitly because of the binary representation of machine code and the properties of the first level bitmap: $fl\ cfg\ =\ \log_2(mem\_size\ cfg)\ -\ sm\ cfg$. Unlike the second level index, one of the validity constraints of the first level index is to be smaller or equal to $fl\ cfg$. The reason for the equal case to be valid will be disclosed when we discuss the function $mapping\_search$.

For the three configuration constraints, the first one does not look intuitive but it becomes clear if we apply exponentiation to both side and reach $2^{sm} \geq 2^l$. This means that the threshold for small blocks must be greater or equal to the length of second level bitmap, otherwise the map between small block sizes and bits in the second level bitmap indexed 0 in the first level bitmap cannot form a bijective relation. For example, if the length of the second level bitmap equals to 256, then the threshold for small blocks should at least be 256B in order to fill up the bitmap, otherwise the state is inconsistent. For the second constraint, if a block with size 0 is allowed, the set of blocks can be infinite, which is thorny to deal with. Moreover, in real world implementations, it is not possible to allocate pieces of memory of size zero. Therefore we prevent such case by introducing that the minimum size of block should be greater than zero. The last constrain precludes degeneration since everything is vacuously true if there is no memory at all.

3.2   System State

In our model, a block is defined by its start address and end address. Accordingly, the size of a block equals to its end address minus start address. A memory state is composed by an allocated block set and a free block bitmap matrix. We then define functions to insert and extract blocks from the matrix at specific indices, collect all free blocks from the matrix, and find the physically previous and next blocks.

```
datatype block = Block (s_addr: nat) (e_addr: nat)
fun size :: "block ⇒ nat" where
  "size (Block s e) = s - e"

type_synonym block_matrix = "nat ⇒ nat ⇒ block set"
record state =
  alloced_block :: "block set"
  free_block_matrix :: block_matrix
```

```
fun free_mat_upd :: "block_matrix ⇒ nat ⇒ nat ⇒ block set ⇒ block_matrix"
where
  "free_mat_upd m i j bs = m(i := (m i)(j := bs))"

fun free_block :: "state ⇒ block set" where
  "free_block s = {b. (∃i j. b ∈ (free_block_matrix s) i j)}"

fun next_block :: "state ⇒ block ⇒ block option" where
  "next_block s b =
    (let s = {bn. bn ∈ alloced_block s ∪ free_block s ∧ is_next bn b}
     in if s = {} then None else Some (THE b. b ∈ s))"

fun previous_block :: "state ⇒ block ⇒ block option" where
  "previous_block s b =
    (let s = {bp. bp ∈ alloced_block s ∪ free_block s ∧ is_previous bp b}
     in if s = {} then None else Some (THE b. b ∈ s))"
```

The set comprehension and logical predicates are commonly used in proof assistants. The predicate "THE" is used in Isabelle/HOL to represent a unique value represented by a predicate P. The uniqueness and existence of a value satisfying P have to be proven in order to use such a unique value in proofs. Taking corner cases into consideration, we use an option in next block and previous block function and it returns None if no such block exists.

3.3   Bitmap Matrix

We model the two-level bitmap following the design in TLSF algorithm. The first-level bitmap divides free blocks in classes that are a power of two apart (16, 32, 64, 128, etc.); and the second-level bitmap sub-divides each first-level class linearly, where the number of divisions is 2 to the power of sli, one of the parameters in system configuration. As a result, the range of sizes of accepted blocks by the segregated list corresponds to each bit in the two-level bitmap can be calculated.

$$size_{i,j} = \frac{2^i}{2^{sli}}$$

$$range_{i,j} = [2^i + size_{i,j} \times j, 2^i + size_{i,j} \times (j+1) - 1]$$

We formalize the specification of the two-level bitmap with regard to the definition of blocks and free block matrix and prove several properties as lemmas for future use. The threshold for small blocks and validity of indices, which are not shown in the formulas, are also considered in our formalization.

Lemma 1. *Properties of the two-level bitmap*

- **Uniqueness.** *Given $(i,j) > (i',j')$, the lower bound of $range_{i,j}$ is greater than the upper bound of $range_{i',j'}$. As a corollary, each range does not overlap with each other. This means that given a block size r, there is at most one pair (i,j) that $r \in range_{i,j}$.*

– **Existence.** *Given an arbitrary block size* r *that does not exceed the total memory size, there exists such a pair* (i, j) *that* $r \in range_{i,j}$.

– **Monotonicity.** *Given* $r \geq r'$, $r \in range_{i,j}$ *and* $r' \in range_{i',j'}$, $(i, j) \geq (i', j')$.

To make it clear, the inequality $(i, j) > (i', j')$ holds if and only if $i > i'$ or $i = i'$ and $j > j'$. The addition $(i, j) + 1$ equals to $(i, j + 1)$ if $j + 1 < sl\ cfg$, or equals to $(i + 1, 0)$ otherwise.

Based on the first two properties, we again utilize the predicate "THE" to get the indices of the segregated list to which the block b belongs.

definition `get_index` :: `"nat ⇒ (nat × nat)"`
  where `"get_index r ≡ (THE (i, j). r ∈ l2_range i j ∧ valid_fl i ∧`
                            `valid_sl j)"`

4   Formalizing the Abstract Specification

4.1   Invariants

We formalize six safety invariants:

1. There are not any two successive blocks that are both free. This invariant follows the strategy in TLSF algorithm that once a memory block is freed it is merged immediately with free blocks that are physically next to it. This invariant holds initially because the memory is initialized with a single free block covering the entire memory space [20].

   definition `no_split_memory` :: `"state ⇒ bool"` **where**
     `"no_split_memory σ ≡`
        `¬ (∃ b1 b2. b1 ∈ free_block σ ∧ b2 ∈ free_block σ ∧ is_next b1 b2)"`

2. There is no intersection between the set of allocated blocks and free blocks. Equivalently, there is not such a block that is both allocated and free.

   definition `disjoint_free_non_free` :: `"state ⇒ bool"` **where**
     `"disjoint_free_non_free σ ≡`
        `alloced_block σ ∩ free_block σ = {}"`

3. There is no overlapping between any two blocks in the memory pool. Equivalently, any byte in the memory pool belongs to exactly one block.

   definition `disjoint_memory` :: `"block ⇒ block ⇒ bool"` **where**
     `"disjoint_memory b1 b2 ≡`
        `e_addr b1 + overhead conf < s_addr b2 ∨`
        `e_addr b2 + overhead conf < s_addr b1"`

   definition `disjoint_memory_set` :: `"state ⇒ bool"` **where**
     `"disjoint_memory_set σ ≡`
        `∀ b1 b2. b1 ∈ all_block σ ∧ b2 ∈ all_block σ ∧ b1 ≠ b2`

```
           ⟶  disjoint_memory b1 b2"
```

4. Every block in the memory pool is well formed. This requires that the start address of each block does not exceed the end address and the size of each block is neither smaller than minimum size nor greater than the size of the total memory pool.

```
definition wf_block :: "block ⇒ bool" where
  "wf_block b ≡
     s_addr b ≤ e_addr b ∧ size b ≥ min_block conf ∧
     size b + overhead conf ≤ mem_size conf"
```

```
definition wf_blocks :: "state ⇒ bool" where
  "wf_blocks σ ≡
     ∀b ∈ all_block σ. wf_block b"
```

5. The segregated list is well formed. This means that the sizes of all the blocks chained in a segregated list lie in the range that corresponds to the bitmap matrix indices of the segregated list.

```
definition wf_adjacency_list :: "state ⇒ bool" where
  "wf_adjacency_list σ ≡
     ∀i j. valid_fl i ∧ valid_sl j ⟶
        (∀b. b ∈ free_block_matrix σ i j ⟶ size b ∈ l2_range i j)"
```

6. The total size of memory does not change.

```
definition sum_block :: "block set ⇒ nat" where
  "sum_block bs ≡
     Finite_Set.fold (λb s. size b + overhead conf + s) 0 bs"
```

```
definition all_block_mem_size :: "state ⇒ bool" where
  "all_block_mem_size σ ≡
     sum_block (all_block σ) = mem_size conf"
```

For the allocation function, if the invariants hold before the execution, the invariants still hold regardless of whether it succeeds or not.

Theorem 1. *Given an initial state s, if s satisfies the invariants, after an execution of memory allocation on requested block size r, the terminal state satisfies the invariants.*

For the free function, its behaviour on request to deallocate a block that has not been allocated is undefined. Therefore, we only specify that the invariants preserve if that condition is met.

Theorem 2. *Given an initial state s, if s satisfies the invariants, after an execution of memory deallocation on an allocated block, the terminal state satisfies the invariants.*

4.2   Specification of Allocation

Following a successful allocation, we expect that the returned address is the start address of one of the free blocks and that the size of this block is larger than that of that requested block. These properties compose the functional correctness of allocation. Moreover, if the result of the size of the block to be allocated minus that of the requested block is larger than a predefined threshold, then it is split and the remainder is inserted back to free block matrix. Otherwise, the allocator simply returns the suitable block to the caller.

Proposition 1. *Given an initial state s that satisfies the invariants, after a successful allocation on requested size r, the returned value addr and terminal state t satisfy the following properties:*

1. *There exists such a free block b in the state s that b starts at addr.*
2. *The size of block b is greater or equal to the requested size r.*
3. *If size $(b) - r \geq$ threshold value, then b is split to b_1 and b_2 where b_1 has size r and the following equations hold:*
   (1) $free\_block(t) = free\_block(s) - \{b\} + \{b_2\}$
   (2) $allocated\_block(t) = allocated\_block(s) + \{b_1\}$
4. *If size $(b) - r <$ threshold, then the following equations hold:*
   (1) $free\_block(t) = free\_block(s) - \{b\}$
   (2) $allocated\_block(t) = allocated\_block(s) + \{b\}$

In the above proposition, $+$ and $-$ symbols represent set union and subtraction.

4.3   Specification of Deallocation

The behaviour of deallocation on blocks that are not allocated is undefined and it is the caller's responsibility to guarantee that an allocated block is passed to deallocation function. Therefore, we focus on the case of well-behaved dealloca-tion and how the block gets merged with its physical free neighbours.

Proposition 2. *Given an initial state s that satisfies the invariants, after deal-locating an allocated block b, the terminal state t satisfies the following properties:*

1. *$allocated\_block(s) = allocated\_block(t) + \{b\}$*
2. *If both the previous and next blocks are not free, then $free\_block(t) = free\_block(s) + \{b\}$*
3. *If the previous block b_p is free while the next is not, then $free\_block(t) = free\_block(s) - \{b_p\} + \{merge(b_p, b)\}$*
4. *If the next block b_n is free while the previous is not, then $free\_block(t) = free\_block(s) - \{b_n\} + \{merge(b, b_s)\}$*
5. *If both the previous b_p and the next b_n blocks are free, then $free\_block(t) = free\_block(s) - \{b_p, b_n\} + \{merge(b_p, b, b_s)\}$*

5 Formalizing the Algorithm

5.1 State Monads

State monads allow pure functional model of computation with side effects. For the purpose of reasoning about the TLSF memory allocator, it is inevitable to keep track of free blocks and allocated block in the memory pool. Therefore, we use state monads [4] in Isabelle/HOL to model the TLSF allocator and the specification can be written in the way similar to imperative programming languages.

Since our TLSF allocator is an abstract behavioural model, it is convenient to express computation nondeterministically. So unlike normal state monads in Haskell, the return type is a set of values and states coupled with a flag represents whether the computation fails or not. Function *return* and *bind* are the fundamental monad functions. The function *return a* simply returns its argument a, does not change the state and does not fail. The function *bind f g*, also written as $f >>= g$, is the execution of f followed by the execution of g. The definition says that the result of the combined operation is the union of the set of sets that is created by g applied to the result sets of f; the combined operation fails if either f or g fails.

```
type_synonym ('s,'a) nondet_monad = "'s ⇒ ('a × 's) set × bool"
return a ≡ λs. ({(a,s)},False)
bind f g ≡ λs. (⋃(fst ' case_prod g ' fst (f s)),
                True ∈ snd ' case_prod g ' fst (f s) ∨ snd (f s))
```

Function *get* is the basic accessor that simply returns the current state and does not change anything. Function *puts* returns nothing, changes current state to s and does not fail. Function *selectA* is the basic non-deterministic function that chooses an element from set A as return value, does not change the state and does not fail. Function *gets* apply a function to the current state and return the result without changing the state. Function *modify* update the current state using the function passed in. These are generic functions that are built on top of the basic monadic operations and are convenient in practice.

```
get ≡ λs. ({(s,s)}, False)
put s ≡ λ_. ({((),s)}, False)
select A ≡ λs. (A × {s}, False)

gets f ≡ get >>= (λs. return (f s))
modify f ≡ get >>= (λs. put (f s))
```

5.2 Formal Specification of Memory Functions

Mapping Insert. Function *mapping_insert* calculates the corresponding indices (i, j) of the given block size r. We verify that the return value and the expected indices coincide.

Lemma 2. *mapping_insert r = get_index r*

Mapping Search. Function *mapping_search* searches for the safe segregated list with the least indices that every block in the list is larger than given block size r. If r lies exactly on the lower bound of $range_{i,j}$, the segregated list at (i, j) is safe. Otherwise, the indices of the safe segregated lists is at least the successor of (i, j). Therefore, we introduce a predicate *on_bound* that takes a block size and returns true if it lies exactly on the lower boundary of the interval where the size itself locates.

Definition 1. *Let pair (i, j) be the bitmap matrix indices of block size r and interval $[s, e]$ be the size range that corresponds to indices (i, j). If a block size r equals to s, then r is said to be on bound*

Besides that, *mapping_search* also rounds up the block size r to the lower bound of the safe size range. So the return value is a triple.

Lemma 3. *Property of function mapping_search.*

– *if r is on bound, mapping_search$(r) = (r$, get_index$(r))$*
– *if r is not on bound, mapping_search$(r) = (r'$, get_index$(r)+1)$, where $r' > r$ and r' is on bound.*

Note that the returned index result $get\_index(r) + 1$ might overflow for a pair of valid indices. That is, $get\_index(r) = (i, j)$ where i equals to the length of first level bitmap and j equals to the length of second level bitmap. Then $(i, j) + 1 = (i + 1, 0)$ according to the addition rules of pairs. Therefore, we relax the constraints of first level index validity as mentioned in Sect. 3.1. Moreover, in the detailed implementation one extra bit is needed to avoid the overflow problem.

Find Suitable Block. Function *find_suitable_block* takes a pair (i, j) and a state s as input and returns the set of all pairs that are greater than or equal to (i, j) and corresponding segregated lists that are not empty.

Malloc. Function *malloc* allocates a block to the its caller. It first searches for a suitable segregated list on which the free blocks fulfill the requirements. If there does not exist such a list, then it fails. Otherwise, it non-deterministically selects a block from the list. If the selected block is large enough, then it is split and the remaining part of block is inserted back to its corresponding segregated list. Otherwise, the block is simply returned.

```
definition malloc::"nat ⇒ (state, nat option) nondet_monad"
  where "malloc r ≡
  let (r,(i,j)) = mapping_search conf r in
   do set_ps ← gets (find_suitable_blocks_opt (i,j));
      condition (λs. set_ps = None) (return None)
      (do p ← select (the set_ps);
          b ← remove_block p;
          (condition (λs. size b - r ≥ (min_block conf + overhead conf))
```

```
    (do (b1,b2) ← gets (λs. (split_block r b));
        modify (λs. s(|alloced_block:= insert b1 (alloced_block s)|));
        modify (add_block b2);
        return (Some (s_addr b1)) od)
    (do modify (λs. s(|alloced_block:= insert b (alloced_block s)|));
        return (Some (s_addr b)) od)) od) od"
```

Unlike other memory allocation algorithms, there is no guarantee in TLSF allocator that if there exists a free block with its size larger than the requested size the allocation will succeed. Instead, TLSF allocator successfully returns an address only if there is such a non-empty free block list that all blocks chained on it have larger sizes than the requested size. In this manner, the allocator simply returns the head element of a suitable segregated list. Since the algorithm does not use loops, one of the merits of TLSF allocator is its bounded response time. Unfortunately, this leads to complexity in formalization and verification.

If the requested size r is not on bound, the TLSF allocator looks for blocks from the segregated list whose indices are at least the successor of (i, j), otherwise a block with smaller size might be returned. On the other hand, if the requested size r is on bound, it is safe to return an arbitrary block on the segregated list at (i, j) if there exists one. Therefore, in such case, the allocation succeeds if there exists a free block that has a larger size than the requested size.

Theorem 3. *Given an initial state s that satisfies the invariants, the memory allocation succeeds on requested block size r if either one of the two conditions is met:*

- *r is on bound and there exists at least one free block such that its size is greater or equal to r.*
- *r is not on bound and there exists at least one free block such that its bitmap matrix indices is strictly greater than the indices corresponding to size r.*

Similarly, we formalize the case when the allocation fails by simply taking the negation of the above theorem. Note that the case when there are suitable blocks but it still fails to allocate is included.

Theorem 4. *Given an initial state s that satisfies the invariants, the memory allocation fails on the requested block size r if either one of the two conditions is met:*

- *r is on bound and all the free blocks are smaller than size r.*
- *r is not on bound and the bitmap matrix indices of all the free blocks are smaller or equal to the indices corresponding to size r.*

Free. Function $free$ deallocates a block. It first finds the block that starts at the given address and removes it from the allocated set. Then $join\_prev$ and $join\_suc$ are called to merged the released block with its physical neighbor blocks if possible. Function $join\_prev$ and $join\_suc$ are analogous so only the former is shown in below. Finally, the merged block is inserted into the segregated lists.

```
definition free::"nat ⇒ (state, nat) nondet_monad"
  where "free addr ≡
    condition (block_alloced addr)
      (do b ← gets (get_alloced_block addr);
          modify (λs. s⦇ alloced_block := Set.remove b (alloced_block s)⦈);
          b ← join_suc b;
          b ← join_prev b;
          modify (add_block b);
          return 1 od)
      (do modify (λs. undefined);
          return undefined od)"
```

```
definition join_suc::"block ⇒ (state, block) nondet_monad"
  where
"join_suc b ≡
  do b' ← gets (suc_free_block conf b);
     condition (λs. b' = None)
       (return b)
       (let (i,j) = mapping_insert conf (size (the b'));
            b_join = join_block b (the b') in
        do modify (remove_elem_from_matrix (the b') i j);
           return b_join od)   od"
```

6 Formal Verification and Results

6.1 Verification Using State Monad

Together with the monad constructors, Isabelle/HOL also provides a verification condition generator (VCG) to reason about programs represented in state monad within the Hoare Logic framework. In our setting, a hoare triple contains pre-condition, monadic computation, and post-condition. A triple is valid if for all states that satisfy the pre-condition, all result values and result states that are returned by the monad satisfy the post-condition.

```
"⦃P⦄ f ⦃Q⦄ ≡ ∀s. P s ⟶ (∀ (r,s') ∈ fst (f s). Q r s')"
"invariant f P ≡ ⦃P⦄ f ⦃λ_. P⦄"
```

To reason about the calculus, backward reasoning rules are used to calculate the weakest pre-condition (WP) that ensures the validity of Hoare triples from giving monads and post-conditions. Rules, as shown in Fig. 2, are proved safe and work directly on the validity predicate. By invoking VCG, appropriate rules are applied automatically to generate the weakest pre-condition for the entire program. The result is a proof goal in higher order logic and can be solved in Isabelle/HOL with all kinds of verification tools.

For example, one of the properties of deallocation is formalized using the validity predicate as shown. The pre-condition says that the invariants hold, the address to be deallocated is valid and neither the previous nor the next block is free. Then we deduce that the free blocks set in terminal state equals that

$$\{\!|\lambda s.\ P\ (f\ s)\ s|\!\}\ gets\ f\ \{\!|P|\!\}$$
$$\text{GetsWp}$$

$$\{\!|\lambda s.\ P\ ()\ (f\ s)|\!\}\ modify\ f\ \{\!|P|\!\}$$
$$\text{ModifyWp}$$

$$\{\!|\lambda s.\ \forall x \in S.\ Q\ x\ s|\!\}\ select\ S\ \{\!|Q|\!\}$$
$$\text{SelectWp}$$

$$\frac{\forall x.\ \{\!|B\ x|\!\}\ g\ x\ \{\!|C|\!\}\quad \{\!|A|\!\}\ f\ \{\!|B|\!\}}{\{\!|A|\!\}\ f \ggeq g\ \{\!|C|\!\}}$$
$$\text{BindWp}$$

$$\frac{\{\!|Q|\!\}\ A\ \{\!|P|\!\}\quad \{\!|R|\!\}\ B\ \{\!|P|\!\}}{\{\!|\lambda s.\ \text{if}\ C\ s\ \text{then}\ Q\ s\ \text{else}\ R\ s|\!\}\ condition\ C\ A\ B\ \{\!|P|\!\}}$$
$$\text{ConditionWp}$$

Fig. 2. A sample of backwards reasoning rules used to reason about Hoare-style valid triples [4]

in the initial state plus the freed block. To verify the property, we first unfold the definition of free function. Then the VCG is invoked and we prove the precondition implies the weakest pre-condition generated by VCG.

```
lemma free_property_2:
  "let b = get_alloced_block addr σ in
 {|λσ'. σ=σ' ∧ inv σ' ∧ block_alloced addr σ ∧
     prev_free_block conf b σ = None ∧ suc_free_block conf b σ = None |}
    free addr
 {|λ_ σ'. free_block σ' = free_block σ ∪ {b} |}"
```

6.2 Evaluation

All the formalization and proofs are done in theorem prover Isabelle/HOL. In total, the model and mechanized verification consists approximately 5000 lines of specification and proof, with 400 lines for specification, 2000 lines for data structure and auxiliary lemmas, 1200 lines for proof of allocation and 1400 lines for proof of deallocation.

During the formal verification, we confirmed a limitation in the TLSF allocator, i.e. sometimes when free blocks that fulfill the requirements do exist in the free block pool but allocation might fail. This case is stated in Theorem 4 and has been verified. However, this is a functional property that TLSF trades to ensure that allocation requests are served in bounded time, which is essential for a real-time system. Except that, the high-level design of the TLSF allocator is correct with reference to the requirements of ordinary operating systems.

7   Conclusion

We present a verified TLSF dynamic memory allocator that is specifically designed for real-time systems. We formalize an abstract model that captures the behaviour of the TLSF allocator. It is represented in Isabelle/HOL under the state monad framework. Then we specify the functional correctness and safety invariants using higher order logic in Isabelle/HOL. Finally, we verify the model implements the specification and in the process of execution invariants preserve.

References

1. TLSF: Memory allocator real time embedded systems. http://www.gii.upv.es/tlsf/
2. Masmano, M., Ripoll, I., Crespo, A., Real, J.: TLSF: a new dynamic memory allocator for real-time systems. In: Proceedings of the 16th Euromicro Conference on Real-Time Systems, ECRTS 2004, Catania, Italy, 2004, pp. 79–88.https://doi.org/10.1109/EMRTS.2004.1311009
3. Masmano, M., Ripoll, I., Real, J., Crespo, A., Wellings, A.J.: Implementation of a constant time dynamic storage allocator. Softw. Pract. Exp. **38**, 995–1026 (2008). https://doi.org/10.1002/spe.858
4. Cock, D., Klein, G., Sewell, T.: Secure microkernels, state monads and scalable refinement. In: Mohamed, O.A., Muñoz, C., Tahar, S. (eds.) TPHOLs 2008. LNCS, vol. 5170, pp. 167–182. Springer, Heidelberg (2008). https://doi.org/10.1007/978-3-540-71067-7_16
5. Nipkow, T., Wenzel, M., Paulson, L.C.: Isabelle/HOL: A Proof Assistant for Higher-Order Logic. Springer, Heidelberg (2002). https://doi.org/10.1007/3-540-45949-9
6. Saraswat, V.A., Jagadeesan, R., Michael, M., von Praun, C.: A theory of memory models. In: Proceedings of the 12th ACM SIGPLAN Symposium on Principles and Practice of Parallel Programming (PPoPP), pp. 161–172. ACM (2007)
7. Yu, D., Hamid, N.A., Shao, Z.: Building Certified libraries for PCC: dynamic storage allocation. In: Degano, P. (ed.) ESOP 2003. LNCS, vol. 2618, pp. 363–379. Springer, Heidelberg (2003). https://doi.org/10.1007/3-540-36575-3_25
8. Leroy, X., Blazy, S.: Formal verification of a C-like memory model and its uses for verifying program transformations. J. Autom. Reason. **41**(1), 1–31 (2008)
9. Tews, H., Völp, M., Weber, T.: Formal memory models for the verification of low-level operating-system code. J. Autom. Reason. **42**(2), 189–227 (2009)
10. Gallardo, M.d.M., Merino, P., Sanán, D.: Model checking dynamic memory allocation in operating systems. J. Autom. Reason. **42**(2), 229–264 (2009)
11. Ševčík, J., Vafeiadis, V., Zappa Nardelli, F., Jagannathan, S., Sewell, P.: CompCertTSO: a verified compiler for relaxed-memory concurrency. J. ACM (JACM) **60**(3), 22:1–22:50 (2013)
12. Mansky, W., Garbuzov, D., Zdancewic, S.: An axiomatic specification for sequential memory models. In: Kroening, D., Păsăreanu, C.S. (eds.) CAV 2015. LNCS, vol. 9207, pp. 413–428. Springer, Cham (2015). https://doi.org/10.1007/978-3-319-21668-3_24
13. Vaynberg, A., Shao, Z.: Compositional verification of a baby virtual memory manager. In: Hawblitzel, C., Miller, D. (eds.) CPP 2012. LNCS, vol. 7679, pp. 143–159. Springer, Heidelberg (2012). https://doi.org/10.1007/978-3-642-35308-6_13
14. Gu, R., et al.: CertiKOS: an extensible architecture for building certified concurrent OS kernels. In: 12th USENIX Symposium on Operating Systems Design and Implementation (OSDI), Savannah, GA, pp. 653–669. USENIX Association (2016)
15. Klein, G., et al.: seL4: formal verification of an OS kernel. In: 22nd ACM SIGOPS Symposium on Operating Systems Principles (SOSP), pp. 207–220. ACM Press (2009)

16. Klein, G., Tuch, H.: Towards verified virtual memory in L4. In: TPHOLs Emerging Trends, Park City, Utah, USA, 16 pages, September 2004

17. Alkassar, E., Schirmer, N., Starostin, A.: Formal pervasive verification of a paging mechanism. In: Ramakrishnan, C.R., Rehof, J. (eds.) TACAS 2008. LNCS, vol. 4963, pp. 109–123. Springer, Heidelberg (2008). https://doi.org/10.1007/978-3-540-78800-3_9

18. Blanchard, A., Kosmatov, N., Lemerre, M., Loulergue, F.: A case study on formal verification of the anaxagoros hypervisor paging system with frama-C. In: Núñez, M., Güdemann, M. (eds.) FMICS 2015. LNCS, vol. 9128, pp. 15–30. Springer, Cham (2015). https://doi.org/10.1007/978-3-319-19458-5_2

19. Bolignano, P., Jensen, T., Siles, V.: Modeling and abstraction of memory management in a hypervisor. In: Stevens, P., Wąsowski, A. (eds.) FASE 2016. LNCS, vol. 9633, pp. 214–230. Springer, Heidelberg (2016). https://doi.org/10.1007/978-3-662-49665-7_13

20. Su, W., Abrial, J., Pu, G., Fang, B.: Formal development of a real-time operating system memory manager. In: 2015 20th International Conference on Engineering of Complex Computer Systems (ICECCS), Gold Coast, QLD, pp. 130–139 (2015). https://doi.org/10.1109/ICECCS.2015.24

21. Fang, B., Sighireanu, M.: Hierarchical shape abstraction for analysis of free list memory allocators. In: Hermenegildo, M.V., Lopez-Garcia, P. (eds.) LOPSTR 2016. LNCS, vol. 10184, pp. 151–167. Springer, Cham (2017). https://doi.org/10.1007/978-3-319-63139-4_9

22. Fang, B., Sighireanu, M.: A refinement hierarchy for free list memory allocators. In: Proceedings of the 2017 ACM SIGPLAN International Symposium on Memory Management, pp. 104–114. ACM (2017)

23. Fang, B., Sighireanu, M., Pu, G., Su, W., Abrial, J.R., Yang, M., Qiao, L.: Formal modelling of list based dynamic memory allocators. Sci. China Inf. Sci. 61(12), 103–122 (2018)

24. Marti, N., Affeldt, R., Yonezawa, A.: Formal verification of the heap manager of an operating system using separation logic. In: Liu, Z., He, J. (eds.) ICFEM 2006. LNCS, vol. 4260, pp. 400–419. Springer, Heidelberg (2006). https://doi.org/10.1007/11901433_22

Author Index

Printed in the United States
By Bookmasters